KAHUNA OF LIGHT

KAHUNA OF LIGHT

The World of Hawaiian Spirituality

MOKE KUPIHEA

Inner Traditions International
Rochester, Vermont

Inner Traditions International
One Park Street
Rochester, Vermont 05767
www.InnerTraditions.com

Copyright © 2001 by Moke Kupihea

Library of Congress Cataloging-in-Publication Data
Kupihea, Moke.
   Kahuna of light : the world of Hawaiian spirituality / Moke Kupihea.
      p. cm.
   ISBN 0-89281-756-9 (alk. paper)
      1. Hawaii—Religion. 2. Kahuna. 3. Kupihea, Moke. I. Title.
   BL2620.H3 K87 2001
   299'.9242—dc21

                                                              00-053563

Printed and bound in Canada

10 9 8 7 6 5 4 3 2 1

Text design and layout by Virginia Scott-Bowman
This book was typeset in Caslon with Block Berthold and Willow as the display typefaces

CONTENTS

INTRODUCTION

IN ANCIENT TIMES IN HAWAII *a kahuna,* as you shall learn in the chapters that follow, was a priest of sorts, a shaman who maintained intimate connection with the spirit world—the realm of the *na `aumakua o ke ao,* or our ancestral spirits of the immediate past, and the *na `aumakua o ka po,* or our ancestral spirits of the distant past. He was a seer who dealt in a currency of mysticism, knowledge, and wisdom not immediately accessible to the common man. Thus in practice the ancient kahuna was more a kahuna of darkness and mystery than of light. But there is another interpretation of *kahuna,* one of light, one who helps us, people of the modern world, to access all that we must know about who we are and where we have come from before we can truly find our opening to both the immediate and distant worlds of the *na `aumakua* (ancestral spirits), our door to their spiritual light and power.

A kahuna today is a living storehouse, a vessel of hereditary knowledge and the knowledge of accumulated personal experience who shares and transfers this knowledge through the telling of stories—stories of places, people, and their entwined history. A kahuna of light is a teacher, in the broadest definition or translation of the role, gifted in his or her humanity and understanding of people and place. A kahuna of light is a teacher who, through his or her spiritual nature, inspires others to awaken to their spiritual nature and to the light of the `aumakua, or ancestral spirit.

By leading us to this spiritual awakening, these modern-day kahuna can provide us with one of the most important pieces of information that can be given to a child, or even an adult, for that matter: who we are. For many of us the first kahuna we know are our parents, our most immediate ancestors, who make vivid for us their history and experience, and in doing so are the first to show us who we are—our kahuna of first light. Beyond our parents are all the *kupuna* (elders) who surround us in our years from childhood to adulthood—our kahuna of expanding light. These kahuna may be other family members such as our aunts and uncles and their elders, or, especially, our grandparents, whose genealogical knowledge and understanding of our home can reach back farther and run deeper than the knowledge of our parents. Family friends may be kahuna; many of them may share our ancestry and culture or have stories to tell about our world as it was. Beyond these, kahuna can be any of those who act as teachers to someone willing to learn—whether a child or someone grown—sharing with this person their time and knowledge and stories.

Far from the ancient sorcerer, mystic, and shaman, these kahuna of light surround us every day, and while many reach out to share their wisdom, still more need only to be asked to share. In addition to telling us who we are, they can tell us where we have come from, and most important, they can tell us of the spirit that carried us here from the past and that must carry us into the future if we are to survive. They connect us to our place of origin, and can help us to develop a deep spiritual tie to this place and to its preservation. Through offering knowledge of our ancestry and an instinctive understanding of the land of our ancestors, kahuna can lead to what is at the heart of my people's belief: the `aumakua—which is not some deceased being or spirit outside of ourselves with whom we communicate but, rather, is that part of our ancestors that still dwells within us.

A belief in the `aumakua must be inherited or passed down from those who have come before and who are willing to connect to those who are to come after. The road, or life, pointed out by our kahuna leads to the world of the `aumakua; more specifically, it is the *journey* on this road—a path reaching behind us into a world of the past, the visions of which we can still recall, and stretching ahead into the future, the visions of which we are able to project—that can lead us to the realm of these ancestral spirits. Or, taking things one step farther, it is the journey on this road that leads us to ourselves, for in reaching the world of the ao `aumakua, we reach its power, or *ao* (spiritual light), within ourselves.

I believe the world of a o `aumakua is a living world; *ao* is the source of energy that all living things need to survive, an energy that exists in two forms: one that takes away darkness, such as the light that comes from the sun, and the light that dwells within us, such as the light of knowledge and the spirit, called enlightenment. When we speak of ao `aumakua, we speak of this second light that exists in the mind and body—which, if it is nurtured, can dispel the darkness outside of ourselves, as it did for me once when I was nearly twelve years old . . . but that is part of the story of my journey.

In this book I will share a great deal of my early road with you. As for most people, my childhood and years as a youth were a time when my beliefs were being shaped and molded through my association with many kupuna while growing up in the 1950s and 1960s in the Waimea Valley on the island of Kauai. These were people of the last century and the early part of this century—people like my mother, a kahuna of first light, and kahuna of expanding light such as Willy Kani, Mr. Roland Gay and George Cliff, the Naumu family, Eugene Makaaila, Kala, and Pipito, to name just a few—who led me to know the `aumakua within myself and to feel its presence growing as I grew.

The Hawaiians have a word to describe what I am sharing with you in this book: *mana´o,* which means thought, idea, opinion, theory, one's mind, one's desire to think and consider, and, most significant of all, one's memory. When you share your mana´o, you share all of these. And if you are Hawaiian, you share them in a unique way: unlike the Caucasian, perhaps, a Hawaiian does not immediately focus directly on the subject at hand, or head directly for the point of view that he is trying to establish. On the contrary, it is very important first to explain everything that he has encountered along the way to arriving at this point of view because thoughts are always woven of memory. How this habit came about I am not sure, but perhaps it is a result of the fact that we had no written language until very recently in historical time; ours was an oral culture in which it was vital to commit everything to memory and to repeat this stored knowledge to others so that it would not become lost over time. If, for example, you were to ask an old Hawaiian where So-and-so lives, in giving you the location he would also tell you the history of So-and-so's house—when it was built, who lived there before, what was located there before the house was built—who So-and-so is related to, and who his parents were. Thus, in addition to finding out where So-and-so lives, you would have a full history of this person and his place, and so it would be for any question you posed about any person, place, or object. In the reply you would learn the story of how, through time, that person or place or object came to be.

This book, as you shall see, is written in this same fashion; it is the only way I know to share my mana´o—and I believe that it is important to record names, places, and legends that we encounter on our journey so that they can be preserved for future generations. Many of the details that you read here about the town of Waimea and of the valleys and ridges of Waimea Canyon have never before been published. I wish to allow the tourists and the dwellers alike to see what Waimea once was, and to give to everyone who reads this at least some picture and understanding of the people who once dwelled in the Waimea Valley, the Makaweli Valley, and beyond. For the Hawaiian reader, some of my mana´o may help you in the future as you trace your own genealogy. For the non-Hawaiian, reading about my journey—especially about my years as a child and youth—may help you to reflect on your own memories of your upbringing and formative years. If you wish to recognize your `aumakua, you must have hold of your earliest memories and the knowledge you have gained along the way. In the process you may recall the elders of your youth who, in your world, were kahuna of light.

This text, in its entirety, I dedicate to the youths and elders of the future who claim descent from the aboriginal people who inhabited the Hawaiian Islands prior to the arrival of Captain James Cook in 1778, and who still see themselves as Hawaiians; and I dedicate it to all others in the world who see themselves as aboriginal, wherever their place of origin may lie.

To the youth of today who, in this changed world and environment, are not able to experience the spiritual knowledge of their kupuna and are not able to reach out to their kahuna, I want to tell you that the ancient people are here today, surviving, and they are within you, waiting to be recognized. In recognizing them you are well on your way to becoming a kahuna for those in the future

The least I can wish for is that this book rekindles the reader's interest in his or her roots. The world today is drifting away from life's source, and so many people use the past only as a gauge of their present or future success. I hope that I can, in some small way, be the reader's kahuna, showing and teaching that the past travels with us into the future, that we were created in the past and we prepared for our futures in the past. I hope that in sharing my journey I inspire you to make your own. To begin, you need only remember; when you are alone, revisit your unique history, your past, and think of all the words of your life's kahuna. If your memory leads you to some ancestor who has touched you in your life, keep this person alive within you as a source of a o —your `aumakua in this world that is both old and new.

CHAPTER ONE

THE `AUMAKUA

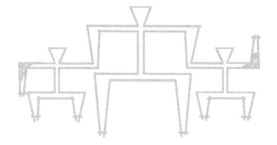

MY STORY HERE IS THE STORY OF A JOURNEY, from boyhood to manhood, into the world of the ao `aumakua. In keeping with the oral tradition of the Hawaiian, in telling this story I am making this journey again, and am inviting you to make it with me. The `aumakua is foreign to many Westerners—indeed, even to many Hawaiians today. For those who do know the `aumakua, there has been a great deal of confusion surrounding what it is, what it is not, and the belief system of which it is the heart. To help you as we travel, I give you first a glimpse of the ao, or light, of my ancestors' ancient beliefs as they were before being dimmed by corruption from within their own priesthood and further extinguished by the Christian tradition that replaced it.

In the past, a descendant of priests and scholars would have been carefully coached in the sacred wisdom of his ancestors, but these are different times. The wisdom passed down to me came in bits and pieces, often from stories told by older relatives and their lifelong friends. This folk wisdom ignited a desire in me at a very early age to associate myself with the few surviving elders of my grandmother's generation. A profound experience in the then wilderness mountains of Kauai when I was not quite twelve transformed that desire into a quest for the truth. In later years, this quest led to further study and to a personal awakening and desire to share these ancient spiritual truths.

While experience made the concepts real to me, scholarship often served to confirm my own conclusions. So here, at the start, I pay homage to the elder William Kapahu kani o lono Goodwin, to all of the elders of my youth whom you shall meet during the course of this book, and to three of Hawaii's prominent native historians: Mr. David Malo Kupihea, who provided other historians with accurate detail and firsthand knowledge in the early 1900s; Mr. Samuel M. Kamakau, who wrote in the 1860s and 1870s; and Mr. David Malo, who in the 1830s and 1840s wrote the original manuscript for the book *Mo'olelo Hawaii,* more commonly known as *Hawaiian Antiquities.* The work of these three men in the absence of the elders of my youth has echoed and strengthened my own experiences, allowing me the confidence to show you firsthand the living history of an all-but-lost ancient belief system that still has much to say to men and women of all races.

Kumulipo (Out of Darkness)

The Ancient Trinity of Hawaiian Gods
Kane nui akea—Kane is the Great Expanse.
Ku nui akea—Ku is the force of the Great Expanse.
Lono nui akea—Lono is the sound of the Great Expanse.

Kane himself is the Great Expanse,
Kane himself is the Universe,
Kane himself created Nature,
Kane himself is Nature.
Kane is God.

Ku himself is the force of the Great Expanse,
Ku himself is the force of the Universe,
Ku himself is the force of Nature,
Ku himself is the force of God.
Kane is God.

Lono himself is the sound of the Great Expanse,
Lono himself is the sound of the Universe,

Lono himself is the sound of Nature,
Lono himself is the sound of God.
Kane is God.

Man himself is the child of the Great Expanse,
Man himself is the child of the Universe,
Man himself is the child of Nature.
Kane himself is the father of Man.

To begin at the beginning, a cosmogonic, or creator-type god, such as the Judeo-Christian Jehovah, was known by my ancestors as an *akua*. Just as Jehovah is credited with the creation of Heaven and Earth, so was Kane nui akea (Kane of the great expanse) said to have created the highest Heaven (Lani Kuaka´a), the Earth (Ao), and all the things that fill them both. While Kane nui akea represented original *lokahi* (unity), two other akuas—Ku nui akea and Lono nui akea—shared his *mana* (power) as the twin forms of nature that exist within a single creation: generation and regeneration. A fourth akua, Kanaloa, is also mentioned in our myths, but his presence is much more mysterious, perhaps because his connection to the Hawaiian people was more remote.

Although akua exist as eternal spirits transcending mortal life, our traditions clearly state that the akua Kane nui akea, Ku nui akea, and Lono nui akea descended upon the earth, where they assumed mortal form. In these earthly incarnations, the gods regenerated within mortals, beginning the three genealogical lines of the Hawaiian people. Because the immortal akua were never truly separated from their eternal source, a new aspect of their being evolved once they had regenerated within humanity: in their offspring they had passed down the divine spirit of god into the living spirit of man, and became *akua ʻaumakua*, traveling upon the earth in their mortal incarnations under the names Kane, Ku, and Lono. They became ancestral gods to the genealogical lines that followed as they sowed their seed among humanity. Thus Kane, Ku, and Lono each existed in two worlds: in one as a seed passed down from generation to generation and in the other as the creator of that seed—as an akua ʻaumakua. In their offspring they regenerated the ʻaumakua, the source of descending divinity in the living spirit of man. The Christian Jesus can be seen only in the light of existence as an akua ʻaumakua because Jehovah's earthly incarnation has no genealogical line.

Ao ʻaumakua (Ancestral Light)

While an akua ʻaumakua, as the procreator of an ancestral line, is indeed an ancestral god, an ʻaumakua, as the ancestral link to the divine, is not, though it has often been described as such. This confusion of an ancestral link to a god with the god itself has led some critics to say that our people worshiped as many as four hundred thousand gods, but this is simply not so. In truth, the ʻaumakua is not worshiped as a god. Perhaps it is the prayer that one uses to acknowledge and contact the ʻaumakua that causes this confusion. But while it is true that the ʻaumakua is treated with reverence, it is not considered some kind of supreme being that rules over creation; rather, it is part of the chain of life that has descended from a god's incarnation. It is not the immortal light of a god but instead a mortal light lit in mortal creation, an ancestral light. It is the part of ourselves that deifies wisdom, love, and ancestry within our own genetic chain. Our parents (makua) are our closest generational link to this endless chain of time known as the au, and each of us represents a temporary end to that chain. As the light slowly fades within us, our descendants come forth to provide the next link. Thus, we never stray from the intent of those who created us, even though our connection to our origins has been largely forgotten.

During the long course of Hawaiian history, a number of shadows have been cast upon our understanding of the ʻaumakua and its role in connecting us to our spiritual source. These shadows mark a distinct separation between what have become known as the realms of the na ʻaumakua o ka po (darkness—our ancestors of the remote past) and the na ʻaumakua o ke ao (light—our ancestors of the immediate past). As a result of this separation, in our most recent history two types of spirits have become commonly, though mistakenly, referred to as na ʻaumakua. These two spirits, one called an unihi pili and the other uhane, are basically the same. Unihi pili refers to a deified spirit in its role in afterlife, either ritualized into a demigod or worshiped as a god after passing over the threshold of death.

A good illustration of the confusion that surrounds the na ʻaumakua o ke ao can be seen in a 1936 interview with my great-uncle David Malo Kupihea, as recounted in a book by Julius Rodman entitled *The Kahuna: Sorcerers of Hawaii:*

> Early in 1936 when I was gathering material for a paper on fish-
> ing methods of the old Hawaiians, I sought out another Hawaiian
> authority, David Malo Kupihea, a descendant of the great David
> Malo, author of *Hawaiian Antiquities.* He served ably in the terri-
> torial legislature from 1901 until 1915, and has since been a fish-
> erman residing in a simple house in the Kalihi kai district on the
> island of Oahu. We had many congenial meetings in years past,
> but I was surprised when he spoke freely of kahuna lore. Kupihea's
> na ʻaumakua were sharks, and he confessed to making offerings to
> his ʻaumakua and to his shark god before each fishing excursion.
> It seemed only natural that this old fisherman would speak of that
> order of kahuna who sent sharks and various other creatures on
> errands of death, saying in part, "That is true, I have knowledge of
> many works of the kahuna, the good and the bad, knowing only
> the results of their ceremonies, but little of how they learned to
> harness the things of the spirit world . . . and talk with the old
> gods, who the missionaries say never existed. I, like you, would
> like to know these secrets. I am in ignorance because in my great-
> grandparents' time missionaries placed tabus on our old religion,
> and in my family the tabu was very strong."

The word ʻaumakua clearly doesn't belong in this passage, unless Mr. Rodman means to say that the ancestors of the Hawaiian people were sharks, for if there is a shark ʻaumakua, then it is an ancestor of sharks, not of men. And so it is that mistakes like this form the divide between us and our ancestors. As my great-uncle states, the tabus on our religion were very strong, and within generations a great deal had been lost. People broke faith with the ʻaumakua, severed their connection to its *kumupaʻa* (fixed origin), and began to attach the original ʻaumakua as an ancestral spirit to different forms. Over time, the original `aumakua lay dormant, replaced by these newfound deities that were called na `aumakua but were really unihi pili. To this day, many older Hawaiians will still answer the question "Who is your `aumakua?" with "Shark," or "Turtle," or "Lizard," or whatever creature their family line has established to serve such a purpose. The younger generation follows today.

To get a better notion of how my ancestors originally viewed the roles and relationships of these various spirits, let us examine Mr. Rodman's "shark god" from the perspective of the heart of the `aumakua belief.

Ao uhane (Light of the Soul)

The uhane, the spirit of the present life in the realm of the na `aumakua o ke ao, has been likened to the Judeo-Christian concept of the soul, but I don't find this comparison useful. For one thing, the word *soul* refers to the same concept whether in life or in afterlife. There is no such continuing, unchanged spirit in the `aumakua belief, where terms often shift meaning at the threshold between life and death. The uhane refers specifically to the life spirit. At death, the remnants of that spirit still cling to the body, but the uhane is not immortal. It dissipates at the end of each generation unless it is held in consciousness by the following generation. Thus it can be said that one's `aumakua in life is the consciousness of another's uhane remnants in death.

What we are talking about is not one entity known as the soul but, rather, three spirits: The first is the immortal light of the akua called kumupa´a ascending into immortality. The second is the mortal light lit by the akua `aumakua. This is the light of the `aumakua descending into mortality through its offspring. Both of these are housed by the third spirit, current life (the uhane), and are held together in unity by the spirit of kumupa´a, which is the fixed connection to one's origin in relationship to a god of procreation.

The uhane is said to still dwell in the bones and hair of a deceased person and can be withdrawn *(unihi)* and lured into another body, creature, image, or object where it will cling *(pili)*. The person responsible for this transfer then becomes the creature's or image's keeper, or *kahu*. Once the uhane is transferred, it is called an unihi pili. Because the unihi pili is the creation of its kahu in its new body, it can turn to cling to the kahu, as it is said to do when a kahu fails to continue to appease his unihi pili with the promises of worship and recognition. At such a time, the unihi pili may turn on its kahu and bring him nothing but misery until it finds the location of its remains and can again rest and eventually dissipate.

In the days of the ancients, those who practiced such arts as luring the uhane were known as kahuna of the class called *ana `ana `aihue* (those who stole the spirit of life; those who attained another's property by the use of sorcery). It was this type of kahuna that Mr. Rodman refers to when he speaks of sending "sharks and various other creatures on errands of death." These kahuna had another name as well. They were called *kahuna po`o ko`i*, meaning "adze heads," because when they were caught practicing their dark arts by the established priesthood, they were frequently beheaded with a stone adze.

Ke unihi pili o po`ele`ele (Deified Spirit of Darkness)

In the case of the shark, possession begins with the kahu using prayer *(pule)* and promises to entice the uhane, to withdraw it from its current bodily remains, and to transfer it to a creature of life, the shark. This unihi pili now clings to the shark's spirit of life and performs only the kahu's desires; the unihi pili can thrive in the shark only by relying upon its kahu and not on the creature to which it clings. When the desired purpose of the kahu is accomplished or the kahu dies, the possession of the shark by the unihi pili, without the offertory memory of the kahu, comes to an end, and the unihi pili dissipates into the world of the sharks. After this, in order for a descendant of this kahu to call on this unihi pili, he would have to pule within his ancestral line until he came in contact with the `aumakua of the particular ancestor who created it, thereby providing the unihi pili a familiar offertory. Clearly only the ancients, those who could reach into the realm of the na `aumakua o ka po, could travel within their genealogical line well enough to reach back into any period of time, call upon the source of one link, and extend into another body thereafter.

Ho´uhane o ke ao (Deified Spirit of Light)

In the oral tradition, a story was handed down to me by my mother, Catherine Mahina Wilson, which she heard while being reared by her grandmother at her grandmother's old Bannister Street home in the Kalihi kai district of the island of Oahu. A sister of David Malo Kupihea, her grandmother also sometimes spoke of unihi pili and uhane. One story she often recited involved a curse that had been placed upon her at the age of sixteen.

In 1891 her grandmother Tutu Kahili lukahi mo´i Kupihea met and fell in love with a foreigner named Charles Samuel Huston Johnson and agreed to marry him. At that time, foreigners were deeply distrusted by the Hawaiian people, and for good reason—a foreign conspiracy known as the Annexation Club was secretly plotting the overthrow of Queen Lili-uokalani and the Hawaiian monarchy. When her grandmother refused to comply with the tabu against having anything to do with the foreigner, she became gravely ill. As her condition grew worse and her doctors could find neither cause nor cure, the family began to suspect she was a victim of a curse. But by whom, and for what reason? These were the questions they had to unravel if the curse was to be removed.

As time passed, many family elders tried unsuccessfully to counter or remove the curse, but none succeeded. Finally, Mr. James Campbell of the famed Campbell estate family suggested that her grandmother be taken to a kahuna who had no direct genealogical connection to her. Mr. Campbell, who was the husband of Abigail Kuaihelani (a distant cousin of her great-grandfather Samuel Kupihea), sensed that the curse might be coming from the family itself, and when her grandmother was taken to Maui to see an unrelated kahuna, his suspicion was confirmed. Almost immediately the kahuna determined that the person responsible for her grandmother's condition was her own mother! As it turned out, Melia Hipa (Mele Kahilulu Kaai Kanaka) had placed the curse on her daughter because she knew that Charles Johnson had associated himself with members of the Annexation Club and she would rather have seen her daughter dead than married to him. It was only through constant pule, recited in unison under the direction of the Maui kahuna, that the curse was finally removed.

What appears to be a simple battle of wills in the placing and removal of a curse illustrates how the uhane and the `aumakua can become intertwined in life and can become deified in the darkness of an unihi pili. Recall that the `aumakua is the spirit of past lives accumulating in the regeneration of life, and that the uhane is the spirit of the present life. In this example, mother and daughter possessed the same genealogical line of na `aumakua, with the daughter having the two additional na `aumakua of her mother and father. Even though the mother was still alive, her `aumakua was already in existence within her daughter, having descended at the moment of conception, as did that of her daughter's father. Upon discovering that her daughter had broken the tabu, the mother became the kahu of her own `aumakua and willed it to pili (cling) to her daughter's life spirit, convincing it to withdraw as a spirit of the afterlife by replacing its will with her own.

Once the kahuna from Maui realized what had happened and who was responsible, he was able to bypass the curse through devotional prayers of dedication (pule) directed to the girl's father's na `aumakua, to his genealogical line. The mother's influence was then removed from her daughter's spirit of life.

Her grandmother, who ended up marrying the foreigner, lived to the age of seventy-nine. When she recited this story to my mother during her later years, she said that many older Hawaiians had converted to Christianity just to avoid experiences like hers. Since Jesus was the only stepping-stone to God, it was thought that such perils on the road to the `aumakua might be avoided. Some Hawaiians even began to refer to Jesus Christ as an `aumakua, though this was incorrect, since Jesus had no offspring.

Kumu ao (Out of Light)

The uhane, as the life spirit, has evolved solely to serve one's current existence. Unlike the `aumakua, it has never lived a prior life, and once this life is done, its consciousness will cease to exist. It has been said that the uhane's constant fear of extinction is what brings about man's fear of death and initiates the ongoing quest by humanity to convince itself that there will be a life after death, a life where the uhane will survive with all of its knowledge intact. But according to the old beliefs, this is a fruitless quest, one that destroys the spirit of kumupaʻa and creates unihi pili within and around oneself, which have been withdrawn and which cling for religious appeasement on a quest for an afterlife.

The ancient kahuna, in the light of the procreators of their race, were taught from birth that their connection to spirit lay in their ancestral links to it. Thus, as the light of the procreators began to distance itself, the three priestly lines—Kane, Ku, and Lono—developed to preserve the origins of the akua ʻaumakua. In time these priesthoods became corrupt and secretive, and during the period we call the na ʻaumakua o ke ao (within the time of our ancestors of the recent past), they replaced the eternal and immortal spirits of our people with the living spirit of man. When the priests elevated the *aliʻi,* "ruling class," to the status of living gods, our true origin became dormant, and misdirected uhane and unihi pili replaced our original ʻaumakua chain. With the spirit of kumupaʻa broken, our beliefs became misguided, and by the time the Christian missionaries arrived, it appeared that our people practiced only heathenism. This is a picture that continues to be painted today by Western authors trying to exploit the mysticism of ancient beliefs in order to cater to those who seek the thrill of supernatural powers.

Kumupaʻa o ke ao (Light of Origin)

To practice these ancient beliefs without corrupting them, one must always remain in a state of lokahi (unity) with one's light of origin, in relation to the ʻaumakua. The spiritual bond that we call kumupaʻa must never be broken, for once torn away, the uhane will seek spiritual light only outside of its true origin. If you are without lokahi—outside of your light of origin and in a state of separation—and you practice telepathy, mind reading, or sorcery that brings harm to others, you destroy the ʻaumakua. Once the kumupaʻa has been severed and lokahi lost, the uhane is left to wander the earth with no directional spirit of origin. In this disconnected state it becomes a *lapu,* or "ghost of one's own creation." This is what happened to my ancestors' beliefs when hereditary rule was established and secured by elevating the ruling class to the status of gods, inaugurating a long period in which the internally derived images of man became replaced by the external images of religion.

Ao o ka ho´omana (Light of Religion)

By the time the great temples *(heiau)* were built and dedicated to the distant akuas, these gods of the great expanse were truly isolated in their highest heavens, unapproachable except through the intervention of the chiefly *kuauhau,* or genealogist of court, and the *mo´o kahuna,* or line of hereditary priests, for only they retained knowledge of the `aumakua pathway to these gods, which was recited in secret at the temple ceremonies performed for the high chief. For the rest of the people, the distant pathway of the `aumakua became lost in an ever-increasing line of lesser temple gods existing beneath the gods Kane nui akea, Ku nui akea, and Lono nui akea.

It was during this period that a change occurred in the hierarchy of the gods:

Kane, the Maker of Heaven, was outranked by Ku, God of Generation, who became God of War and was now seen as predominant among the four major gods. In earlier times the sun was said to be the light of Kane; now it was Ku who caused the sun to rise and set, thus earning him the title God of the Darkest Heavens.

In this religious order, which required the spoils of war to maintain wealth and power, Lono, God of Regeneration, became God of Peace, Agriculture, and Fertility and was ranked second. Lono was connected to the sounds of such natural phenomena as the winds, rain, and the ocean. Lono also presided over the season of the *makahiki,* a time for sports, games, and tournaments and also a time when taxes were collected. Lono, translated as "to listen, hear, and obey," reminded the people to be obedient and attentive.

Kanaloa, who was known as Lord of the Ocean and the Ocean Winds, is said to have caused strife among the ancient gods of Hawaii and among the Hawaiian people by showing them how to heal with sorcery. The change in the hierarchy of the gods of Hawaii is said to have occurred during the period of the priestly and chiefly migration to Hawaii of the Tahitians, who introduced the practices of Kanaloa to elevate the order of Ku. According to legend, Kanaloa was once a noted healer who usually traveled on earth in the company of the god Kane. Kanaloa had no genealogical line that connected him directly to the Hawaiian people, although he is mentioned as the pro-creator of the Tahitians, Samoans, Tongans, and Marquesans. Even though Kanaloa is considered one of our four major gods, little attention seems actually to have been given to him prior to the migrations of the Tahitians. His primary legacy appears to be that he was the god who is said to have brought the gift of death and sickness to the Hawaiian people.

So it was that the major orders of the *oi'hana kahuna* (office of the priesthood) and the *mo'o kahuna* (line of hereditary priests) secured their power by replacing the memory of the `aumakua chain among their people with grand symbols of immortal gods. Thus, religion was used not to enlighten the masses but to keep them ignorant. In the great heiau dedicated to Ku and Lono (the procreators of these two powerful hereditary lines), Kanaloa remained in a cloud of secrecy and Kane was reduced to a minor presence, although worship of him still took place in lesser shrines, some as small as a single stone. From the day the great temples were built, the `aumakua ceremonies were reserved strictly for the *ali'i nui* (high chief of a district) and *ali'i ai moku* (high chief or king of the island), and their highest of priests, for as in all other civilizations of the ancient world, only the king could be associated with a god by genealogical line. The priesthood vigorously protected this belief, for it ensured its role as *ali'i ku'i*, the power behind the throne.

Once the ali'i and the kahuna inserted themselves into the genealogical line, severing the connection between the commoner and his distant ancestors, the na `aumakua o ka po, they effectively stifled the `aumakua beliefs. From that time on, only the ali'i and high priest were to be possessed of the hereditary power and wisdom to contact the akua by channeling their prayers through the na `aumakua of their genealogical line. All other participants, such as the lesser chiefs and commoners, were relegated to worshiping the akua through unihi pili, idols that spoke only to the ruling class. At these lower levels, understanding of the `aumakua was primarily limited to one's immediate ancestors, the na `aumakua o ke ao.

There was, however, one additional area of common society in which the `aumakua practices continued to flourish, though in a truncated form, and that was within the trades. Since religion dictated the trades each class was allowed to practice, and because these professions were hereditary, the na `aumakua turned out to play a major role in every form of education throughout the classes. This happened because the Hawaiian language, as an oral tradition, depended on memorization to pass down its legacy. From the beginning of Hawaiian culture, specialized knowledge of the trades had been connected to the ancestors who had practiced those trades, and apprenticeship was as much concerned with memorizing these connections as it was with strictly practical applications. It was common practice that any omissions that might occur in the training of an apprentice could be acquired later through the contacting of one's `aumakua. Because such occupational knowledge was too important to be eliminated, the na `aumakua continued to be influential, if only at this level, as the following ancient prayer illustrates:

> *Enter deeply, enter to the very origin,*
> *Into the very foundation of all knowledge,*
> *Thou of the hidden face!*
> *Gather as in a great and lengthy net*
> *In the inner recess of the ear.*
> *As also in the desire, the preservation,*
> *Of these thy offspring, thy sons.*
> *Descend on them thy memory, thy knowledge,*
> *They the learned! Thou the determined,*
> *Thou the self created.*

It had taken our people more than a thousand years after the fall of Egypt, Greece, and Rome to develop their beliefs into a religious form resembling that of the medieval popes. And just as it was in the churches of Europe, canonical law was enforced by intimidation and fear, with strict punishments awaiting those who broke scriptural tabus.

Na ao ka poʻe (Light of the People)

The *papa kanaka*, or people of Hawaii nei (all of Hawaii), were now divided into classes, the highest being the *aliʻi nui* class consisting of the *papa aliʻi* and the *papa kahunaʻpule*. It was here that the line of chiefs and priests descended from the upper level of the ʻaumakua belief.

The *makaʻainana* class, or commoners, supplied food, clothing, and housing. They were the caretakers of the land and provided warriors to the aliʻi. For the makaʻainana, education was simple. They were taught by their parents or other experts within the family the hereditary trades, such as farming, fishing, *kapa* (cloth) making, and house building. The elder expert (kupuna) would pass on to an apprentice all the knowledge he had accumulated about his particular occupation during his lifetime; the apprentice would then commit it to memory, along with the names of all ancestors who had practiced the same occupation. At this lower but personal level, the tabus were less stringent and the gods (who consisted mainly of deified family members because the ʻaumakua was worshiped as a family god) were of lesser stature.

More specialized fields of knowledge were practiced by the upper level of the makaʻainana class, which consisted of lesser chiefs as well as artisans who had mastered genealogies, songs *(mele)*, chants *(oli)*, the hula, herbal medicine, canoe building, and many other skilled trades and cultural practices. An expert in one of these trades was considered a kahuna of his profession. The ʻaumakua chain began to enter its higher and impersonal levels here, as tabus became more stringent and the gods more important. At this level, it was taught that the na ʻaumakua were beings who possessed great intelligence and specialized knowledge. At the mainstream of the makaʻainana level, nature was the primary force; here, canonical law dictated practical application because the ʻaumakua was worshiped as a god who possessed supernatural powers.

For the high chiefly and priestly classes, those destined to become the future aliʻi and kahuna of the hereditary line, education was provided and controlled by the high priests of the two great orders of Ku and Lono. These teachings were kept secret, as were the identities of the people selected to become high chiefs and priests. This was the level of greatest separation, the highest level of the `aumakua belief, and it contained the strictest tabus. Here the `aumakua line was taught to lead directly to the akua. Although teachings at this level were kept secret, the results were not, for it was through the control of the upper level of the `aumakua belief that the people were ruled: the ali`i was made to be an earthly incarnation of an akua `aumakua, or a living god.

In addition to the ruling classes and the maka`ainana class who supported them, there was another caste, known as the *kauwa*. As described by nineteenth-century scholars such as Kamakau, the kauwa were born as outcasts. This caste was so despised that its members were regularly sent to the great temples of Ku to be used as human sacrifices. The kauwa were known by a variety of pejorative names, among them: *kauwa kuapa`a* (load-carrying outcasts), *kauwa laepuni* (outcasts with tattooed foreheads), *kauwa makawela* (red-eyed outcasts), and *kauwa `ainoa* (free-eating, godless outcasts). Malo mentions three other names applied to them. The first two—*kauwa lepo* (base-born slaves) and *kauwa ha`alele loa* (despised things)—reflect their low position and lack of regard. However, the third name suggests something entirely different, for Malo says they were also called akua, which means "superhuman" or "godlike." Although at the bottom of Hawaiian society and regarded by all above them as dirt, I suspect that the kauwa was the only class outside of the priesthood who truly possessed the knowledge of the `aumakua belief, and because members refused to relinquish this belief and break their faith, they were made outcasts by the powerful and jealous priests.

Ao panina (Closing Light)

I have gone to some length to describe the `aumakua, its complicated relationship to other spiritual entities, and the various roles it has occupied during different periods of Hawaiian history in order to help you to understand why so many natives of the same place of origin see this belief in so many different lights of existence. What I have discovered in my own life is that, though broken, the chain is not gone. All its links exist within me as they do within you. At this point you should realize that you too have na `aumakua, regardless of your heritage. And though you may not know how, you can communicate with them, for the descending spirit of your heritage is a living part of you. Finding that spirit is a challenge, for it dwells so deeply within you that you may never truly discover it, even though you spend your life searching.

One key to awakening the dormancy of the `aumakua is to keep in mind that the word *spirit* means not only "soul" but also "frame of mind." And remember, too, that an `aumakua is not a god who works miracles. While your `aumakua can provide knowledge and guidance, visions of the past, and even lead you toward a higher being, it can help you only with things of the living world. Thus, always focus on unity of self because it is only in this that the `aumakua can truly awake. Now, with the heart of the `aumakua belief in your memory, I invite you to follow me as I recall the journey that led me to discover the inner pathway to my own na `aumakua. In our travels we will encounter my ancient ancestors, my early childhood, and the days of my youth. Although the road map of memory upon which we travel is my own, the journey belongs to us all, for you have a parallel path that is capable of reconnecting you to your own na `aumakua. It is my hope that this story inspires you to walk it. Ka´ahele, ka´apuni, hua ka´i.

CHAPTER TWO

THE ʻAUMAKUA DESCENDS

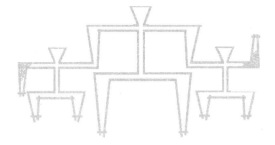

EVERY CULTURE ON RECORD HAS CONCERNED ITSELF with two fundamental questions about life: Who am I? and How did I get here? Ancient Hawaiian tradition answers these questions with the image of a luminescent path stretching through time, its steps composed not of stone but of generations. On this path, we are linked to those before us by blood, common experience, and the land upon which we have lived and will one day die. When our lives are over, we too will take our place upon this path, connecting future generations to ourselves and to those who came before us. But ultimately the path opens always to the living, for only in life can the ao, or light, be experienced.

To know who we are and who our children will be, we must know who we have been. Here are the stories of those from whom I descend.

As living human beings, we exist within a body of light. Without it we are nothing, yet long after we have returned to dust, our light can live on in our progeny, both in memory and in the flesh, for our ancestors do indeed inhabit our present bodies. It is their blood and their DNA that formed us. Our bodies are the living memories of our ancient ancestors, and only we, the living, can awaken our forebears to the ao.

For Hawaiians of previous generations, this ancestral connection was synonymous with spirituality. Although recent generations may have lost touch with this connection, I found it resurrecting quite naturally in myself. Partly because of my heritage, partly because of the circumstances of my upbringing, and partly because of my personality or character, I began to acknowledge the existence of the `aumakua within my inner world of thoughts as the remnants of my ancestors revealed themselves to me without benefit of formal training or ritual. The na `aumakua, like an inner voice, speak within my mind because I truly acknowledge their existence. I have found them to be a reliable source of information beyond my scope of knowledge; they clarify and amplify many of my thoughts and guide me along paths of our ancestral history. Such a source of an age-old past can still act within modern man if he is made aware of it, experiences it, and acknowledges it.

In writing this book, I have expressed many thoughts that have surfaced from this deep world within me. One revelation I have had concerns the development of the na `aumakua within a child who is their host.

I hear the voice of the `aumakua:

When living in a child, our strength is but that of a child, for we must continually start life over again from infancy. Our growing strength and cohesion are dependent upon the newborn who hosts our hereditary chain of descent. We possess no physical entities of our own. We are pure memory and must rely on you, the living generation, to determine through self-recognition and acknowledgment our future fate. Only you can awaken us and bring us to the surface of your awareness, so that we can once again experience the ao—the living world of light.

ʻAumakua o ka po (Ancestral Darkness)

For thousands of years, Hawaiian priests have memorized and passed down sacred creation chants of their lineage. The genealogical compositions of these chants were continually recast onto descending generations in the dedication ceremonies performed for a newborn chief of the *naiupiʻo* class (a child of the mating between a brother and sister). A birth of a niaupiʻo child was regarded as a repetition of the first human birth.

One such chant, the Kumulipo, was last recomposed by the seventeenth- to eighteenth-century kahuna Kekoauliko okea kalani for the consecration ceremony of the newborn chief Lonoikamakahiki, also known as Ka I i mamao. The baby's name was bestowed on him at the heiau (temple) of Kueku at Kahaluʻu in Kona, Hawaii, in the year 1700 by his paternal grandmother Keakea lani wahine, who was a high chieftess of naiupiʻo rank. The baby was consecrated and given the tabu while his navel cord was cut. Ka I i mamao would become known in history as Kalani nui I i mamao because the kahuna Kekoauliko inserted the *lani nui* (greatest of heavens) into his name while composing the chant.

Kumulipo, the title of the chant composed and transmitted entirely in the oral tradition, literally means "beginning in deep darkness," and its 2,102 lines provide an extended genealogy of the high chief Kalani nui I a mamao's divine origin from the beginning of the world, as first passed down by the ancient Hawaiian priesthood over two thousand years ago. The chant descended orally from the priesthood of Lono and was brought from Oahu (where Lono worship was most active) to Maui, the genealogy of whose ruling chiefs, down to the seventeenth-century high chieftess Piʻilani, occupies the chant's last section. From Maui it was brought to the island of Hawaii through the marriage of Piʻilaniʻs daughter, Piʻikea, of the lineage of Lono, to Umi a liloa, of the lineage of Ku. Umi a liloa was usurping chief over the island of Hawaii after the death of his father, Liloa, last of the ancient line of kings. Umi a liloa's marriage to Piʻikea temporarily ended the ruling lineage of Ku on Hawaii. This lineage was replaced by the lineage of Lono with the birth of Kalani nui I i mamao, the sixth-generation heir descending from their union.

The birth of Kalani nui I i mamao in 1700 can be celebrated as one that resurrected the existence of genealogical prayer chants. His birth and the chant preserved for all time not only the link of one royal family to the primary gods of the whole people and of allied Polynesian groups, but the link of an entire race from the other two chains of lineage to their primary gods as well. In addition, his birth also preserved links to the past (the ancestors of his race who were born of intermarriages with chiefs and deified chiefs of the living world) and to the future (the family lines of every descendant of the race today). Finally, his birth preserved the people's connections to migrational stars, to past homelands, and to the plants and animals that are the earthly embodiments of the hereditary gods.

When Vassar College scholar Martha Warren Beckwith began her thirty-three-year quest to translate and research this genealogical prayer chant in 1918, she turned to my great-uncle David Malo Kupihea to advise her. He continued to help her until the chant was finally published in 1951. It wasn't until Martha Warren Beckwith was eighty years old that she could open a book and see this ancient wisdom in print. The first two lines read:

> *Hanau ka po i ka po, po, no,*
> *[Things born in the night are of the dark,]*
> *Hanau mai a puka i ke ao, malamalama—*
> *[Things born from and sprung up in the day are of the light.]*

Dark and light, po and ao—these, my great-uncle would say, are what separate mankind's intellectual faculties from those of less developed animals and plants. That this knowledge took time to develop is illustrated by the 594 lines of the chant preceding the point at which the light of reason begins to shine in man.

> *The night gave birth*
> *Born was Kumulipo in the night, a male*
> *Born was Po'ele [deep darkness] in the night, a female.*

And so creation existed in darkness until man recognized his part in it. Until this point the chant concerns itself with the matings of creatures of the sea, sky, and land, including a mute, brute sort of mankind whose existence is in complete darkness. These are the forms assumed by the gods before the period of the ao, when the gods were finally birthed in man, thereby enabling our rational powers and endowing us with culture and art. While the po is a world of spirit, the ao is the world of living men inspired by gods who immersed themselves in matter and illuminated the world. The opening three lines of the ao read:

> Well-formed is the child, well-formed now
> Child in the time when men multiplied
> Child in the time when men came from afar.

Ao kahea (Call to Light)

Chants like the Kumulipo provided living generations a means to enter into the world of ao `aumakua and to recall their ancestors into their living light. For thousands of years these chants existed only in the memories of those who held them sacred. Today, they live in memory no longer, existing only as words on paper, strange symbols that those who originally spoke them would not recognize or be able to read. This does not mean that the world of ao `aumakua is necessarily closed, for the chain of births continued, even after they stopped being included in the chants. If one is aware, as I was, the stories told by elder relatives and their friends can serve a role similar to that of the chants and awaken one to the living part of the past. My ancestors, noted among the first scholars of the Hawaiian race, have left our family a literary pathway that places our lineage with the ao of the Kumulipo.

An early-twentieth-century scholar of Hawaiian history named Theodore Kelsey, author of the 1932 work *The Prayer of the Gourd of Lono*, used my great-uncle extensively as a native source in his research on native Hawaiian navigation and based the following on information from him.

> Mr. Kupihea is a relative of the noted historian David Malo.
> Kupihea's great-grandfather, Holo wai (some people called him
> Holoaʻe, and some Ka wai holo), was konohiki nui o kiholo,

Kona, Hawaii, principal lord over the ahupua'a, the "land district" of Kiholo, Kona, Hawaii, and principal keeper of the temples under kings Kalani 'opu'u and Kamehameha I, providing all fish, pork, and dog for ceremonies. . . . Holo wai was [descended from] a high chief on the side of both father and mother. His father was Hiapo (Iapo in history) or 'I o ka po a i ka lani (his full name), who was Konohiki nui under King Kalani 'opu'u. He was the chief who stripped the bones of Captain Cook and returned the remains to the *Resolution*. The father of Hiapo was Kaleikini, who was also known (by the name Ahu kini) as a demigod. His mother was Akahi II or III, daughter of Akahi a kuleana, [a] wife of Liloa [and] mother of Umi a liloa.

With Umi a liloa's marriage to the Maui chieftess Pi'ikea in the sixteenth century, the Kumulipo and the lineage of Lono reenter the lineage of Ku and the ruling line of chiefs on Hawaii Island. David Malo, our earliest ancestral scholar, would record for all generations the affair of the king Liloa and his mistress of chieftess descent, Akahi a kuleana, in the traditions regarding the ancient kings of Hawaii nei as recounted in the book *Hawaiian Antiquities*.

The Birth of Umi

Umi was the son of Liloa, but not his first son. The name of his first son was Hakau, whom he begot by Pinea, the regular wife of Liloa. Hakau was considered a very high chief, because Pinea was of the same ali'i rank as Liloa, owing to the fact that Liloa's mother, Waiolea, was the elder sister of Pinea. Umi was the child of Liloa by a woman whom he seduced, named Akahi a kuleana. She has often been spoken of as a person of no ali'i blood, but the fact is that she was of the same ali'i line as Liloa himself. They were both descendants of Kanipahu, thirteenth-century king of Hawaii and Molokai Islands, who was himself a descendant of the eleventh-century king Hanala'a nui, elder brother of Hanala'a iki and ancestor of Pi'ikea (whose births appear in line 2,071 of the Kumulipo chant).

The genealogies of Akahi a kuleana and of Liloa, from Kanipahu, are as follows: Kanipahu first took as his wife Ala i kaua koko, as a result of which Kalapana, the ancestor of Liloa, was born. Afterward Kanipahu took as his wife Hualani, who gave birth to Kalahumoku, the ancestor of Akahi a kuleana. These two genealogies met in Umi, and here is the story of how he was born.

Liloa, the father of Umi, was at that time the king of all Hawaii and had fixed residence in the Waipi'o Valley when he made a journey through Hamakua toward the borders of Hilo to attend the consecration of the heiau of Manini. This heiau, which Liloa had been pushing forward to completion, was situated in the hamlet of Kohola lele, Hamakua. When the tabu had been removed, he waited for a while, till the period of refreshment *(hooma hanahana)* was over, and then moved on to the north of that place and stayed at Kaawikiwiki, where he gratified his fondness for *pahee* (dart throwing) and other games. While staying at this place he went to bathe in a little stream that runs through Hoea, a land adjoining Kealakaha. It was there and then that he came across Akahi a kuleana. She had come to the stream after her period of impurity and was bathing in preparation for the ceremony of purification, after which she would rejoin her husband, that being the custom among women at the time. Her servant was sitting on the bank of the stream, guarding her *pau* (wrap cloth).

When Liloa looked upon her and saw that she was a fine-looking woman, he conceived a passion for her, and taking hold of her, he said, "Lie with me." Recognizing that it was Liloa the king who asked her, she consented, and they lay together.

After the completion of the act, Liloa, perceiving that the woman was flowing, asked her if it was her time of impurity, to which she answered, "Yes, this is the continuation of it."

"Then you will probably have a child," said Liloa, and Akahi a kuleana answered that it was likely. Liloa then asked her whose she was and what was her name.

"I am Akahi a kuleana," said she, "and Kuleanakapiko is the name of my father."

"You are undoubtedly a relation of mine," said Liloa, and she agreed that it was quite possible.

Then Liloa instructed her regarding the child: "When our child is born, if it is a girl, name her from your side of the family; but if it is a boy, give to him the name Umi."

"By what token shall I be able to prove that the child is yours, the king's?"

Then Liloa gave into her hands his *malo* (loincloth), his *niho palaoa* (royal necklace; a whale tooth pendant hung from multiple strands of human hair), and his *laau palau* (club), saying, "These are the proofs of our child, and when he has grown up give these things to him." To this arrangement Akahi a kuleana gladly assented, and handed the things over to her maid to be taken care of for the child.

Liloa then made himself a substitute for a malo by knotting together some leaves with which he girded himself. On returning to the house, the people saw that he had a covering of ti leaf, which was not his proper malo, and they remarked to each other, "What a sight! Liloa is out of his head. That isn't his usual style; it's nothing but a ti leaf, makeshift for a malo." Liloa remained at this place until the hooma hanahana was over, then went back to Waipo´o, his permanent residence.

A short time after this, Akahi a kuleana found herself to be with child, the child Umi. Her husband, not knowing that Liloa was the true father of the child, supposed it to be his own. When the boy was born his mother gave him the name Umi as she had been bidden to do by Liloa at the time of his conception, and they fed and took care of him until he was grown to good size. The story is told that on one occasion when his foster father *(makua kolea)*, the husband of Akahi a kuleana, returning to the house after having been at work on his farm and finding that Umi had eaten all the food that had been prepared, gave the lad a beating.

Umi was regularly beaten this way every time it was found that he had consumed the last of the fish and poi or any other kind of food. This was the way Umi's foster father treated him at all times, because he in good faith took the boy to be his own son. But Umi and Akahi a kuleana were greatly disturbed at the treatment he received. Umi privily asked his mother, "Have I no other father but this one? Is he my only makua?"

"You have a father at Waipi´o," answered his mother, "and his name is Liloa." "Perhaps I had better go to him," said Umi.

"Yes, I think you had better go," said his mother.

After that, on a certain occasion when Umi had consumed the food and his foster father had given him a drubbing, Akahi a kuleana reasoned earnestly, "My husband, it is not your own son that you are beating all the time."

Then her husband flamed into passion and sarcastically asked, "Who, pray, is the father of this child of yours? Is it King Liloa?"

"Yes," she said, "Liloa is the father of my child."

"Where is the proof of the fact that this son to whom you, my wife, have given birth belongs to Liloa?" he demanded.

Then Akahi a kuleana called to her maidservant and ordered her to bring the things that Liloa had left for Umi. "You see now," she said, "who is the real father of the boy."

And the man was satisfied that he could not claim the paternity of the child. Some time later, Akahi a kuleana carefully instructed Umi as to his going to Waipi'o and Liloa.

She girded him with Liloa's malo, hung about the boy's neck the lei niho palaoa, and put into his hands the laau palau, after which she explained to Umi how he was to act.

"Go down into Waipi'o Valley," she said, "and when you have reached the foot of the *pali* [cliff], swim to the other side of the stream. You will see a house facing you; that is the residence of Liloa. Don't enter through the gate, but climb over the fence; nor must you enter the house in the usual way, but through the king's private door. If you see an old man and someone waving a *kahili* [a feathered standard representing royalty] over him, that is your father, Liloa; go up to him and sit down in his lap. When he asks who you are, tell him your name is Umi."

Umi assented to all his mother's instructions.

Akahi a kuleana ordered her brother, Omao kamau, to accompany Umi and to wait upon him. Omao kamau readily agreed to this and followed him as a servant. She also directed that Omao kamau take charge of the club that had been Liloa's. When all arrangements had been made, Umi and Omao kamau started off on their journey by themselves. On reaching Keahakea they came across a little boy named Pi'imaiwaa, who asked him where they were going.

"To Waipi'o," they replied. "I will adopt you as my boy, and you may go along with us," Umi added.

"Agreed," said the lad, and they proceeded in company.

On reaching Waipi'o, they descended into the valley by way of Koaekea, and coming to the foot of the pali, they all swam across the Wailoa stream. Gaining the other side, they saw before them the residence of Liloa at a place called Hau no ka maaa hala, with the entrance to the house facing them.

On nearing the house, Umi said to the others, "You two wait for me. I will go in to Liloa. If, in my going to him, I am killed, you must return by the way we came; but if I come back alive, we all shall live."

With these words, Umi left them. He climbed over the fence that surrounded the residence and entered the house by Liloa's private door, as his mother bade him do. When Liloa's officers standing guard saw that the lad had forfeited his life (laa) by climbing over the fence, which was a sacred and tabu thing, they chased after him to kill him. Then Umi ran up to Liloa and made as if he would sit down in his lap; but Liloa spread his thighs apart so that Umi sat down upon the ground. As he did so Liloa saw the lei niho palaoa on Umi's neck and his own malo about Umi's loins and asked, "What is your name? Are you Umi?"

"Yes," he answered, "I am Umi, your son."

Then Liloa took Umi upon his lap and embraced and kissed him and inquired of him, "Where is Akahi a kuleana?"

"It was she who directed me to come to you."

Then Liloa showed to the people the things that Umi had, saying, "This is my malo and my palaoa, but where is my club?"

"It is outside, in the hands of my companion," answered the boy.

Then Liloa sent for Omao kamau and Pi'imaiwaa. And he said to all his people, "When we went to consecrate the heiau you called me Crazy One because I wore a malo of ti leaf. But here is that malo of mine, and that niho palaoa, and my club. I left them for this one. He is my son Umi." Then all the people saw that Umi was the son of Liloa. The king then ordered his idols, that the ceremony of oki piko (cutting of the navel cord, reenacted here) might be performed on Umi, and it was done.

When Hakau, Liloa's first son, heard the sound of the drum, he asked what it meant and the people answered, "It is the drum at the oki piko of Liloa's newfound son, Umi."

On hearing that Liloa had a new son, Hakau was full of wrath, and he came to Liloa with the question, "Is this your son?"

To this Liloa assented and at the same time tried to placate Hakau, saying, "You will be king, and he will be your man. You will have authority over him."

With words like these Liloa tried to soften Hakau's anger toward Umi. Hakau was outwardly appeased, but there was a hypocritical reservation within him.

While Umi lived in the court of Liloa he gave the strictest obedience to his father's commands, and Liloa, on his part, took the greatest care of his son Umi. This was noticed by Hakau, and the very fact intensified the hatred he felt toward Umi, so that he always treated him with rudeness; and thus it was so long as Liloa lived. Hakau's anger and constant hectoring of Umi continued through Liloa's life and caused the king much pain and sadness.

When Liloa drew near to death he announced it as his will that Hakau inherit all the land, but that the idols and the house of the gods be given to Umi, to be under his care. The result was that Hakau acted very insultingly toward Umi and constantly abused and found fault with him, until finally it came to war between them and Hakau was killed by Umi. Umi a liloa (Umi, son of Liloa) then ruled in place of Hakau.

The Priesthood and Hereditary Duty

With Umi's marriage to the high chieftess Pi'ikea, daughter of Pi'ilani, ruling chief of Maui, two houses of the gods were under his care. The first was the priesthood order of *pa'ao*, whose visible symbols were the hereditary feathered idols of the gods Kuka'ilimoku, Kuho'one'enu'u, Kukeolo'ewa, and Kukalani'ehu, the hereditary gods of Liloa. The second was the priesthood order of *kuali'i*, meaning "Ku the chief," whose visible symbols were the hereditary idols of the gods Lonoika'ouali'i and Lonoikamakahiki.

Ka lei kini, "garland of the multitudes," was then appointed caretaker of the temples of Lonoika`ouali`i under the priestly order of kuali`i to serve the hereditary line of Umi, his brother-in-law. Ka lei kini was the descendant of Ahukini laa, the son of Laa mai kahiki, the legendary thirteenth-century chief of Oahu and Kauai. Laa mai kahiki had introduced image worship to the Hawaiian people in the shape of the feathered figure Lonoika`ouali`i, along with the coconut robe called Lanalana wa`a. Ka lei kini wore a garland of bird feathers about his head and neck and used an *auku`u* bird (a black-crowned night heron; it appears in line 353 of the Kumulipo chant, referred to as an `aumakua by the scholar Kamakau) for an ensign and flag of privilege. From then on Ka lei kini was called upon as the demigod Ahukini, because he was the holder of the sacred hereditary garland of Ahukini laa, and was a living altar of sacred genealogies.

Thus Ka lei kini followed the destiny that he had been consecrated at birth to perform. The priesthood was a hereditary office, descending from priestly lines: not one that could be chosen, but one that was entered only by birth heritage.

A Cloak of Black and White Feathers

Hiapo I ka po ai kalani (Hiapo—meaning "firstborn son"—was a hereditary name that was often given to the first offspring of one who was believed to have been an `aumakua god, as was the deified Ahukini o kalani) followed then in the hereditary duties as the keeper of the god Lonoikaouali`i. In this position he served under the hereditary line of Umi a liloa, from the reign of Keawe i ke kahi ali`i o ka moku to the reign of Kalani `opu`u. He now occupies a permanent part of Hawaii's history as the chief who returned to the *Resolution* the remains of the British explorer Captain James Cook after he was slain by the chiefs of Kalani `opu`u on February 14, 1879, at Ke ala ke kua (pathway of gods) Bay, Hawaii Island. Lieutenant James King aboard the *Resolution* left a written account of the details supplied by the Hawaiian chief "Eappo" (King's pronunciation of Hiapo):

> The skull and long bones were distributed among three chiefs including King Terreeoboo [King's pronunciation of Kalani

`opu´u] and the rest of the body burnt. The skull and long bones were later returned to Captain Clerke by Eappo, wrapped in a quantity of fine tapa cloth and covered with a spotted cloak of black and white feathers. In addition to the skull and long bones, the bundle contained the two hands which were recognized as those of Captain Cook by a deep scar between the thumb and forefinger of one hand. The hands had the flesh intact but cuts had been made in several places and were crammed with salt for preservation. Thence was the use of a cloak of black and white feathers a testament to the hereditary line of Hiapo i ka po a i kalani.

Thus Hiapo followed the destiny that he had been consecrated at birth to perform. The priesthood was a hereditary office, descending from priestly lines: not one that could be chosen, but one that was entered only by birth heritage.

The Passing of Hereditary Gods

Holowai, meaning "to flow as in a course of water," was consecrated as Lono hauoli mai kini nui a i mamao, which, like I ka po a i kalani, was a hereditary name given to one who was believed to have been the offspring of a first `aumakua. Holowai followed as the keeper of the god Lonoika-ouali´i, serving under the hereditary line of Umi a liloa, from Kalani `opu´u to the death of Kamehameha I, and to the death of the high chief Kekua o kalani (the chief of the gods). He occupies a permanent place in Hawaii's history as a chief who witnessed the passing of hereditary gods and the arrival of the adopted God of Christianity. Following are the details of this history.

While Kekua o kalani lived in the court of Kamehameha, he gave the strictest obedience to his uncle's commands, and Kamehameha, for his part, took the greatest care of his favorite nephew. This was noticed by his two queens—Kaahumanu, his favorite, and Keopuolani, mother of his son Liholiho—and intensified their hatred of Kekua o kalani so that they always treated him with rudeness. Thus it was, so long as Kamehameha lived, causing the king much pain and sadness. The prophet Ka pihi made the following prophecy to Kamahameha of the life of the kingdom that was to come: "There shall be a long malo [here, royal loincloth] reaching from Kuamoʻo to Holualoa. The islands shall come together, the *kapu* (religious laws) shall fall. The high shall be brought low, and the low shall rise to heaven."

In 1819, when Kamehameha I drew near to death, he announced it as his will that Liholiho, his son, should inherit the kingdom, but that the idols and the house of the gods should be given to Kekua o kalani, his favorite nephew. (These two, the kingdom and the gods, were considered of equal importance in ancient days, and previously Liloa had passed down one to each of his sons, but Umi later came into possession of both the kingdom and the house of the gods because Hakau failed to rule aright.) The result was that Kamehameha's two queens acted very insultingly toward the house of the ancient gods belonging to Kekua o kalani, and constantly abused and found fault with the system of kapu that was upheld by the house of the gods.

The kapu was a system of laws of a religious nature that regulated the privileges and prohibitions of the commoners and the aliʻi alike. The best known of these affecting all classes was the `ai kapu,* the one forbidding men and women to eat together. This kapu was broken by the queens the day after the death of Kamehameha on May 12, 1819, although its abolishment was not announced officially until five months later, by which time tables were being set in the European fashion at the residence of the king. On November 5, 1819, Kamehameha II (Liholiho) in the twenty-first year of his life and at the will of the self-proclaimed *kuhina nui* (queen regent or vice king) Kaahumanu issued orders that the eating kapu was officially abolished. This order also officially abolished all other kapu and temple worship. Liholiho then issued orders to destroy the heiau and burn the idols, and this was to be done from one end of the kingdom to the other.

When Kekua o kalani heard that the ruling chief, Liholiho, had been made to practice free eating, he was angry with Kaahumanu and with the whole family of chiefs for forcing this upon the young chief and ending the kapu of chiefs. To show his support for kapu eating, he left Kailua (the old capital of Hawaii) and sailed to Ka´awaloa and lived there, shunning free eating. He was joined by Kuaiwa and Holo a lena, soldiers of the kahuna lines of Ka uahi and Na hulu, and Holo wai, caretaker of the gods, who made the journey from Kiholo after worshiping at the ancient heiau of Mo´okini to preserve the ancient religions. These three said, "The ungodly chiefs of old who lost their lands never sinned like this!" and urged Kekua o kalani to take over the rule, for it was an ancient saying in Hawaii, "The chief who prays to the god, he is the chief who will hold the rule." Kekua o kalani, thus encouraged by the kahuna and orators, stood for kapu eating. Many of the commoners and chiefs, even those who had participated in free eating, and the brothers of Kaahumanu themselves wanted kapu eating. Few of the chiefs were in favor of free eating. Ke kua i pi´ia, the sister of Kaahumanu and foster mother of Kekua o kalani's father, was sent to get him to come to Kailua and preserve his kapu, but he refused.

Disorder arose; in the district of Hamakua one man took up arms against the government. A lesser chief named Lono akahi was sent by Liholiho to see what was going on, and in a scrimmage in Mahiki he and two of his men were killed. The king and his chiefs held a council of war to determine how they could send assistance to their men in Hamakua. Kalanimoku, commander-in-chief of the warriors under Liholiho, and one who had received baptism from a visiting Roman Catholic priest aboard a ship from France and had proclaimed himself pope over the islands, said, "There is no use sending men to Hamakua. The cause of the uprising is in Ka´awaloa in the person of Kekua o kalani. Hew down the trunk and the limb will wither." This brought about the Battle of Kuamo´o, in which Kekua o kalani, his wife, Manono, and all of his priests and followers were slaughtered.

Holo Deifies Christianity

Holo wai was fortunate enough to escape with his life. With the help of Ke kua i pi´ia he hid out in the countryside on the island of Maui, where he was called by the name Holo, meaning "to run; the running water." He returned to his beloved island of Hawaii only to die after the departure of the monarchy to Oahu. In the 1927 book *History of the Catholic Mission in the Hawaiian Islands,* Father Reginald Yzendoorn records the final account of Holo's life:

> In the early part of 1821, Liholiho and his chiefs removed to Honolulu. Mr. Loomis accompanied Kalanimoku. The missionary who had settled at Kailua also soon left his station. Previous to the King's removal, Mrs. Thurston had been insulted by a vile heathen priest, whilst her husband was occupied in his school. Instantly breaking away, she fled to her natural protector, who, "himself a host" was not slow in teaching the assailant a practical lesson in Christian morals. After the departure of the chiefs they did not feel secure on the Big Island and joined the brethren on Oahu. About this time Mr. Bingham [a Boston missionary] records the following: "About the middle of August, Holo, a chief of low rank, being ill, was visited by Mr. Loomis and Hopu, to whom he gave some evidence that he believed the truth and loved it. Hopu, at one time finding an English Bible, which, though unintelligible to the sick man, was lying on his bosom, asked him [Holo] the reason for it. He replied, 'I love Jehovah, and wish to be with Him.' This is the first recorded case of bibliopathy in the Sandwich Islands [Hawaii]."

Thus Holo followed the destiny that he had been consecrated at birth to perform. The priesthood was a hereditary office, descending from priestly lines: not one that could be chosen, but one that was entered only by birth heritage. Holo had a son through Heone, mother of Malo, to whom he bequeathed the name Nahupu.

The Arrival of the Adopted God

Nahupu (the silencing—*pu*—of the *nahulu* priesthood as a collective body) was born in south Kona, reared in the land of Kaulana at Ka´u, Hawaii, and educated in Lahaina, on the island of Maui, where he adopted the name of Joshua Malo. Contrary to popular historical belief, the Kupihea family traces the name Malo (loincloth) to a Spanish priest who, they say, arrived on a French vessel and baptized a few family members, giving them the Spanish name Malo (in Spanish, "one of those who has fallen from grace"). The immediate descendants of these baptized, in the light of Christianity, adopted the Hawaiian meaning of *malo*. Thus was the name Joshua Malo tied to the ancient cloth of the biblical Joshua, and David to the biblical David.

The Kupiheas recount that as old religious alliances were abandoned and new ones made, the family became a battleground. While Joshua Malo chose Catholicism, if only superficially, the hereditary line of practice still existed, though it had gone underground. David Malo, on the other hand, whose father, Aoao, had served as a warrior under Kalanimoku, allied himself with Queen Regent Kaahumanu, who supported the Protestant Boston Missionary Company's bid to become the sole Hawaiian church. Kaahumanu went so far as to persecute any Hawaiian who was found practicing Catholicism. Just as these two factions tore the Christian religion apart in Hawaii, so did they rend my family into two opposing clans: the Malos of Joshua and the Malos of David. Nahupu witnessed the kingdom ushering in a new religion, a Western base for learning, the deaths of the feudal generation and rulers of pre-Western contact, and the establishment of the monarchal heirs of post-contact Hawaii.

In 1832, eight years after the death of Liholiho, Kaahumanu died. However, her uncompromising devotion to Protestant Christianity continued till the death in 1839 of Kinau, one of the wives of Kamehameha II, who, as the succeeding kuhina nui, held joint rule with Kamehameha III. In July 1839 France interceded on behalf of Hawaiian Catholics, and, under threat of war, Kamehameha III granted permission to the Roman Catholics to share equal rights of worship with the Protestants. By May of the following year all persecutions of those who practiced Catholicism ceased and pardons were given. In the years that followed, the Great Mahele and the issue of landownership in the kingdom would overshadow everything, but for Nahupu the ending of the persecution of Catholicism stood above all else.

Ka Mahele

Ka Mahele, the great land division of 1848, is recorded in history as the most revolutionary and far-reaching legislation involving landownership ever enacted in Hawaii. It was instituted to give the descendants of the chief *konohiki* (lord over a land district or fisheries) who had served under the reign of Kamehameha I the title to the land that they claimed, and to satisfy the foreigners' demand for outright ownership of land. During the reign of Kamehameha I, the existing land system was essentially feudalistic in character. The land belonged to the conquering king, and under the powerful kuhina nui who reigned long after his death, the system was unquestionable. However, after the death of Kinau, in 1839, the Council of Chiefs became very powerful, and it was declared in the constitution of 1840 that though "all the land from one end of the islands to the other" belonged to the Kamehamehas, it was not their private property. It belonged to the chiefs and people in common, of whom the Kamehamehas were the head. Below the king the konohiki, who theoretically received his land from the king, was next on the feudal scale. Beneath the konohiki were the tenants. The lands apportioned to the landlords were commonly called konohiki lands, and those claimed by the king, crown lands.

During meetings held from late January to early March 1848, some 245 konohiki, of whom Nahupu was one, came forward to arrange and divide their lands with the king. A separate division, or *mahele*, was made by the king with the chief or konohiki who hereditarily ruled over a large tract called *ahupua'a*, a land division usually extending from the uplands to the sea, so called because the boundary was marked by a heap *(ahu)* of stones surmounted by an image of a pig *(pua'a)*, symbolically an altar to the god Lono. The division was then recorded in a book called the Mahele Book, in which appears the name of Joshua Malo, also called Jacob (or Nahupu), and the following transaction: relinquished one half of the ahupua'a of Kaulana, and received one half of the ahupua'a of Kaulana, (N.) Kona, Hawaii, Book 85–86 (90–91) of Na Mahele.

Thus Nahupu followed his destiny as a descendant of one who had been consecrated to perform the works of the gods of old, descending from priestly lines. He followed one of his choosing, not one that he entered by birth heritage. Nahupu had a son through Ku nui akea Makakau, of Lahaina, Maui, whose common ancestors were Liloa and Akahi a kuleana, and they gave him the name Kupihea.

The Gourd of Stars

Kupihea is a name synonymous with the ancient prophet Kekiopilo, *kaula* (seer) of Kupihea, (meaning "to translate or read the clamorous noises of the god Ku that reverberate from the darkness of clouds in the heavens"), who prophesied the coming of the white man. Nahupu's son Kupihea was born and reared in the ahupua'a of Kaulana at Ka'u, Hawaii, and was given the biblical name Samuel; he became the first of the hereditary line to be dedicated into Christianity at birth. Kupihea then became his surname, a name held in common by the family since. Samuel, also called Holowai, or Holo, was later removed from Ka'u, Hawaii, to Ka haka 'aulana, Oahu, by Kamehameha III, in the time of Nahupu, to perform the work of a *kilo hoku*, or "stargazer," for the head fisherman and konohiki, or "head of fisheries" for Kamehameha.

Ka haka 'aulana, or "the floating oracle," today called Sand Island in Kalihi Basin, Honolulu, once the beach residence of Kauikeaouli (King Kamehameha III), later became the house of the kingdom's head of fisheries. Major William Moe honua was the first konohiki under Kamehameha III, followed by He'u and an old man named Noa, who had charge of the fishing *ko'a* (shrine) on the Kona side under the kings Kamehameha IV and V. Noa was followed by Wai'ea (water of life) under the kings Lunaliho and Kalakaua. Wai'ea and his wife, maternal grandparents of David, also became the konohiki of the *limu* (seaweed) gardens of Ka ma'e (named for King Kalakaua's grandmother), and the keeper of the gourds of Lono, ancient navigational gourds that Wai'ea called *ipu hoolele waa* (gourd of stars) that exist only in stories today.

My great-uncle David Malo Kupihea said that when he was a young boy he saw these gourds many times at Ka haka 'aulana when he visited his grandfather Wai'ea, konohiki of all fisheries but especially of Ka haka 'aulana. The gourds themselves were of all styles and kinds. Small ones were placed on shelves within easy reach, while heavy ones were hung from three spears or poles serving as a tripod. Some were decorated with human teeth and set on a table, and some were placed in corners of the house on white cloth and were polished every day with dry *lau'ulu* (leaves of the breadfruit tree). The men at Ka haka 'aulana chanted about the gourds, with Wai'ea chanting alone and then, at certain times, all of them chanting together. His grandfather died when he was seven or eight years old, and was succeeded by Ka ili anu, who died around 1885. Following were Tom He'u and Lokana of the same family, both born in Moanalua. David said that he believed the gourds were taken away in Ka ili anu's time. And they haven't been seen since.

Holo, or Samuel, and the old men of the island used these navigation gourds for trips to Kuai he lani, which included Nihoa, Nector, and the islets beyond, such as Midway. They were gone on their trips for six months at a time, including the special sailing season of May to August. They fished for 'opelu and *aku*, attracting some back to Kona, Hawaii, and Kona, Oahu, through a *ku ula* (fish god) or *oahi*, which was a stone used to lure 'opelu. Thus fish were brought to the ko'a at Ka haka 'aulana. On such trips, one of the gourds was partly filled with water to catch the reflection of the stars when two sight holes on opposite sides were in line with the North Star, thus setting the "needle" of the Hawaiian compass. The reflections of other guiding stars and constellations, such as the morning and evening stars and the Dippers, would now be in correct position. The gourd was hung on the mast or elsewhere when not in use. In a single canoe it might be fastened to the covering piece over the bow *(kuapo'i)* by placing over it a calabash net with mesh about one-half-, three-quarter-, or one-inch wide and tacking down the extending cords around it. The man in the bow would then be the *kilo*, or observer who used the instrument. On a double canoe the extending cords of the inverted calabash net could be tacked down to the *pola,* or raised platform of light poles bound together between the mast and the steersman.

Thus Samuel followed his destiny as a descendant of one who had been consecrated to perform the works of the people of old, descending from priestly kilos: not one that could be chosen, but one that he entered only by birth heritage. Samuel had a son and a daughter through Melia Hipa, also known as Mele Kahilulu Kaai Kanaka, daughter of Wai´ea, whose common ancestor was Heone, mother of Nahupu (Joshua Malo), David Malo, and Henry Malo. The boy, born February 7, 1872, at Ka haka `aulana, was named David Malo Lono hauoli mai kini nui a i mamao Kupihea, and he was my great-uncle; the girl, born August 29, 1875, in Kalihi´uka, was named Kahili lukahi mo´i and was called Kahilulu after her mother, or simply Lulu, and she was my great-grandmother.

The Western Path

Kahili lukahi mo´i, meaning "to shed the feathers of the royal emblem," spent her childhood on the inlets and islands of Ka haka `aulana and the adjacent Moku o`e`o, in an era of rapid change. As Hawaii distanced itself from past and ancient bloodlines, Western ways displaced old traditions. Her brother David once recalled to Theodore Kelsey the dim remnants of ancient Hawaii that surrounded the first ten years of their lives, only to disappear, like the gourds of Lono, within the following decade.

As David and Lulu entered the second decade of their lives, the 1880s, the islands continued to become more and more Westernized. The king, David Kalakaua, was the second to be elected by the Hawaiian people. His opponent, Queen Emma, wife of the late King Kamehameha V, was already of part-English descent. A descendant of the Kumulipo´s Kalani nui I i mamao through Kapaihi a ahu, Kalakaua was known as the Merry Monarch because of his love for music and the hula. He was also a scholar who ordered the ancient Kumulipo chant to be transcribed and preserved in Hawaii's brand-new written language. American, European, and Chinese sons-in-law were also becoming very common, as wave after wave of immigrants flooded the islands. Among these new settlers was the Blackstad/Andreas family from Oslo, Norway.

A kinsman of the Blackstads' named Valdemar Knudsen had first arrived on the neighboring island of Kauai in 1852, and over the years had made his fortune raising longhorn cattle on a ranch he leased from the Kingdom of Hawaii. As was customary for successful immigrants of the time, Knudsen looked outside Hawaii to his homeland when he needed help running his enterprise, and in 1880 he summoned his twenty-six-year-old kinsman

Martin Olaus Blackstad to join him. Martin made the six-month journey along with his wife, Maren Christine; son Theodore; daughter Anna Gurine Marie; and in-laws Balser and Inge Margarette. Upon arriving in Koloa aboard the *Windjammer* in the spring of 1881, the Blackstad family was taken by horse and carriage to the Knudsen ranch at Wahiawa, just outside the little town of Kekaha, on the western side of the island above Mana Flats. Here they would settle, having five more children in this new land. Their last child, born January 12, 1889, was christened Lena Katarine (Katherine) Blackstad.

As the 1880s progressed, the Blackstad family learned to master a land that was foreign to them, while the Kupihea family, in their native island home, were being mastered by foreigners. Both Kupihea children were educated in the English language by Soren McQuibbert, who had married their paternal grandmother, Ku nui akea, after the death of Nahupu.

David, thereafter under the guardianship of James Mea, who was the first Hawaiian bandmaster of what later became the Royal Hawaiian Band of Iolani Palace, attended the Royal School, originally the School for Young Chiefs founded in 1839. Later he attended the Punahou School, where he would first become associated with Joseph M. Poepoe, an expert on ancient Polynesian genealogies who later wrote the text he called *Kamokuiki's Genealogy of the Kumulipo* and acted as an informant to the scholar Rivers in his early works on Melanesian society. Lulu was sent to St. Andrew's Priory School for Girls, founded in 1867 by the dowager Queen Emma, who was also responsible for the establishment of the Episcopal or English Catholic Church in Hawaii.

January 1, 1890, ushered in a decade that would forever change Hawaii and the hereditary line of the Kupiheas. David was afforded the opportunity to attend Yale University, and after a brief stint there decided to tour Europe instead, following Robert W. Wilcox, a descendant of the Kamehamehas. He would later became Hawaii's first delegate to the U. S. Congress (1901–1902). Upon returning to Hawaii, David was appointed konohiki of Ka haka `aulana, Moku`e`o, and the remains of what were once the Royal Fisheries by King David Kalakaua. Occupying the house of Wai´ea, the house of his birth and the beach house of former kings, he would remain there for the rest of his life.

In 1891, shortly after David's return to Ka haka ʻaulana, the king died. Two years later, in 1893, conspirators seeking to annex Hawaii to the United States succeeded in overthrowing Kalakaua's successor and sister, Queen Liliuokalani, bringing home rule to an end. In the same year, Lulu became a part of the first senior class to graduate from St. Andrew's Priory, and, after a lengthy illness, married Charles Samuel Huston Johnson, an immigrant who had arrived aboard the USS *Oceanic* from San Francisco, California, in the 1880s to work on the Oahu Railroad. Lulu and Charles had four children. The oldest, Catherine, was also given the name Mahina Oʻhoku Malamalama—meaning "the glowing light of knowledge," or referring to the moon at its brightest when it seems to have a huge halo around it—by the elderly Tutu Mu, one of the last remaining wahine kahuna of the period.

In the meantime, on the neighboring island of Kauai, the Blackstad family had founded a ranch of their own, and purchased a homestead at Waiahole in the Waimea Valley, just above the present-day location of the Menehune Ditch. By the century's end, because of the constant flooding of the Waimea River, they were forced to sell their homestead and move closer to town. The new residence would be the family's home for generations to come. The house, originally built by the Reverend Rowell (1843–1865), came with two parcels of land. One was known as Namahana, meaning "the two or twin branches," as in the twin stars, Pollux and Castor, called respectively Na mahoe mua (to travel ahead) and Na mahoe hope (to travel behind). The other parcel, Papalekoa, was the site of an ancient fishing shrine.

January 1, 1890, ushered in the time period of two branches since the mating of those who possessed ancestors in common all but ceased. On Oahu David Malo Kupihea was elected in 1901 as a representative in the Territorial Legislature, a position he held until 1915. In the meantime, on Kauai, Lena Katherine Blackstad married Frank L. Wilson in 1906. Originally from Kentucky, Frank was a member of the U.S. Army, and when World War I broke out, he was part of a squadron deployed to Waimea to prevent uprisings by German immigrants still loyal to the Fatherland. Lena, who now went by the name Lena K. B. Wilson, had only one child by her husband, though she would have six more out of wedlock. Her third son, whom she named Martin Olaus Wilson in honor of her father, was born on June 12, 1912. His father was Clem Gomes, who would later become a senator representing the island of Kauai in the Territorial Legislature.

On Oahu in 1914, the first Kupihea to marry a Caucasian was about to become a grandmother. Kahili lukahi mo´i's daughter, Catherine, married Ernest Wilson (no relation to Frank) earlier that year, and by year's end had delivered him a son. Marrying a man named Wilson was just one of several coincidental similarities Catherine shared with Lena Blackstad. Like Lena's husband Frank, Catherine's Ernest was a member of the U.S. Army. Like Lena, Catherine would have seven children, of which only the first would be fathered by her husband. On March 26, 1925, Catherine died while giving birth to her last child, a girl named Catherine Mahina O´hoku Malamalama in her honor. Little Catherine was raised by her grandmother Lukahi among the remains of the old royal fishponds in Ke´ehi Lagoon, spending her childhood wading the shallow inlets between Ka haka `aulana and Moku`e`o Islands under the watchful eyes of David Malo Kupihea, who continued to reside on the island.

While Catherine M. Wilson was being taught the traditions of her Hawaiian ancestors by her grandmother at Ke´ehi Lagoon, Martin Olaus Wilson was learning the traditions of his Norwegian ancestors from his grandfather on the island of Kauai. When war broke out with Japan in 1941, both Martin and Catherine ended up at the Kaneohe Naval Air Station on Windward, Oahu, where Martin managed the commissary and Catherine prepared meals for aircraft crews flying missions into the Pacific. Here, Martin and Catherine fell in love. They were married in 1945, after the surrender of Japan to the United States. Between 1945 and 1949 they had three children: Leslie, Lanis Gaye, and Martin Jr. In 1949 they moved to the old Blackstad estate at Waimea, on the island of Kauai, where Martin was born and reared. By coincidence, they resided in an old rooming house that was situated upon the parcel of land known as Papalekoa, the site of an ancient fishing shrine.

On November 5, 1950, Martin and Catherine had a son. They named the boy Herman Alexander Wilson in honor of an uncle who had been named after a Father Herman, an early Catholic priest of the district. The old Waimea Hospital in which Herman was born was built on the grounds of what had once been the site of Keali'i Heiau (the temple of fair chiefs), an ancient temple dedicated to the god Lono and the first heiau visited by Captain Cook in 1778, resulting in his being mistaken for the god Lono. Herman's first visitor was William Kapahu kani o lono Goodwin, an old man whose Hawaiian name means "the sounds of the drums of the god Lono." He arrived carrying a large bundle of red roses just as Herman was born.

Herman was raised in the land of Namahana and Papalekoa in Waimea. He was dedicated in the old Hawaiian church built by George Rowell in 1872. Not long after he was born, his mother had a visitor from Honolulu. This visitor, a second cousin, was the oldest grandson of David Malo Kupihea. John Kaena Tremane Sr., whose Hawaiian name means "to glorify," was an ordained minister of the Congregational church of Hawaii, the Church of Kaahumanu. Upon setting eyes on Herman, he turned to Catherine and said, "This is not the image of a Herman. His name shall be Moke." The name Moke is a variation of the Hawaiian word *moki*, which means "to shoot forth." It is a name the early creators of Hawaii's written language used to refer to the biblical Moses, which in Hebrew means "to take out, remove, or extract."

I would be known as Moke from that day on, and I am destined to shoot forth, to proclaim what is ancient or past.

Ao ho'i'ho'i (Return to Light)

So now you know the stepping-stones along my ancestral pathway. These are just a few of the men and women who exist in my inner world of thoughts, and as the spiritual remnants of past lives they serve to guide my way into the world of ao `aumakua. With the acknowledgment of their existence, I will take you on the journey of my self-realization, and as I retrace my encounter with this inner world, it is my hope that you will be led to the entrance of your own hereditary existence. At the beginning of the rest of the story, I hear again the voice of the `aumakua:

First light for us in him would begin at an early age because of two things: First, our descendants are aware of their priestly heritage, and second, the traits necessary for our descent into his body of light are already in place, legacies inherited from those who came before. This boy is destined to enter our ancestral consciousness. His mother was raised within grasp of these hereditary forms of expression, but the thoughts were dormant within her. The physical appearance of her child reawoke in her memory the words once spoken by those who reared her, and the memory of their image reopened a pathway within her that allowed her to pass down her ancestral chain to her son. The word `aumakua *was mentioned to him at an early age, allowing us the opportunity to stir his inner senses of past realms and to plant the seed of acknowledgment. Our beginning would have to be his, and with us in place, he would look out into the modern world and see an ancient one.*

CHAPTER THREE

THE EYES OF THE `AUMAKUA

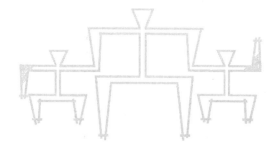

FOR A YOUNG CHILD, the sense of sight is powerful. Through his eyes he studies and takes in the faces of those around him—the lips frowning or smiling, the eyebrows raised, the eyes angry or laughing. And he takes in the sights of home—the walls he can touch, the floors he stands on, the colors, the light. And the world around him—the earth, the paths, the waters, rocks, and sky—he takes all of it in through his eyes. His ancestors are alive in all of it, in all the places where they have walked and talked and thought. In making the world around him part of his memory, he takes in the light of his ancestors.

When I recollect the first five years of my life, I imagine myself looking very much like Mowgli, the native Indian boy of Rudyard Kipling's 1894 classic, *The Jungle Book*. My thick curly brown hair, large brown eyes, and Polynesian complexion made me an acceptable novelty in my family—I recall many blue eyes peering at me from beneath braided blond hair. Even my closest kin, including my brothers and sister, mirrored in appearance and traits their Norwegian ancestors. There existed only one pair of brown eyes in which my image was truly reflected: the eyes of my mother. My immediate family called me Moke Boy, the town merchants and teens called me Curly Q, but to my mother's circle of friends I was known as Kanaka Boy, "little Hawaiian man."

Seeing with the Eyes of the ʻAumakua

The house we lived in was situated upon the parcel of land known as Papalekoa, just a few hundred feet below the site of my birth. A dilapidated wooden structure of three rooms in a row connected by a partially screened-in wooden corridor, the building was the remnant of a rooming house built by my great-grandfather, M. O. Blackstad, in the days when the old Waimea Landing still served as a port of call for the island. Just eighty feet away into the valley, like a mission post outside of our little village, stood the Blackstad house, a memorial clinging to the past. From its faded Victorian ornamentation to its cracked and peeling paint, everything about the house pointed toward better days. I haven't been there since I was nine years old, but my visions of that house are so strong that I can close my eyes even now and see it clearly. It sits on six-foot stilts in anticipation of the regular flooding of the Waimea River. Wide wooden steps rise from the ground to the spacious porch, which extends eight feet from the house and runs its entire length. A row of light green columns faces our old house and the ocean to the south, and connecting each column is a railing, the balusters of which are made to resemble flower vases.

After years of family feuds, the estate had come into the sole possession of old man Blackstad's youngest daughter, my grandmother Lena K. B. Wilson. She was a year younger than the elder William Kapahu kani o lono Goodwin, my first visitor at birth, and had been his childhood playmate and lifelong friend. She seemed to accept me with open arms and heart, and my life in the beginning was divided between my grandmother's sense of joy and my mother's instinct of love. However, my auntie Frieda, who lived there with her illegitimate son, was always lurking out of sight and earshot of my grandmother to remind me never to enter the house or yard. I was not to trespass into the light of her mother's eyes, or into the house, or upon the grounds.

On Sundays the surviving members of the Blackstad clan's second generation were always sure to attend the services at the Waimea Foreign Church, which was more a weekly social event than it was spiritual worship for the Caucasian community that lived in the district of Waimea. It was also a sure thing for the clan to undertake their Sunday automobile ride—with everyone still dressed in his or her glorious Sunday best—to the south shore of the island, to dine with the Christian family. The clan would be gone for the entire afternoon, not returning until sunset. My grandmother's house would lie temporarily dormant, inhabited only by voices of the past. Unknown to all, the house was often visited by a child with a pair of big brown eyes that glowed beneath golden brown curls. In the emptiness of such Sunday afternoons he entered into its solemn spaces through a broken screen door.

Thus began my habit of disappearing, only to reappear in a world where remnants of the past lay temporarily unseen and unheard by the people of the present. I would wander through it, calling on its voices, creating images of it within myself.

As I close my eyes today and turn away from the outer world, an inner eye begins to open and I see my own past stretching out and winding through memory like the solitary paths I used to walk as a boy in Waimea. I have a memory of two worlds, and of two ways of existing in the world: one that leaned toward embracing life with arms wide open and one that leaned toward isolating oneself from the complications of life by hiding in stuffy rooms of bygone eras. Both are my heritage and each has helped to awaken the `aumakua within me in different ways.

I reappear on my grandmother's broad front porch. The main entrance to her house is through a large French door, which is covered by an old homemade screen door to keep out bugs, but the screen is torn in the corners. Surrounding the door on either side is a double-hung window of six nine-by-twelve-inch panes. Each of these panes has a thick gray halo, the result of lead leaching in from the corners of the aged glass.

The French door opens to the parlor, a room twenty feet by twenty feet with a twelve-foot-high ceiling. Wainscoting of one-by-two-inch tongue-and-groove Douglas fir painted light green rises to a height of about four feet, where it is separated from the now faded vine-patterned wallpaper by a crown molding. Another crown molding meets the wallpaper at the ceiling. All the furniture in the parlor is lined against the walls, leaving the center of the room open, like a dance floor. The linoleum, which as always is well mopped and waxed, is of a grayish color imprinted with a white grape-leaf design. The dark green wicker chairs and love seats against the walls are covered with homemade pillows and pieces of crochet. There are also wicker tables with marble and little wooden lamp tables with carved legs. Sitting on the wicker tables are beautiful kerosene lamps with etched-glass chimneys and brass and porcelain bases. There are also displays of ancient Hawaiian calabashes made from milo wood, as well as numerous Hawaiian stones, poi pounders, salt pounders, and medicine bowls and pounders. Pushed into the corners are small tables holding the clocks my great-grandfather brought with him from Norway. These clocks are fairly large (about twenty inches tall) and quite decorative, with gabled roofs and etched-glass doors. They are also loud. The noisy click of the pendulum paces every conversation, and when the chimes sound, conversation stops.

My most vivid memory of this room is of standing in its middle, my eyes closed and my arms outstretched, spinning around and around and then coming to a stop, opening my eyes, and discovering which of my relatives' portraits would meet my gaze. It didn't matter which direction I ended up facing, for each wall was hung with photos in dark, wooden frames. Most of these were old, and the chemicals used to produce them had reacted to time in different ways. As I see them now in my mind's eye, some are eerily white and ghostlike from the heavy concentration of silver in the developing bath. Others have oxidized into a sepia tone. Still others have a blue-gray cast. On one wall there is a picture of my grandmother and her brothers and sisters, taken when they were young. Nearby hangs a portrait of my great-grandparents taken in their native country of Norway. There are even portraits of my great-great-grandparents. Though most of the photos are of relatives, there are also pictures that speak of my family's strong allegiance to the United States and their respect for the great figures of their times. Portraits of Franklin Delano Roosevelt, William Howard Taft, Woodrow Wilson, and Theodore Roosevelt seem oddly at home in the company of my Scandinavian relatives.

The most amazing thing about all of these portraits is that there is not one smiling face among them. Even the Merry Monarch, King David Kalakaua, whose portrait hangs over the corridor entrance to the dining room, wears a stern face. The serious expressions on all of those in these portraits create an eerie mood in the room. The eyes behind the dour faces seem to follow you, as if their spirits still dwell here.

The only time the parlor was used was when my grandmother had guests—usually family members or friends of her own age. I remember how, sitting in the presence of all the portraits, they would naturally start to reminisce about the individuals displayed. Sometimes the pictures would take them back to the days of their youth; sometimes much farther, leading them into discussions of the family's genealogy. As little as I was, it seemed that I knew personally each individual in these pictures. I knew where they came from, how they arrived, for whom they worked, where they lived, how they died, and where they were buried. I knew their successes and their failures, their virtues and their vices. I also knew their dark, personal secrets, for the extramarital affairs and illegitimate children of the people in these portraits were also part of the conversations.

One of the oddest things about the parlor discussions was that often the people recalling the intricate details of the lives of those pictured looked remarkably similar to their forebears. Although I was too young to fully understand what an ancestor was, I do remember having some vague appreciation for the fact that the natural feelings of trust and belonging that I associated with my mother and grandmother somehow extended to the people in these images. And just as some of the people who sat in this room looked like those pictured on the walls, so did it seem that this family resemblance should stretch beyond even the oldest portrait, so that when my grandmother and her friends discussed relatives who had lived and died in much earlier times, I had only to find their counterparts on the wall to be able to see their faces. I now believe that this natural familiarity with my ancestors derives from the existence of the `aumakua within me, but back then I did not yet know what the word meant. Though my grandmother would not have approved of talk of the `aumakua, her ancestral family was very much a part of her household. It had been there so long it was as if it had been built into the walls. Its voice could be heard in the stories told in the parlor, and its heartbeat in the ticking of my great-grandfather's many clocks. It was what comforted me when I wrapped myself in hundred-year-old quilts and sat on furniture that had been passed down for generations. It would take many years to appreciate what all this meant, but even back then, when I would open my eyes after spinning around and around and the first thing I'd see would be the familiar faces hanging on the wall, I felt secure. It was as if all those faces were there to remind me that I would never be alone in this world.

Now that I'm old enough to leave the parlor and its portraits behind, I've come to realize that it never was the photographs that gave me the comfort. They were material things that would, in time, disintegrate and disappear. No, what comforted me was my own `aumakua, which stirred in response to the genealogical cues of this house and these portraits, as if awakened by the knowledge that the past was so welcome here that both the living and the dead seemed to share the same rooms.

Looking toward the west wall of the parlor, I see the door leading to my auntie Frieda's room. We were never allowed to enter this room, and it always seemed very mysterious to me. The wooden door is made with a screen inset in the top half, where a curtain was hung for privacy. Sometimes this curtain would have a slight opening on one side, and I would peek into the room and be able to see the wooden furniture inside, all of it covered with pieces of crochet. The large bed is also covered with crochet, as well as with several of the quilts my grandmother used to make. Everything about the room is old and dark, including the oil-stained dresser and carved bed. This room was where my great-grandfather died, and I remember my grandmother talking about how, days after his funeral, he could still be heard rummaging around inside. She said they could hear him sometimes, late at night, walking through the parlor and onto the porch. This would be followed by the rhythmic groan of his old rocker and the smell of his pipe tobacco drifting in through the screen door.

On the east wall of the parlor, another door leads to a smaller room where everything is plain and simple, including the faded, washed-out furniture. This was my older cousin Melvin's room. It was also the room in which my uncle Frank died of convulsions in 1917, when he was only eleven years old. According to the stories my father used to tell, Frank had fibbed to his grandfather about something another one of his brothers had done, and this brother became angry and beat Frank pretty badly. Not long afterward, Frank had an attack and died. The brother who beat him was so shamed he was shipped out on a steamer by his grandfather to serve as a cabin boy. He was only fifteen when he left, and he did not return to Hawaii for fifty-six years.

From the center of the parlor's north wall, facing the mountains, a long corridor about twenty feet in length leads to the dining room. As I step into this corridor, I hear my grandmother's voice admonishing me not to run, and I remember the clatter I would make when I ignored her and ran anyway. Looking at this hallway now, it occurs to me how peculiar it is. It was built by my great-grandfather to connect the parlor with the dining room, which, as in most traditional Hawaiian homes, was originally separate from the main house. For some reason the corridor was never painted, leaving it with a raw, unfinished look. Perhaps it didn't make sense to my grandfather to waste paint on a room that was always so dark. The only light filtering in to illuminate the one-by-six-inch tongue-and-groove boards that line floor, wall, and ceiling comes from a window in the east wall at the end of the corridor, just before the entrance to the dining room, where the house brightens.

Just after entering the corridor from the parlor, a door on the right leads to my grandmother's cozy little room, where as a child I often snuggled up beside her for the night. There is barely enough space for her large hand-carved bed and dresser. The bed is covered with embroidered pillows, thick colorful quilts, and crochet pieces, all made by her own hands. Hanging from the dresser's mirror are numerous pieces of jewelry—chains and brooches as well as various leis made of shell, *kukui* nut, glass beads, and glass. The top of her dresser is also piled with old jewelry boxes and ornaments, many of which have been passed down for generations. It was in this room that my grandmother gave birth to all of her children, and rumor has it that hidden somewhere within it is a pouch of uncut diamonds that my great-grandfather brought with him from Norway.

Directly across the corridor from my grandmother's room another door opens into a storage room. As a boy I must have explored every box in here, and there were a lot of them. The room is so full of the packaged-up belongings of every person who ever lived in the house that its contents spill out into the hall in boxes stacked on either side of the door. In this room I would wind up the old crank-style phonograph that sits on a wooden stand and play records from a large collection of 78 R.P.M. recordings from the early 1900s to the 1940s. Alongside the phonograph is an old wooden Zenith stand-up radio that resembles a jukebox in size and shape. There are also boxes of clothing; an assortment of memorabilia from World Wars I and II, including helmets, uniforms, and even gas masks; and a collection of old rifles. I remember one in particular: a long black-powder rifle called a rice gun that was said to have been used by the early Chinese to ward off birds from their rice fields. When I was a boy the main attraction of the room was the box of toys saved from my father's childhood, toys such as cars made from empty cigar boxes, with empty thread spools for wheels. And of course there are the toys that my auntie Frieda reserved for only her son Melvin: a miniature farm set, complete with a barn, animals, tractors, and a fence, all made of tin; and a very large collection of wooden Tinker Toys. On my Sunday visits I would play with these forbidden toys for hours.

At the end of the dark unfinished corridor sits the dining room. Well lit by windows in its east and west walls, the dining room looks much like the parlor, except that it is larger, approximately thirty feet long by twenty feet wide, and the floor, which has obviously been repaired many times, is bare wood rather than linoleum. The middle of the room is dominated by a large handmade dining table with chairs that seem to have come from several different dinette sets. The most noticeable thing about this room is its unintentional resemblance to a turn-of-the-century Hawaiian tavern, thanks to Antoinette Ashe, my grandmother's sister.

Antoinette and her husband used to own and operate the Waimea Saloon during the 1890s, and when Antoinette closed its doors in 1902 to move to the mainland United States, she left its contents here. Framed liquor and beer signs occupy every space on the wall, as though mimicking the portraits in the parlor. Today these advertisements are made mostly with neon lights on a reflective background, but back then they were painted on tin and made to resemble large oil paintings, complete with heavy frames. There are stately portraits depicting bottles of Bohemia beer,

New beer, Budweiser lager, and Blue Ribbon beer. The most memorable one is a large portrait of a lion promoting Burghermeister beer. A painting of two spotted hound dogs promotes Black and White whiskey and black and white Scottie dogs promote scotch. A painted likeness, molded in tin, of a pack of Chesterfield cigarettes holds a thermometer. There are also several saloon chairs pushed against the walls. On the north wall, next to the door leading to the kitchen, is a four-foot-high locked wooden cabinet, which used to be the liquor cabinet at the Waimea Saloon. Inside are my grandmother's antique china, silverware, and lace tablecloths, and on its top is an extensive collection of decorative beer mugs of nineteenth-century European origin. It was in this room that my grandmother spent most of her time sewing, crocheting, and reading. The dinners she served here were always very formal, with starched white tablecloths and porcelain dishes and real silver that she inherited from her parents. As in the parlor, conversation seemed directed by the wall decorations, as if my grandmother and her friends were seated not in her dining room but at the old Waimea Saloon.

A strange thing that I would not realize until many years later was that my mother was never present at any of these gatherings. In fact, she never even entered this house. I eventually would learn that this was because she was Hawaiian. Although my grandmother had spent her entire life on the island, she still regarded Hawaiians as beneath her. Even her lifelong friend William Goodwin never went beyond her front porch during his visits, while my auntie Frieda stood pouting out of sight in the parlor. I would later realize that this was because William Goodwin, like my mother, was Hawaiian. When I found this out at about nine years of age, I promised myself I would never return to this house again, and I haven't until now, and now only in memory.

Before leaving the house and its memories for the last time, I would like to take a final look around my grandmother's kitchen. Entering through the door at the end of the dining room, I see a room about ten feet long and twelve feet wide. Like the corridor, it was built by my great-grandfather and left unpainted. At the north wall, beneath a window that looks out on the base of a fifty-foot cliff upon which once stood the ancient temple of Keali´i, there is an old wooden table with two homemade benches. Like the room, they are unpainted. The only light fixture is a bare bulb hanging from the ceiling, its pull cord dangling above the table. My grandmother's hearty meals were cooked on the old-fashioned kerosene stove that sits against the opposite wall beside the dining room door. The big metal box sitting on the floor next to it is the oven, which is completely separate and placed atop the burners only for roasting or baking. It was in this oven that my grandmother made the bread she was so proud of. It came from an old Scandinavian recipe and would keep for months without spoiling or molding. When baking the bread she would always add a few sardine cans for baking pans, so that we children would have our own special loaves. I spent many an afternoon sitting on one of the benches, watching the flames flicker through the oven's tinted cellophane windows as the aroma of home-baked bread filled the room.

Passing through a door located in the west wall, I enter a small room, really little more than a shed with a corrugated metal roof. On the east wall, jutting out a few feet beyond the end of the kitchen, there is a little sliding window, a double-hung installed sideways rather than up and down to accommodate the kitchen sink below it. The sink is set in a rough wooden frame made of cast iron coated with what once was white porcelain. The drain boards on either side are covered with tin. On the west wall there are exposed nails for hanging pots and pans, and everywhere there are cats. When I was young, twenty-one cats called this room home, and I can't picture the room without them.

Of course, the cats are gone now. All of it is gone, actually. The house was torn down in 1968, shortly after my grandmother's death. Some would say it no longer exists. Others might argue that it requires only a living memory to come to life. If, while traveling with me through my grandmother's house, you found yourself traveling back to your own places long gone, then you have experienced how something that no longer exists in space can still exist within the mind. And if this memory caused you to reflect on your own childhood, then you are beginning to see through the eyes of your most immediate na `aumakua.

My solitary journeys years ago through my grandmother's house on Sunday afternoons were the journeys of one who is different. Unlike a child who is naturally accepted to dwell comfortably within a family circle,

I was placed outside of it to watch life's spinning. Only through the eyes of heredity can one recognize the turning motions of the circle from this view, the spiraling of time through generations. Long ago, to see through the eyes of the `aumakua was a natural occurrence. Each family circle prepared children by teaching them their genealogy at an early age, placing their ancestors among the living and not the dead. It was believed that if the eyes of one's `aumakua were not opened early enough, they would never open at all, and so part of every child's education, though taught more stringently among the priestly and chiefly class, involved being taught how to establish the *aha* cord in order to connect with his or her ancestral lines.

The aha (a meeting or gathering point) is the remnant of the umbilical cord, the cord of life, like the knotted cord that preserved the genealogies of the ancient Kumulipo chant; and the *piko* (the knotted navel) is a knot on the cord of life that preserves its present link. The aha is important because the `aumakua is the living link of family immortality. Unlike the Christian, who refers to his ancestors as being dead and lights candles to entreat an external God to look after their souls, the Kupihea line has believed that the spiritual component of one's ancestors, called the `aumakua, exists within all those with a direct biological connection. By outwardly acknowledging an ancestor, by entreating it with food and gifts, this indwelling `aumakua can contact the balance of the departed's ancestral spirit line. It's an extension, really, of the way in which the spirit of my grandmother's house still dwells within me. Just as I can turn within and walk through a house that was demolished in 1968, so can I travel among ancestors who lived hundreds or even thousands of years ago. Of course, you can't converse with a house, but images such as the house create the state of memory that you must enter into in order to see, with the eyes of the `aumakua, the ancestor you seek. Once in this inner world, you can interact with this relative regardless of when he or she actually walked the earth.

The whole point of heredity is that we owe our lives and our bodies to those who have gone before us. Without them, we wouldn't exist. The `aumakua belief pulls this truth around so that its tail faces its head and says that to exist after death, we are equally dependent on our progeny—for the spirit, it seems, has a genetic component and cannot survive without it. It has been said that the body is the temple of the spirit; the belief of the ancient Kupihea line accepts this truth in its most literal interpretation.

Although traditional Hawaiian spirituality had no place in my grandmother's house, the house itself—indeed, the whole environment, including my grandmother's preoccupation with family heirlooms and history—instilled in me exactly the kind of genealogical understanding and vision that would, in time, allow me finally and forever to open the eyes of the `aumakua that had always existed within me. This vision and understanding would begin to develop fully not in my grandmother's house but in the company of my mother.

Maha and the Huki lau

By the time I was five years of age, we had moved from my grandmother's estate at the mouth of the Waimea Valley to an old house just a few hundred feet away. This house adjoined the land of Pana´ ewa, meaning "a place to wander in time," where the Waimea River flows into the ocean and the site where Captain James Cook first stepped ashore in Hawaii. The house had formerly served as a mission school and as church parsonage for the old Waimea Chinese-Hawaiian Church, an affiliate of the Waimea Hawaiian Church. It was still active when we lived there and Sunday services, along with periodic funerals, were held just fifty feet from our front door. Over time it seemed we had witnessed the passing of the church's few remaining members, and the structure was later torn down, leaving only the slowly disappearing markers to the many grave sites that surrounded our old house. These eventually became patches of native shrubs surrounded by small stones that were planted and laid in place by my mother.

Here, among what seemed to be remnants of a Hawaii long past, my mother lived in a world of Hawaiian history that had its foundations in the geography of her native land and genealogies of its people. Among the many differences between my mother and my grandmother was the fact that my mother's house was rarely the center of her life. She had no memories of a foreign land to isolate within a house's walls. Like most Hawaiians of her day, my mother's life was lived outside the house—in the yard raising native plants, many of which were medicinal herbs; at the river; in the valleys and uplands; and along the beaches—all the time interacting with both nature and the people who descended from it. Sometimes it seemed as though the entire island of Kauai was her home, and in essence it truly was: she possessed at least some knowledge of the history of every Hawaiian family on the island. My most memorable moments of early life at our new home are of my mother packing up a few belongings for a one-day outing that sometimes turned into three because we often followed the local fishermen as they, in turn, followed the seasonal schools of fish that continually moved around the island.

One of my mother's neighbors, a man by the name of Maha Leoiki, was renowned for his skill at harvesting these fish. (Interestingly, *maha*, meaning "temple" or "the side of the head," also refers to the gill plate of a fish.) He followed them around the island, moving on as the fish left one inlet for another, conducting at each location a fishing ritual known as a *huki lau*, which my mother was often invited to take part in when she traveled with him.

Huki lau is a traditional way of catching large amounts of ocean fish using a series of gill nets connected by ropes. The name means "to pull ropes," and it not only harvested enough fish to feed a village in the days of old, but also requires almost that many people to work the nets. It demands a skilled fisherman to coordinate the effort. I was barely in kindergarten the first time I watched Maha set up the nets. First he would direct the men from his lead boat just offshore to arrange the nets in a large semicircle to head off the school. Next, he'd wade into the shallow waters to secure one end of the rope to shore, thereby creating a large seine. The men, upon his signal, would then paddle their smaller wooden boats a few hundred feet offshore, stretching the collection of nets into a great arc that would cut off the school's access to the open sea. Finally, the far end of the rope was brought ashore a few hundred feet down the beach from its beginning so that the fish could be hauled in. Although only Maha and his immediate family would set up nets, he required a small army of volunteers on shore to complete this feat, most of these to man each end of the rope and others to wade out and strike the water between the shore and the nets. Maha's men on the boats did this as well, thrashing the water with homemade plungers and often diving down to release large sharks that had been caught so that they would not damage the nets. All this splashing and disturbance scared the fish into the nets. Then, at his discretion, Maha would signal to his leaders on shore to begin pulling the ropes. As the net was slowly hauled to shore, the huki lau truly began—a huge tug-of-war that pitted community against the ocean. As the semicircle started to tighten, the net, now heavy with fish, grew more and more difficult to pull. Women and children rushed to the edge of the surf to collect fish from the nets and shallow water.

Maha took his traveling huki lau from Waimea to Kekaha to the Polihale beaches on the far western side of the island. Since the fish he sought always circled the island during each season, it seemed as if he, too, was always moving about. He spent the summer months at Polihale, where he had a beach house constructed of driftwood and coconut leaves, complete with fresh water supplied by an underground spring. There he would fish for *moi, halalu,* and *akule.* At other times of the year, he traveled to Niumalu, Hanamaulu Bay, and Waialua Beach, and sometimes as far as Kalihiwai on the north shore. In each area Maha supplied the boats, nets, and the expertise, while the people who lived there provided the muscle.

When word got out that a huki lau was taking place, people came from as far away as the inland valleys to help. Whole families would come running down to the beach to join the pulling. When the net was finally hauled to shore, the fish were removed and divided equally among everyone who participated. The *mahele* (division) of the fish was overseen by Maha and his family crew members. Then, after the nets were gathered and cleaned and the boats loaded onto the trucks for the trip home, an all-night celebration began. Everyone who participated began enjoying drinks, taking turns at playing and singing to the many ukuleles, and, of course, eating a lot of *ono* (deliciously) prepared fish, both cooked and raw. Because people came from far away to participate, the huki lau often became a time of reunion for friends and family who had not seen each other in over a year. It was also a time to meet new people. I remember everyone introducing themselves, first by name, then by the Hawaiian family they descended from. The topic of family would prompt elaborate discussions about who had relatives where and what their skills and trades were. Inevitably two strangers would discover a connection, whether it was by blood, marriage, or a traditional skill handed down through a hereditary line.

This sense of belonging and of having some kind of intimate connection with everyone you encountered was a result of the preservation of the many genealogies and traditions that had been orally handed down to the Hawaiians of my mother's day. Maha's huki lau was just one of many events of this era that acted as a catalyst for sharing these traditions.

Another of my mother's friends, a woman named Maile Naumu, had an impact similar to Maha's huki lau on those whom she brought together. Her maiden name, Kupau, like Kupihea, was connected to the ancient god Ku. She had met my mother through her husband, Nahuka, who had been a childhood friend of my father. She was probably my mother's best friend; I called her Auntie Maile, and I adored her.

A Journey with Auntie Maile

Just as for many Hawaiians' real names, there is a story to Auntie Maile's real name given to her at birth. According to tradition, when someone introduces him- or herself and offers the full story of his or her Hawaiian name, it is expected that you will respond in kind, with your name and story. The foundation for the conversations to come is thus laid in place at the beginning. As I can recall, Maile was only my mother's friend's nickname, acquired over the years. I called her Auntie Maile even though she was not an acknowledged blood relative. Her real name was Lydia Aha O Moku Puni Kupau, and she was a descendant of the Kupua family of Waianae, Oahu. She was born November 5, 1921, inside a Hawaiian church called Liliuokalani Church (after the last queen of Hawaii) at Waialua, Oahu. Her mother was there to attend an *aha moku puni,* or "island conference" of Hawaiian churches, when she suddenly gave birth to Maile and gave her the name Lydia Aha O Moku Puni, or Lydia of the island conference, Lydia being the English name of Queen Liliuokalani.

It was with Auntie Maile and another Hawaiian woman named Maraea

Kaialau Cox that my mother and I hiked through what seemed like every mile of the Waimea and Makaweli River valleys, visiting old friends and distant family members and exchanging with them stories and legends of the people and places whose ancient paths we crossed on our impromptu movable feasts.

A typical visit would start out at the Menehune Ditch in the upper Waimea Valley, about a mile and a half outside the town of Waimea. You may have heard of the Menehune Ditch if you've ever read a Hawaiian guidebook, for it is part of the colorful lore of old Hawaii. The ditch is said to have been built in ancient times by a race of people only slightly larger than dwarfs. Known as the Menehune, they were said to be able to accomplish major feats of construction, but only late at night, under cover of darkness. To me there seemed nothing miraculous about the ditch, other than the odor of the ancient that drifted from its moss-covered stone walls. However, it always signaled that our journey was about to begin.

Auntie Maraea would park her gray and white 1953 Chevy sedan as close as possible to the stone walls of the Menehune Ditch because only the narrow road separated it from a steep drop to the river. We would all get out of the car, and I would run up and down the bank of the ditch while they unloaded their booze and *pupu* (snacks). Each of the women usually carried a bag of pupu and belongings in one hand and a gallon of wine or vodka in the other.

Standing at the Menehune Ditch, I could look out across the Waimea River and see the mouth of the Makaweli Valley toward the east. The fertile delta lands called Kakalae on the northern bank joined the fertile lowlands of the western bank of the Makaweli River. Toward the west curved the Waimea River to its source, the Waimea Canyon, a huge gorge that has been compared, when viewed from high above, to the Grand Canyon of Colorado. It was created by millions of years of water erosion since its beginning as an ancient volcanic fissure. The gorge intersected the western slopes of Mt. Waialeale, Kauai's single pyramidal volcanic mass that towered more than five thousand feet above. There the gorge took all streams into its own channel, moving southeast to become the Waimea Valley meeting the sea below. Similarly, the Makaweli River, which had its beginning in the Olekele Canyon, had worn away the intervening ridge between it and the Waimea River, and was now a branch of the Waimea.

From where I stood, the northern face of Poki'i Ridge rose steeply above the ditch behind me. The river below me was narrow and deep, its flowing waters having just completed a tight turn that curved against its rocky bank, allowing the delta lands to accumulate across it. It was here that a crude handmade suspension bridge had been built to make these lands accessible during the rainy season, when crossing the bed of the Waimea River by foot was impossible. As the river straightened out after a final turn toward the south, it grew wider; and as both ridge and water made their final descent to the ocean below, the high ridges grew farther apart. In looking toward the mouth of the Makaweli Valley, still about a mile above the ocean, I could envision our destination—taro fields situated beneath Mokihana, the intervening ridge of Waimea's northern walls, and Nonopahu, the intervening ridge of Makaweli's eastern walls. It was there that the Makaweli River flowed into the Waimea River, joining the two valleys into one great, fertile plain. Those taro fields had been there for centuries, and many of the friends and family we visited there could trace their histories back to well before Cook's arrival in 1778. But to get to the mouth of the valley, we first had to cross the rickety old suspension bridge.

Crossing the Swinging Bridge

The bridge, which hung groaning and creaking in the wind about thirty feet above the river and spanned some three hundred feet, was constructed of two large cables about three feet apart that were stretched across the water. Suspended from these two cables was a walkway made of one-by-twelve-inch boards, with an inch gap between each board. The rails on each side were about three feet high and made of two-by-fours and wire mesh. It was known as the Swinging Bridge, and for good reason: every step caused the bridge to bounce up and down and sway back and forth, creaking and groaning ever louder the closer one got to its center.

By the time we got to the Swinging Bridge, my mother and her friends would be laughing, joking, and—if the wine had already been opened, which it usually had been—not exactly walking straight. The landing of the bridge was twelve feet above the road, and was reached by a rickety set of wooden steps that were so narrow we had to walk single file. I would usually be last, tagging along behind my mother. At the top of the steps, just as we started across the bridge, I would always stop and look down, through the wire mesh, at the top of a huge boulder known as Pohaku lani, meaning "the stone of a high chief," which was said to sit upon four smaller stones in the riverbed below. According to legend, it was the ill-fated son of an ancient Waimea king who, along with his sister, was turned into stone for breaking a tabu. The sister was a slightly larger boulder about a hundred feet farther upstream, on the hillside above the Menehune Ditch.

It was Auntie Maile who first told me the legend of Pohaku lani. In ancient times a king named Ola struck a bargain with the king of the Menehune to build an aqueduct that would divert water from the upper Waimea River to the village of Pe´e kaua´i at the base of the eastern slopes of Poki´i, just beyond the pinnacle of Kikiao la and the gorge of Paliuli in the lower Waimea Valley. Without water, taro could not be grown, and without taro, Ola's kingdom would never prosper. The king of the Menehune agreed to perform the task and in return Ola would supply all the *opae* (small freshwater shrimp) his people could eat during the course of their work. Opae were a delicacy especially enjoyed by the Menehune, and the king demanded that each night two thousand large calabashes filled to the brim with them be delivered to a hilltop on the southern slopes of Puka pele, the intervening ridge that separates Waimea Canyon from the ocean. Then the king of the Menehune added one final condition: It was important that no one within the district venture outdoors at night while the work was being performed, for the Menehune would work only at night, and only in complete secrecy. Ola agreed, and work began.

All went well at first. The stones that would make up the aqueduct were cut from secret quarries deep in the Mokihana Valley, and handed from one Menehune to another in a chain of Menehune that spanned the miles between quarry and project site. Each night the aqueduct snaked closer and closer to its destination, and each night the opae were delivered to the hilltop some ten miles away. In fact, progress was so rapid that it took only a few nights for construction to reach the site now known as the Menehune Ditch, below the northern cliffs of Poki´i. Then, upon the final night of work, the son and daughter of King Ola gave in to their insatiable curiosity and decided to sneak a peek at the Menehune magic. But while hiding on the hillside above the ditch, they were spotted by some of the Menehune workers, and as punishment for breaking one of the kapu (laws) of the agreement, the two were turned into stone right where they stood—the sister where she hid up on the hillside, and the brother in the river, where he tried to flee.

If you are ever in Kokee, on Kekaha Road, just before the entrance to the Kokee State Park, you might notice a ditch that crosses the road to feed a nearby reservoir on the right. If you take the time to stop here and look toward the northwest above the green valley, you will see a lonely hill-top in the direction of the island of Niʻihau. The name of this hill is Puʻu opae, which means "hill of opae." This is where King Ola delivered the opae to the Menehune king. The region of the green valley is called Poʻpae, meaning "to arrive in darkness," and the region of the deep valley toward the southeast is called Hau Ola, "act of Ola," where once, a long time ago, the meeting of both kings took place.

Lost in my thoughts about Pohaku lani, I wouldn't at first hear my mother telling me to come along. She was a few steps ahead of me, and my aunties Maile and Maraea were even farther ahead. Already the bridge began to sway and bounce, and with their hands too full of bottles of booze and packages of pupu to grasp the railings, my mother and her friends seemed to be having some problems keeping their balance. Though it took us awhile, we finally made it across the river, and at the Mokihana side of the bridge we took our last look at the Waimea River, for it would soon be out of sight. As our eyes followed along the bank of the river in the direction of the Waimea Canyon, the river made a turn about three hundred feet upstream. Just beyond that it disappeared into the base of Mokihana Ridge, where it flowed alongside a rocky ledge until the bank formed once again at Waiahole farther up the Waimea Valley.

This ledge gave the area its name, Pili a moʻo, which, to the travelers of my day, meant "a place that lizards *(moʻo)* cling to." And Pili a moʻo, like the boulder Pohaku lani, has a story. It was in this vicinity in the days of old that Manoʻeha, the shark man of Pili a moʻo, was said to have swum out through a secret tunnel to feast on human flesh. According to the story, Manoʻeha was a *kakuʻai*, which is a type of demigod that can change shape or form at will. For Mano´eha this form was that of a shark, or *mano*. He was not a threat as a man, for he was old and hunchbacked, but as a shark he was said to be agile and deadly and was to be avoided at all cost. Though no one had ever seen the man Mano´eha's back, everyone agreed that the reason he was so careful to keep it covered was because it showed the clear image of a shark's head and mouth. It was rumored that Mano´eha reached his prey through an underground tunnel that ran from a pond called Puna wai mano, or "spring of the shark," located at the bend in the river just prior to Pili a mo´o, all the way to what is known as Kau lima, commonly called Pipito's Point today, at the junction of the Makaweli and Waimea Rivers. Mano´eha would enter the river at Pili a mo´o, change into a shark, and wait at Kau lima to attack and devour some unsuspecting swimmer. Once his belly was full of human flesh, Mano´eha would then swim back home through the tunnel, shift back into the form of an old man, and act as if nothing had happened.

In the days of Auntie Maraea's youth, sharks would still venture up the Waimea River and could be seen frolicking at the Makaweli junction. In the vicinity of Pili a mo´o lived Kalipo Kamake and his family, Kalani Nawahea, and a Hawaiian blacksmith named Nahino. But all of this was in the past by my day, with only ancient stone walls and remnants of shacks remaining to remind us of the stories.

Kanikula

Once across the Swinging Bridge, the trail narrowed. We were now heading inland, toward the mountains. A thick wall of *haole koa* grew up on both sides of the trail, rising to a height of about ten feet and leaning inward so that it seemed as though we were walking through a tunnel. We walked single file about a quarter of a mile alongside an ancient *au wai*, or "irrigation ditch," lined with stone before reaching the base of a high hill that resembled an ancient volcanic cinder cone. Here the trail turned toward the Makaweli River. The area we were now walking through was known as Pu´u lima, which refers to a joint that pivots, such as the human wrist or finger, though the hill itself was called Kanikula, or "school bell." Evidently the name of the hill was changed when the children of the

Makaweli Valley started to climb it to listen for the bell being rung at the schoolhouse more than two miles away. Kanikula was the center point for the delta lands of Waimea that started at Pili a moʻo and ended at Peʻe a moʻo in the Makaweli Valley. Long ago on Kanikula stood Lae, the last high chief to rule over these ancient lands that came to be called Kakalae, meaning the "arch of Lae," in his honor. From atop this hill, which later became a burial mound for the descendants of these lands, Lae pointed to the two ends of his kingdom.

Once at the base of Kanikula, we continued to walk along the irrigation ditch for another quarter of a mile before turning into the Makaweli Valley. As we made the turn, we were forced to walk a single twelve-inch-wide plank to get across the ditch. Up ahead of us was Barney Holt's house, a dilapidated board-and-batten building with paint that was weathered away to almost nothing and a corrugated metal roof that was rusted to a dark reddish brown. Many of the windows were broken or had panes missing, and the perpetual shade from the giant hau bush behind the house made the place seem gloomy even during the day. The ladies would stop here and visit with the Holt *ohana* (family) before moving on, sharing a drink with Barney and his wife, Eunice Kamai (also called Mamala), a sister-in-law of the elder William Kapahu kani o lono Goodwin, whose own family home was located just below in the land of Kau lima at the junction of the two rivers. Conversation always began the same way: with inquiries into the well-being of each other's families, which often turned to the sharing of their histories. Then, once everyone knew how everyone else was faring, the discussions became more lively. The travelers shared everything that they brought with them, and the temporary host offered all that surrounded him. After a few shots of vodka or wine and a few jokes, the ladies bade Barney and Eunice aloha. Everyone was still laughing as we waved good-bye and continued on our journey.

Moving deeper into the valley, about ten minutes away from the Holt house we came across a large circular millstone next to an abandoned well. The millstone, well, and a few rusted pieces of metal flume were all that remained of an old rice mill that once operated in the valley. From here we followed the trail for another quarter of a mile along the eastern base of

Kanikula. Passing beneath huge tamarind trees, we could look up and see caves on the ledges above us that were ancient burial sites; some of the bones were quite visible from our location on the trail. These caves were considered sacred, and out of respect, no one entered them; the elders say that trespassing in them was strictly tabu, for it offends one's own `aumakua.

We now approached the remnants of an old abandoned house that last belonged to Kaleilani Kauhi and his ohana. It was also the childhood home of one of Hawaii's most talented artists, Linda Dela Cruz, in the 1940s. Continuing farther along the trail, we came to the old Makuaole house, its once elevated wooden floor now sagging pitifully to the ground. No one had lived there since Tole and Cecilia Kamai moved away in the 1940s. A little farther still, we came to the remains of the old Mormon church, which was dismantled and moved to where its congregation had resettled, in lower Waimea Valley. Here the ladies would stop and reminisce about how the Mormon Church had changed the valley by convincing families to abandon their properties and move to Oahu near the Mormon temple located there. Years later, many of these families denounced the Church and returned to the valley, only to find their property had been confiscated and reoccupied. Leaving the site of the Mormon church behind, we next came to the old Manini family home, where once again the ladies stopped to visit and trade stories.

Here in 1830 was born Nawai ekolu, which means "the third waters," who was also known as Malaea Wahapaa and who died in 1945 at the age of 115. She was the grandmother of Puni lei Mahu iki Manini, whom we visited, and one of the earliest native converts to Mormonism, having been baptized in the waters of Kau lima in 1853. In the years that followed, she served as a chief source for George Quayle and J. W. H. Kauwahi in their monumental task of translating the Book of Mormon into the Hawaiian language.

Just beyond the Manini house lay the old Kanikula Road, which crossed the Makaweli River at two forges: the upper forge was called Ku ula (or Ka ula), which refers to the gods of foods from sea and land; and the lower was called Waikai´a, which means "from fresh water to salt water." There the road ran alongside the eastern bank of the Makaweli River and eventually along the Waimea River, passing through a district known as Mahaihai, after an ancient clan who dwelt there (today called Mahiʻai), on its way to joining the highway at the eastern end of the Waimea Bridge. The district of Mahiʻai, when it was still heavily populated by Hawaiians, was cultivated primarily with taro and *akala* (Hawaiian raspberry) trees. Then, during the Rice Era, American and European entrepreneurs leased large tracts of land to the early Chinese immigrants, who planted rice instead to feed themselves and the newly arriving Filipino, Korean, and Japanese immigrants. At present the area is cultivated with sugarcane fields owned by the Robinson family, which also owns most of the Makaweli Valley, including Kanikula, and controls the entire Mokihana Ridge.

The Kanikula Road was built by the U.S. Army during World War II. The ridge was used as an artillery range, and replaced the old Mokihana Trail at Pʻee a moʻa (also called Peʻe a moʻo), which was used by the Robinsons to get their cattle to market twice a year. Since it was used for little else, the road was barely maintained. Only four-wheel-drive vehicles could make it up the steep and rocky slope, at the top of which sits an old Hawaiian graveyard. As a little boy, I once attended a funeral there for Old Lady Makuaole, who lived in the house we had passed, with the sagging floor. I remember the wooden coffin was secured with chains onto the back of an old World War II weapons carrier. The carrier was driven by Maha Leoiki, the neighbor who conducted huki laus. Maha had bought it as military surplus after the war and had volunteered its use to get Old Lady Makuaole to her final resting place in the remote cemetery.

As the weapons carrier slowly climbed the steep road, it was accompanied by the sound of rocks being crushed beneath its wheels. You could also hear the coffin scraping against metal as it shifted from side to side. The mourners walked slowly behind, covered with the bright red dust kicked up by the makeshift hearse. When the funeral procession finally made it to the top of the hill, the mourners began singing some of the old Hawaiian songs that had been favorites of the deceased. The emotion in their voices was raw and powerful, full of deep feelings of sorrow and spiritual longing. It seemed to me their songs were like tears that flowed from the lips rather than the eyes. After the burial, the mourners stood solemnly for a while, remembering the deceased, before proceeding back down the road to the traditional Hawaiian gathering waiting below. Some of these gatherings were known to last as long as three days.

On top of Kanikula, not far from the old cemetery where Old Lady Makuaole rests, there is an imprint of a large right foot (size 16, at least) embedded in solid rock. It sits on a perch overlooking the mouth of the Makaweli Valley and is said to have been left there by a retreating tribal warrior during an ancient military rout. According to legend, a clan from the Hanapepe Valley, the next large valley to the east of Waimea, decided to wage war on the people dwelling in the Makaweli Valley to make their own temple of Ku ula the sole place of worship for their gods. The offensive army determined that the best place to attack would be from the flatlands of Nonopahu, directly above the area known as Waikai´a. From Nonopahu they would be able to overlook the entire Makaweli Valley below. The plan was that they would descend the gorge of Makaweli's Ku ula, desecrate the temple there, and then cross the Makaweli River into the village of Pe´e a mo´o.

The people of Makaweli were few in number back then and when their high chief, Naulii, heard rumors of the attack, he set about developing a plan for the defense of his people. Anticipating that the attacking force would outnumber his own small group of warriors, Naulii first gathered his clan and persuaded them to evacuate Pe´e a mo´o and follow him on a long march up Kanikula. From Kanikula they climbed onto the central plain of Mokihana Ridge, which they then followed to the bright red slopes of Kalua o kalani. Here they hid in the safety of the forest of Poki´i pua.

Camped high above Mokihana Ridge, Naulii could look out across the rolling hills of Nonopahu and see all the way to the district of Kaumakani (place of the wind) below the hill of Pe´a pe´a. From his position, he could see the invaders as soon as they crossed the ridge of Kaumakani, which they soon did. When Naulii noted the enemy's superior numbers, he realized he would be unable to defeat them in hand-to-hand combat and would have to outwit them. He also knew that there was little time. Although the advancing army had stopped for the night to make camp atop Po´o pueo (hill of the owls) on Nonopahu Ridge, Naulii knew they would attack at first light. That night Naulii ordered his warriors to cut down all the *lehua* trees that grew on the upper slopes of Mokihana Ridge just below his camp and to pile them up in one location for their quick use the next morning.

At sunrise, the warriors from the east descended the gorge of Ku ula into the Makaweli Valley to find the temple and village of Pe´e a mo´o abandoned. In search of Naulii's men and priests, they then followed the trail up Kanikula to Mokihana Ridge. By noon the harsh sun had baked the bare red soil of the rolling hills of Mokihana into a powdery dust. This was exactly what Naulii had been waiting for. He now ordered his warriors to drag the felled lehua trees by their trunks, turning their branches and leaves into huge brooms that swept up great clouds of dust, which the attacking force mistook for the dust of an advancing army. The trees were also dragged through the various gullies that ran down Mokihana, making it appear as though many warriors were arriving from different directions to counter the attack. The chief from Hanapepe, afraid of being caught in a trap so far from home, ordered a retreat, which soon turned into a rout. As the warriors from Hanapepe fled, Naulii ordered an all-out attack, instructing his men to make as much noise as possible. By this time the warriors from Hanapepe were in full panic, scrambling down the ridge to Kanikula, running across the Makaweli Valley, flip-flopping through the river, scrambling back up the gorge of Ku ula, onto Nonopahu, and beyond to Kaumakani.

As Naulii´s warriors came storming down from Mokihana, they captured one of the warriors from the east, whose name was Kanaka opu´u nui. They dragged their captive to a dirt mound on the central plain of Mokihana and then slowly slaughtered him. The screams and yells elicited by the slaughter of Kanaka opu´u nui created even more fear in the retreating warriors. One of them was so terrified that he jumped from the top of Kanikula with such force that his foot sank into the rock from which he leapt, leaving its print behind. Apparently he made it all the way across the Makaweli Valley, for on the edge of Nonopahu Ridge, above Waikai´a, where the warrior is said to have landed, there is another flat rock imprinted with a left footprint.

Even today the landscape carries names associated with this battle. High above Mokihana Ridge, atop the western rim of Kalua o kalani near the entrance to the forest beyond, there is a small knoll of bright red dirt known as Naulii. It is said that this is the spot from which the Makaweli chief planned and directed the battle below. The shallow ravine below Naulii is known by the name of Ka lehua hakihaki, which means "the breaking of lehua branches." About halfway across the central plain of Mokihana, heading back toward Kanikula, there is a little hill of red and bluish dirt called Kanaka opu´u nui—the spot where the warrior from the east was slaughtered.

Gathering at the Apo House

As we left the Manini house, we crossed Kanikula Road and continued up the Makaweli Valley. The trail now became very rocky, and there were many *keawe* trees and thorns; we had to watch our step to keep from tripping. Just before reaching the Char family home in the land of Pe´e a mo´o, we came across an odd site: an old Hawaiian lady tethered to a big mango tree. She had long gray hair and was dressed in a white muumuu. The tether was just long enough to allow her to wander about twenty feet away from the tree. As she moved toward us, I started to run, causing my mother and aunties to laugh hysterically, for they knew she was really harmless, and they reminisced about a big man named Benny Holt, whom they had once witnessed running from this same woman.

Old Lady Char was tethered to the tree every day to keep her from wandering off or burning down the house while her family was away working in the taro patches. Though grown men had been known to run when Old Lady Char came out from behind the mango tree rattling her chains, my mother and aunts treated her like anyone else, stopping to chat with her and exchange stories. The old lady's maiden name was Makuaole. The Makuaole family had farmed taro in the district since the time of the ancients, and now Old Lady Char's three sons continued the family tradition. The oldest boy, Barney, supervised most of the taro fields in the district, and though neither of his younger brothers, Ernest and Nani, could read or write, they too were experts at cultivating taro. Also living at the Char home was a man named Albert Kekua Makuaole, known simply as Pipito. Pipito was one of the greatest mountain men of his time in this district. From the Makaweli Valley to the very top of Mt. Waialeale, there wasn't a trail that he did not know. Pipito was always thirsty, and once my mother and aunts shared their liquor with him, he was then ready to accompany us to wherever we were heading next.

It was only a short walk from the Char house to the Apo house. On the way we crossed the upper source of the same au wai (ditch), straddled by a large flat rock this time, just before we passed what was left of the old Pa'alua house, which had collapsed years before. The Apo house was typical of the other valley homes we had walked past on our way. It was small and built above ground to avoid flooding during the district's long rainy season. Its four rooms (a parlor, a kitchen, and two bedrooms with blankets for partitions) were all quite small. There was also a front porch facing the mouth of the valley far below; it was usually cluttered with horse blankets and old Hawaiian saddles. We entered the yard from the side that faced the ancient au wai; the other three sides were surrounded by taro fields that separated the site from the Makaweli River. Like all other houses in the valley, this one had no electricity or plumbing and water had to be fetched from the nearby ditch. Its exterior was constructed of one-by-twelve-inch board-and-batten painted dark green, and its roof was made of corrugated metal. Directly in front of the porch was a small yard, which was bordered on two sides by taro patches. In the middle of the yard, a very large logan tree stretched its branches over a wooden table, providing shade for the lively discussions that were always taking place beneath it.

Like the celebration following Maha's huki lau, the Apo house was where everyone gathered to share stories about the way life used to be. Discussions would always start with someone remembering his or her own childhood experiences, and before long everyone was reminiscing. Extended genealogies were compared and family ways were examined and passed on like heirlooms. There was always a great deal of food, and most of it was fresh from the aina (land). Among the pupu sizzling on the grill were mountain goat and pig (including their internal organs), chicken, opae, frog, and plenty of fish from both the river and the ocean. There was also plenty of poi and, of course, taro, since we were in the midst of its source. Visits that were intended to last only a few hours often turned into two- or three-day affairs as one old-timer after another arrived to enjoy the Apo family's hospitality. Each guest brought pupu and drink with them, and once the gathering started, it would go on day and night.

I was never in a hurry to go home. The Apos had nine children, and we made our own entertainment. We had to, since we weren't allowed to hang around the adult table while they were drinking. As soon as one of us children approached, some adult would say, "Kuli kuli," which means the equivalent of "Be quiet" or "Go play." And play we did. We spent our days swimming in the river or, if we wanted to stay close to home, the nearby ditch, passing the day beneath the rocky ledge of Pe´e a mo´o. Sometimes we would follow the older children to a swimming hole located farther up the valley, just beyond the source of the ditch. Gilman Apo and his sister Anne would lead us along the irrigation ditch past the remnants of the old Naholoholo house, which lay collapsed, and on into a huge tunnel of haole koa trees till we reached the ancient intake *(mano wai),* a wall of stone that diverted water from the river into the au wai.

Once we crossed the Makaweli River, the swimming hole was only a short distance away. The area in which it was located was known as Waitolu, which means "the third water." Towering above the swimming hole was a twenty-foot cliff called Ka ena manu, from which the older children jumped.

During our excursions, we'd snack on Hawaiian oranges, bananas, guavas, and mangoes, all of which grew wild right there in the valley. At night, we'd return to the Apo house to find the adult gathering still going strong. Sometimes we'd creep up to the table, sneak pupu, and eavesdrop on the adults' conversation. When at last we grew tired, each of us would find a spot where we could sleep. Some of us would be spread out in the yard; others would hunker down along the riverbank, or on ancient *lo´i* (terraces) in the midst of ancient taro patches. This was where I and a childhood friend named Kaeo always chose to sleep. We stared up at millions of stars and at the shadowy images created by the giant ridges on both sides of us. It was nights like these that stirred our imagination, transforming in darkness the forms of nature that we were unafraid of in the light.

It was only after the gathering was over that I'd really get to know what had been shared at the adult table, for as we'd leave, the ladies would start talking about what a good time they'd had, and recall all the memorable experiences that had been passed around the table over the past several days in the age-old tradition of sharing thoughts, ideas, and experiences, or mana´o. While they reminisced about people who had come and gone, I pictured them in my imagination. Each one had his or her own unique character, and each one was an expert in some traditional Hawaiian skill that had been handed down for generations. These were the family historians, proud keepers of the traditions that their brothers and sisters so often abandoned. Most of the children growing up in the valley moved away as they grew older. Of a family of nine, perhaps only one child would remain to act as a conduit for the family traditions, first receiving knowledge from the elders and then passing it on to the next generation. Many times the brother or sister who stayed was criticized by those who left for not adjusting to the times or to a way of life that they deemed better.

Years later, those who had left would recognize what had been given up and would try to return to reclaim the treasures they had lost. Sometimes their return was met with unforgiving silence. And often treasures could not be reclaimed.

Those Who Gathered

As we continued walking along the trail, I occupied myself with thoughts of all the people who gathered at the Apos' at a moment's notice to make these visits such a memorable experience—especially people like Sam Apo. Sam was originally from Hanalei, on the other side of the island. A descendant of the native Maluna family there, with ties to the famed Trask family of Kauai and Oahu, he also had some Chinese ancestry. His wife was a big Hawaiian woman named Ka´luna, meaning "the high." She was the older sister of Pipito and was descended from the Ku a pahi and Makuaole families, both original inhabitants of the Makaweli Valley. Many people were afraid of her. Auntie Maile said it was because the pebbles she would *hapai* (carry) in an old Bull Durham bag hanging from a cord around her neck were said to have mana, or power. Within these stones swelled the source of her ´aumakua and the spirits of unihi pili, which could be called upon for favors through prayer.

Sam was a remarkable man with many talents. One of them was cooking mountain meat on an outside fire. Using an old five-gallon cracker can as an oven and steamer, he could concoct a feast equal to that of any world-class chef. Sam was the local authority on preparing the traditional Hawaiian feast known as a luau. He not only knew how to prepare all the dishes but also was an expert in the construction of *imu,* or underground ovens, in which to bake *(kalua)* them. Finally, Sam was an expert at preparing graves according to Hawaiian traditions. He was indispensable if you were having a funeral, since he could not only dig the grave and prepare the burial site with sacred palm leaves, but could also cook the feast to follow the ceremony.

Sam's luaus were elaborate affairs. Since all the food was gathered rather than bought, a luau represented a huge group effort that required each family's particular area of expertise. The only imported items were salted salmon, salted butterfish, and booze; everything else was local. Farmers harvested taro to make poi and *kulolo* (a pudding of coconut and taro that is either steamed or baked in an imu) and provided the leaves for *lau lau,* which is the dish that gives the traditional luau its name. (*Luau* refers to the young taro leaves that are steamed with pork, meat, or fish in a package of ti leaf.) Also participating were fishermen, who supplied salt made from seawater, and returned from the ocean and rivers with fish, crabs, *opihi* (limpets), and many different types of limu (seaweed) used to mix with the raw fish. Hunters went to the mountains and brought back wild pig and cattle to bake in the imu, and goat to grill and smoke for pupu.

These mountain men were the proudest and strongest men in the valley. Their skills had been passed down from generation to generation, and each man began learning his skill the moment he learned to walk. They knew every valley and mountain in the area, and they brought back the mountain meat that was the main source of food in the valley at the time. Besides Albert Pipito Makuaole, Eugene "Capri" Makaaila (also Makaila, meaning "scorch eyes") was a mountain man too. In addition, Eugene was a medicine man who was sought after for his skills at healing horses with herbs. Then there was William Kualu (or Kuwalu), who was a retired cowboy from Niʻihau Ranch. William was in his nineties at the time, but he could still ride and rope—and would live to be well over one hundred years old.

Never far from William were his two sons, Kanaka nui and his younger brother Waitata, also pronounced *Waikaka*. Both had colorful names: Kanaka nui, whose name means "big man," was really quite small, and Waikaka, meaning "water duck," was named after a waterfall in the valley of Kahana, where the Kualus once possessed land, although by their time the family had moved to an island of sand known as Mokuone in the upper Makaweli Valley, about three miles beyond the Apo house. They were one of the families that had followed the Mormon ministries to Laea on Oahu and later returned to Kauai to find their lands under different ownership.

Manny Naholoholo, meaning "evening star," was another of these mountain men, though he considered himself more of a shoreline fisherman than a hunter. His old family home lay collapsed just across the ditch. John Keuma, who moved to the valley from the Hule'ia Valley after marrying a local girl named Jenny Kahalekomo, was known as a sportsman. He had been a boxer in his younger days, proclaiming himself the Bull of Lihue. He was also a disabled veteran of World War II, and was always ready to play a game of *kumau*, the Hawaiian version of trumps. Philip Fortardo, who was Portuguese, had once lived with my great-uncle David Malo Kupihea in his youth, and became known as One Leg Philip after he lost a leg in the old Waimea stone crusher at Akia. Despite his wooden peg leg, Philip was an expert hunter. He also had a sense of humor. When anyone asked him what race he was, One Leg Philip would answer, "Half Portuguese and half stick," and when asked his age, he would reply, "The Portuguese side is forty-nine, the stick, a hundred fifty."

Older mountain people, Tole Kamai and his wife, both of whom came from families that had dwelled in the Makaweli and Waimea Valleys since ancient times, preserved many of the old ways. Tole, meaning "sweet eye" because he possessed only one good eye, was the last person in the valley still practicing the ancient tradition of cooking dogs in an imu, kalua-style, or baked underground. When properly prepared, you could not tell the difference between dog and kalua pig. Cecilia Kamai, who I believe was of the Mokukea line on her father's side, was an expert in the ancient healing art known as *kahea*, meaning "to call." By reciting ancient prayers to family na 'aumakua and applying unselfish touch, Cecilia could heal broken bones, remove muscle aches and strains, and cure most fevers and stomach disorders. Many of the people drinking at the table had been healed by her at one time or another. In the words of Jumbo Taniguchi, nephew of Auntie Maile's husband, when Cecilia passed her hands over you, it felt "as though a fireball was rolling over your skin."

Another old cowboy in attendance at these gatherings was Kale Kuapahi, who lived just below the old A´ana house on the west bank of the Waikai´a river crossing. The Kuapahi name, which means "the knife of the god Ku," like the Kualu family, has been associated with the valley since it was first settled, and by coincidence both families at one time or another have lived upon the same sites. Kale was a hunter, taro farmer, and an expert in the tradition of Hawaiian saddle making. His wife, Miriam, who was originally from the Namakahea (or Namaka´eha) family of Anahola, had been previously married to a Kahalekomo and was the matriarch of that valley clan as well. To the ancient traveler, Namakahea was the daughter of Ola, the ancient king of Waimea who had bargained with the Menehune.

Also present were Barney Char, a true master in all the traditions of the valley, and his two brothers, Nani and Ernest, descendants of the Makuaole family on their mother's side. Nani was said to be moonstruck; during the full moon he would forget who he was and wander the valley, communing with ancient spirits. He was often seen roaming Mokihana Ridge, walking and whistling in the night. Both brothers were known to sleep in burial caves and possessed no fear of ancestral spirits. Nani would often line up skulls at a cave's entrance so they would have a view of the valley below.

Auntie Maile, her husband, Nahuka Naumu, and his brother, Ka´ili, were expert entertainers who brought these gatherings to life with their music. They knew all the old Hawaiian songs and were masters of the guitar, steel guitar, ukulele, and auto harp. The elder William Kapahu kani o lono often joined in with his mandolin. Both Nahuka and Ka´ili—descendants of the ancient Mu people, who were the legendary inhabitants of the Waimea Canyon and the ancient land of Kane huna moku—were expert hunters and they excelled in the tradition of *ha* (sluice) building.

A ha, which is a sluice that passes water or air, is a trap built in the river to catch *o´opu* (black goby), a seasonal fish resembling catfish. The o´opu live most of the year in cold mountain streams, deep within the gorges of the Waimea and Olekele Canyons, but during the rainy season, which begins in September and lasts through October, when the Java plums fall like purple raindrops, the rivers flood, carrying the o´opu to the lowlands, where the adults spawn and die. The young, known as *hinana*, then swim back upstream to start the process again. Ever since ancient times, large traps have been built across rivers to catch the o´opu as they ride the floodwaters downstream. This was the tradition that the Naumu brothers kept alive.

Ka´ili would build the mano, which diverted water to the ha located at its lower end. The mano, which had to withstand raging floods, was made of large stones and resembled a dam. It was built at a slight angle in the direction of the current, just a bit lower than the anticipated height of the river. While Ka´ili was busy building the mano, Nahuka would cut trees to construct the ha, which was a large platform held up by huge posts driven into the riverbed. The ha, which could be up to twenty feet wide, sloped like a ramp from beneath the riverbed just upstream from the mano. It was constructed of long timbers placed against the current and spaced about four feet apart. On the top of these timbers, small branches of haole koa were spaced a finger's width apart and lashed with cord horizontally to the main timbers below to resist the force of the oncoming floodwater. As the mano diverted water to run over the ha, the o´opu would get caught on the latticework. For as long as the flood lasted, people would stand on the ha and collect fish.

Ha´ha—Journey's End, Memory's Beginning

As my mother, Auntie Maile, Auntie Maraea, and I made the final turn at Pu´u lima, we left Makaweli behind. Ahead of us was the Swinging Bridge, and beyond it Auntie Maraea's car. As I took one last look at Kanikula, I couldn't wait for our next visit.

The people of the Makaweli Valley will always be special to me, perhaps because they were so intimately connected to the land on which they lived. Their families had been here for centuries, and most of them could still recall the origins of their ancestral names. Pipito, for example, often spoke of the past glory of the Makuaoles as high chiefs, descendants of the ancient Mano ka lani po and rulers of the valley prior to the arrival of Captain

Cook. The story of the Makuaole family name had been passed down from generation to generation: lesser chiefs, jealous of the high chief's power and priestly image, killed off the chiefly line and his family. Only a few of their children managed to escape by hiding out on the hill of Po´o pueo. These orphaned children were later secretly adopted by other tribal members. Because they would be killed if identified, they could no longer safely use their hereditary name and became known as the Makuaoles, which translates as "children without parents." In time, the Makuaoles (whose last ancestor was Ke´tua, the ancient name of the god Kane), the Kuapahis (whose last ancestor was Makawela, or "glowing eyes"), and the Kualus (whose first ancestor was Ku alunui kini akua, or "Kualu of the multitude of great gods"), would be all who remained of the Makaweli Valley's original families.

Weary but content, we climbed into Auntie Maraea's car for the drive home. On our way we passed my grandmother's house, and like the fleeting view of it from the moving car, the house seemed strangely temporary and impermanent, especially compared to where we had just been. At my grandmother's house, history was confined to a few rooms and visions of the past were limited to faded photographs. But out in the valley, traveling in the open air beneath blue skies, surrounded by ancient rocks and flowing water, the spirits of our ancestors are everywhere, waiting only for our memories to bring them to life. When these memories are triggered by the familiarity of the sight of mountains, the sky, and the rivers that tell our origins, then our ancestors become part of the eternal landscape itself. And whenever we meet someone on our journey and speak with him of those who have died, we prepare the way for our own descendants to stop and remember us on their journey through this same landscape, the landscape of life. Wherever they look, there we will be, for the eyes from which they see are the entrance to the world in which we will, at that point, dwell. And whenever they stop to talk and remember us, our names will leave their mouths, travel upon their breath, and enter into the ears of yet another descendant. There is a Hawaiian word—ha´ha—that means to both inhale and exhale. When we share our mana´o, or our thoughts, our ancestors travel out upon our life's breath—and as long as we continue to breathe, they will live on in the world of ao `aumakua.

CHAPTER FOUR

THE SOUND OF THE `AUMAKUA

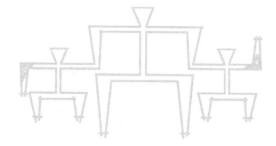

THE PAST DOES NOT DISAPPEAR; it is merely silenced. But a boy of nine or ten or eleven who listens very closely can hear the sound of feet scrambling on rocky ledge; the sound, rebounding from a cave's stone walls, of sand shifting underfoot or pebbles skittering; the strange, resonant bell-like sound made by rock striking rock. These are the sounds of the past. They are the notes of an ancient ancestral time, notes that evoke the spirits of ages and years gone by, and a boy growing closer to the cusp of manhood can hear them and, through them, the past.

Our visits to the Makaweli Valley as a family contingent continued for several more years and then stopped when the Apos, like many families in the district, moved across the Waimea River into the valley below to be closer to the modern conveniences available there. Ironically, in the years to come, the house they finally settled in was itself an ex-resident of the Makaweli Valley, it being the Mormon church whose pulpit had been packed up and moved from the Makaweli Valley in the early 1940s, or about twenty years before. As fate would have it, the Apo children would be the last people to be born in the Makaweli Valley, and their departure seemed to signal the beginning of a new era. As children we still returned to play there, but the sounds of the joyful generations that had just preceded us seemed to have disappeared into dust.

It was 1959, Hawaii had just become a state, and like the Apos of the Makaweli Valley, we all became the last to be born into a territorial way of life, which was departing. While some looked to statehood as their only economic salvation, a traditional way of life of the native Hawaiian population in Waimea and throughout the islands was changing in ways that no one could have anticipated. This way of life, like the kingdom that had preceded it, was to be a sacrificial lamb. A new state bureaucracy absorbed all county jurisdiction over fishing and hunting. Maha Leoiki's traveling huki'lau was outlawed by the Department of Land and Natural Resources. The Division of Fish and Game began destroying the sluices (ha) that were built annually by the Naumu brothers, and hunting for game became a seasonal sport permitted only by fee. Ancestral journeys into the mountains were now made in secrecy, out of sight of the law, by elders who traveled alone in the interest of protecting those of the younger generation from being caught in illegal activity. With the elimination of the right to fish and hunt freely, once proud traditions of strong men began to disappear.

The kind of impromptu outdoor gatherings like those at the Apo house, where people could share their stories and common histories, also became a thing of the past as common bonds and traditions were lost. Instead, small groups made up of former inhabitants of a single district met at individual homes; town bars, like the Lucky U, Buka'tuu, and Gracy's, slowly replaced the inns of the valley—the Mango Tree Inn and the Pine Tree Inn—named after a tree in someone's yard beneath which a few tables had been placed. As they had beneath the longon tree in the Makaweli Valley, the Apos continued their tradition, first beneath a pine tree, then a mango tree (which became the Mango Tree Inn), but the more formal these gatherings became, the more removed was the young ear from the old mouth. The young became removed from the voices that talked about the old days and encouraged them to perform things as a group, as it used to be done.

The more people concentrated on the future, the more they talked about things that only an individual could do.

The ʻAumakua Stirs: Willy Kani and the Caves

My mother's house in Waimea became one of the few places where people of different districts still gathered to talk about the past. Our home was an interesting place in which to live, surrounding us as it did with traces of its former life as first a mission school and then a parsonage. The flagpole from its original incarnation as a school still stood towering over the trees in the yard. The house had a large dining room, which was accessed from the living room through a grand arched entryway. The shedlike kitchen had a small door that faced the ocean, and directly opposite there was a wooden lanai that ran the length of the dining room and living room and faced the old church. Countless gatherings took place within these rooms; a steady stream of old-timers passed through our house, sitting on pews that my mother had salvaged from the old church along with a large wooden cabinet that had once served as its altar and was now fill with her most cherished antiques. Most of these elders came to enjoy each other's company, except for one of them, who seemed to appear alone, when there was no gathering taking place. His name was William Kapahu kani o lono Goodwin, but he was also known as Willy Kani (*kani* meaning "reverberating sound"). This, as you may remember, was the same man who was present at the time of my birth, and he was to continue to be an important influence on my young life.

Willy Kani was born on June 6, 1889, in the Waimea Valley in an area known as Paliuli, where the ancient village of Peʻe kauaʻi, birthplace of kings, was once located. His craggy features and seriousness of purpose always reminded me of a Hawaiian version of the 1950s Western star Randolph Scott. Born of a Hawaiian mother and a German father, he was reared, as were many racially mixed children of the time, by his Hawaiian grandparents. He was already in his seventies when I got to know him. A master of Hawaiian culture and history, he spoke the language in the old tongue of those who had taught him as a child, and his knowledge of the mountains around Kauai was legendary. It was said that he knew every trail in the region and that there wasn't a cliff too steep for him to climb.

Though he was much older than my mother, they obviously treasured one another's company, for they would sit around the dining room table, which he himself had made, and drink beer and talk for hours. At other times they could be found sitting out in the yard under a large mango tree, at a table that once belonged to his grandfather. Ancestry was often the subject of their conversations. Like my mother, Willy Kani came from a priestly line (Kapahu kani o lono translates as "the sounds of the drums of the god Lono"). Their conversations also included talk of ancient Hawaiian spiritual beliefs and accounts of Willy Kani's explorations of ancient Hawaiian burial caves and temples. The stories would soon come to dominate my imagination and set the course for the next period of my life.

At first, when I tried to eavesdrop on their conversations my mother would shoo me off with the usual "Kuli kuli," but after a while, seeing my keen interest, she allowed me to sit with them and listen. In time Willy Kani began to share more and more of his stories with me, and even invited me for private visits to his house at Paliuli, in the Waimea Valley.

Willy Kani's house stood at the base of Paliuli, the gorge located between two cliffs—the pinnacle of Kikiao la and the heights of Pe´e kaua´i—that rise to form the lowest and the highest peaks of Poki´i Ridge. According to Willy, *poki´i* refers to "different images in the nether world that could be attained in life only through dreams." He recalled another ridge that bears the name Poki´i, on the eastern side of the Waipao Valley beyond the town of Kekaha, over five miles from Waimea. This use of one name for two different places having geographical alignments, Willy said, often indicated an underground traveling cave used by the ancients as a secret passageway to get from one spiritual site to another.

In Hawaiian myth, Paliuli refers to a legendary land of plenty and joy. It is also a name frequently applied to places where young chiefs were raised in seclusion. Willy Kani told me the name derived from a large black face of stone that protrudes from the northern slopes of the heights of Pe´e kaua´i. To me it was a place of mystery, spiritual power, and inner strength. From my first visit to Paliuli, I was enthralled. Walking through the gate onto Willy Kani's property was like walking back in time to a different world with different priorities.

There was only one other house in Paliuli. It was the home of Mr. Roland Lalana Kapahu kani o lono Gay. Mr. Gay was a descendant of the original Captain Gay, who, together with the Sinclairs, started Gay and Robinson Plantation on Kauai in 1865, and was a cousin of Willy Kani through his Hawaiian mother.

A narrow road known as Gay Road led into Paliuli. It started about a quarter of a mile before the Menehune Ditch and ran past the old Waimea Poi Factory before reaching the base of the gorge and the gate of Mr. Gay's property, shrouded beneath giant monkeypod trees. From here, a narrow dirt lane followed the riverside fence line around Mr. Gay's land, bordered by taro fields, until it turned back toward the gorge and Willy Kani's gate. Upon approaching this wooden gate and entering Paliuli, I would be met by seven snarling hunting dogs. The only way I kept the dogs at bay was by staring them down as I walked. Then, when I got close enough to the house for Willy Kani to hear me calling, he would come out and shout "Ho'i ho'i! Ho'i ho'i"—meaning both "Return" and "Come"—and the dogs would follow me quietly to the house, where they settled again in their resting spots.

Walking from the gate to the house it was easy to tell that this was once a beautiful estate, though it was now sadly neglected. Willy Kani had, over the last thirty years, spent the majority of his time tracking in and out of the mountains of Kokee. Except for the road and a small area just around the house, the property was overgrown with weeds. A huge pasture that had once been planted to taro now sat empty, except for giant monkeypods and more weeds. Even the fence surrounding the pasture was falling to the ground. Various aging outbuildings and small structures were scattered around the estate, and there were many specimens of beautiful native plants, though they too had become scraggly and overgrown with weeds. The house was built sometime before 1895 and had a floor plan similar to the home of my grandmother, though only a portion of Willy Kani's house was still livable.

Once the dogs settled down, I would sit on the front steps and wait for Willy to launch into whatever topic he had chosen for the day. Sometimes he would share his extensive knowledge of Hawaiiana; at other times he was reflective, comparing life today to life in the past—it all depended on his mood. Some days he would hardly talk at all. On those occasions I just followed him around the yard as he did his chores: feeding his dogs, chickens, ducks, and his one remaining horse. On these days the sight of different objects in the yard seemed to make him nostalgic.

During one of my first visits to Paliuli, Willy Kani told me how Hawaiian burial cists, or vaults, were made. First, a rectangular hole was dug. Then the bottom and sides of the hole were layered with large stone slabs. The body and all the personal belongings that were to be buried with it were lowered into the cist, and finally a large stone slab (or several of them) was placed on top of the crypt. When future burials were required, these tombs could be opened to add more individuals and then resealed, though never covered completely. The covering slabs were instead always visible, flush to the ground, and regularly swept. This type of burial, I was told, was more common for priests, who were often buried within the temple grounds, than for the powerful aliʻi (royalty), whose remains were often hidden in complete secrecy, though such cists were also constructed for commoners living in deep valleys far away from the sea.

Willy Kani claimed he had opened several cists at Mokuone, in the upper Makaweli Valley, that contained individuals of aliʻi rank. One in particular contained a skeleton wrapped in a feathered cloak, with a feathered helmet beside it, both of which were still in good shape when he found them. Although he disclosed its location, I never ventured to find this crypt. He said he also found weapons and personal artifacts, such as necklaces made of human hair and the teeth of dogs and sharks. Willy Kani then walked with me to an area of his property that contained four such cists. The large stone slab covers were clearly visible and were swept clean. Though he spoke only of his grandparents once there, I believe these crypts held the remains of his priestly ancestors.

On one of my visits, he started talking about Hawaiian stones and artifacts. Seeing my interest, he led me to a small shed at the edge of the pasture, the floor of which was being slowly lifted by the roots of a great monkeypod tree close by. When he opened its door, I was awed by what I saw inside, for this ten-by-twelve-foot shack was packed from floor to ceiling with Hawaiian artifacts. It was so crowded we had to stand at the doorway while Willy Kani rifled through the treasure, pulling out one object after another and explaining their uses.

The items made of wood were what initially caught my eye. There were beaters and large wooden anvils made from the logs of the kauila tree, tools that were once used in the process of making kapa, or *tapa*—meaning "the beaten thing"—a native fabric similar to papyrus cloth from which the commoners made simple clothing, bedding, and special garments for the aliʻi class. The wooden anvils, called *kua kuku* or *kua la au*, were seven to eight feet long and eight to ten inches wide, rectangular in cross section. Each kau kuku had a long groove hollowed out on the bottom, the sole purpose of which was to lighten its handling load. On these kua kuku Willy's ancestors placed the bast fibers that had been scraped from the bark of the *wauke* (paper mulberry) tree, the akala (Hawaiian raspberry) tree, and the *mamake* (a member of the native nettle family) and soaked in salt water. The commoners beat the fibers, slowly adding more bast and a resin they had taken from the stalk of a young banana tree to bind the mash together. As it slowly lost its water content, the mixture was pounded into a sheet on which the person pounding placed her watermark. The *iʻekuku* (beaters) used to beat the fibers together on the kua kuku were rods about two inches thick and sixteen to eighteen inches long. They were made in many different patterns. The iʻe kuku that Willy Kani possessed were of the designs known as *pepehi* (deep groove), *maka upena* (net mesh), *hoʻopai* (sharp ridges), *lau maʻu* (fern leaf), and *lei haka* (pandanus leaf). He also had round beaters known as *hohoa*, which were used at the beginning of the process to make the pulpy mash.

Other wooden items in the shed included numerous *papa kuʻi poi* (poi boards), on which taro was pounded to make poi. Made of *ohia* wood, these boards were anywhere from four to six feet long and three to five inches thick. They were oval in shape, and the top was slightly hollowed out to retain some water and also to hold the mixture as it was pounded. (My mother would later tell me that the smaller boards were also used for birthing.)

The collection of stone artifacts in this shed must have numbered in the hundreds. There were poi pounders, salt pounders, medicine stones (Hawaiian pestles), and stone bowls used to burn mashed kukui nuts as lamp oil. There were also adzes, stone chisels, and axes of all sizes. We would return to this room on many occasions, whenever Willy Kani wanted to show me some *pohaku pa'ahana* (implement) that wasn't available in his house.

Even more intriguing to me than these artifacts were those found in burial caves or at the site of the ancient village of Pe'e kaua'i. I knew this from conversations I had overheard between Willy Kani and my mother, and from walking the ancient site of Pe'e kaua'i with Willy as my guide. It was at this time that the word `aumakua` began to impress itself on my imagination with visions of curses, spirits, and ghosts seeking revenge for the theft of their property. You see, many times at our house I had heard about the consequences of removing artifacts from burial caves, but always when Willy Kani was not there to hear the lecture. However, my mother didn't seem too concerned as long as I confined myself to looking at the artifacts, but when I later started entering the burial caves myself, she became anxious and reminded me that my `aumakua was watching over me. (It was clear she meant my ancestral spirit, or else she would have used the word *akua*, which is sometimes used as a reference to the Christian God.) In that period of my life I had no concept of ancestral gods or deities. My idea of an `aumakua was of some sort of invisible spirit with supernatural powers.

It was also at that time that I started to take notice of a large auku'u, or black-crowned night heron, rising out of a ditch that ran not far from Willy Kani's front porch whenever I arrived and again whenever I left, as though it were announcing my arrivals and departures. Ka'ili Naumu, one of the traditional ha builders, once told me that the auku'u was believed to conspire with the spirit world, standing unnoticed along watercourses and listening in on people's conversations until recognized, whereupon he would flee to a secluded spot so that his memories could be transferred to the realm of the spirit world.

Willy Kani must have been aware of the gossip I had heard about curses and superstitions because one day he brought me back to the shed and told me the story of how his collection began. He was about thirteen years old when he first entered a few burial caves in the area of Poki'i Ridge, close to Paliuli. In these caves he came across a large number of sheets of kapa cloth that were in excellent condition and of beautiful design. Upon leaving the cave, he took the sheets of kapa with him and brought them home, where he cleaned them and hung them on his grandparents' clothesline to air out. When his grandfather saw the kapa cloth hanging from his clothesline, he grew very upset. Willy Kani argued that these beautiful sheets would only rot away if left in the cave, but his grandfather was firm: The possessions of the people buried in those caves were not to be removed by anybody, regardless of the reason. His grandfather then ordered him to return the kapa cloth to the exact place he had found it and to pray in Hawaiian both to those he had aggrieved and to his own 'aumakua to understand what he had done and forgive him. Willy Kani did as he was told and returned the kapa to the cave in which he found it. He then offered prayers, just as his grandfather had instructed him to do. When he returned to these caves years later, the sheets of kapa cloth were gone, as were the other artifacts that had previously been placed there. Someone had looted the grave.

From that time on Willy Kani started seeking out other caves along Poki'i Ridge in the Waimea Valley, collecting artifacts and storing them in Paliuli, where they would not be removed for sale or profit. The way he saw it, these artifacts at least remained in the homeland of their rightful owners and not in some distant museum or private collection. Before removing any artifact from a burial cave, Willy Kani always offered a prayer in Hawaiian in which he explained his intentions and asked the owner's 'aumakua to be at peace with his own. When he told me all this that day, I instinctively understood what he was talking about. He believed he was saving the artifacts on behalf of their owners, whereby he brought peace to their na 'aumakua. After that the idea of some kind of curse never crossed my mind, and thoughts of the many superstitions I had been told seemed to be replaced by a growing faith in this 'aumakua that my mother had said watched over me.

After telling me this story, Willy Kani offered to take me to the caves in which he had found the sheets of kapa cloth fifty years before I was born. We left his yard and walked along the dirt lane that followed the perimeter of the Gay property. Upon passing the Gays' front gate, we turned onto an old trail that began at the base of the pinnacle of Kikiao la and led directly into the inner reaches of the gorge. This old trail was overgrown with haole koa, huge poinciana trees, and a jungle of weeds, which hid many sharp rocks that lay scattered beneath. At first the trail was level, but as we left the pinnacle of Kikiao la behind us, it abruptly climbed steeply upward, winding its way through the thick *malina* (sisal) and *panini* (cactus) where the rocky slope separated itself from the growth below. The caves were located in a cleft that separated a second tier of cliffs from a third course above. At first the climb looked difficult, but because there were plenty of places to get a handhold or foothold, making the ascent was like climbing a steep stone ladder carved by nature.

There were three caves, all within ten feet of each other. The first cave, the one farthest to the left, was the largest. It was about four feet high in the opening and sloped down to about two feet high as its rear. It was roughly twelve feet square and contained the remains of several individuals wrapped in *lau'hala* mats (mats woven from the leaf of the pandanus tree). The other two caves were similar but smaller, and the skeletal remains within them were laid out on the ground without being covered, though whether they were laid to rest that way originally or had their coverings removed by looters I couldn't say. Clearly the graves had been tampered with, for bones were scattered all over the dirt floors. I remember feeling surprised that the sight of these remains had no particular effect on me. Apparently Willy Kani's discussions had erased the fear and awe they might otherwise have instilled in me. Instead, I was filled with peace and was aware only of the profound silence of the tomb.

As we stood on the ledge outside the caves, Willy Kani told me how the openings had once been sealed off by rock walls to discourage looters. These walls were constructed from the debris of nearby landslides and matched the cliff in color and texture. The stones were held together with mortar made from clay soil mixed with *pili* grass, a native grass that turns to straw and takes hundreds of years to decay. Even this mortar was colored with dust to blend in with the stone of the cliff. A wood frame made from ohia wood (also filled in with rock) was set in the middle of the wall so that when future burials required the tomb to be opened, this "door" could be removed or resealed without disturbing the rest of the wall. By the time Willy Kani showed the caves to me, the walls were already in ruins, though a few sections were relatively intact.

As we left the caves and walked back to his house, Willy Kani was silent. This was the first and the last time we would visit a burial cave together, though I would search out many more by myself. For more than a year after, I spent all my free time exploring the caves of Poki´i Ridge, reporting each find to Willy Kani. I secretly hoped to find a cave he had not already discovered some fifty or sixty years before I found it, but I never did. Still, I was always on the lookout, scanning the cliffs along the ridge for that one cave whose seal was not broken.

The Traveling Cave

Searching Poki´i Ridge for caves was no easy matter. I had to climb steep cliffs and scramble up tiny ledges to get to most of these burial places, but because I felt protected by the kahu (in this use, guardian) of my ´aumakua, the sense of fear that would ordinarily have accompanied such exploits never troubled me.

Although I wasn't concerned, others were, and it wasn't long before my mother started hearing reports from people who had seen me scaling sheer cliffs and dangling from narrow ledges. Even so, she never attempted to stop me. She even conceded that maybe an ´aumakua really was drawing me to the area for some purpose, though she insisted that I be careful and made me promise that if I did come across any artifacts, I would not remove or disturb the remains in any way. I believe the reason my mother didn't interfere with my activities was that they reminded her of her great-uncle David Malo Kupihea.

When my mother was a girl, he often told her about his exploration of the burial caves on the island of Maui. As a youth searching for caves near Ka´anapali, he came across a startling sight. In one of the caves he found several skeletons, but rather than lying flat on the ground, they were bound in a sitting position. Their long black hair was dressed in braids and still clung to the fleshy skulls. He always believed these skeletons were the remains of Indian natives from the Americas, and when he later worked on developing his theory of the migration of the Polynesians to the Hawaiian Islands, the memory of this cave convinced him that at least a portion of the ancient stock that made up the Hawaiian race (especially those coming from Oahu, Molokai, Maui, and Hawaii) migrated to the islands from South America. He thought the Hawaiians of Kauai and Ni´ihau had a different ancestry, probably from the Marquesas Islands. In his later life David Malo Kupihea returned to Maui, but he was unable to relocate the cave that would prove his theory. After telling me this story, my mother instructed me to take note of the burials I encountered, just in case I happened to come across one from a different culture. I suspect she believed that my great-uncle David Malo Kupihea was kahu to the guardian `aumakua watching over me.

I entered a number of burial caves during this period, and as my mother instructed, I was always careful not to move or disturb anything. Except for the many lau´hala mats that lay scattered on the ground, I didn't see any artifacts, though there were many human remains. Most of the caves were just small cavities in the cleft of the cliff—less than two feet high with interiors that were twelve to sixteen feet deep and of about the same width. Only a few of them displayed remnants of having had a concealing rock wall. In each of the caves I explored there were no more than five or six adults; most of the remains were children and infants, who were usually found in the company of an adult. Of the adults, several appeared to be in what I at first thought were small canoes, but when I later mentioned this to Willy Kani, he told me they were just ohia logs that had been split in half lengthwise and hollowed out to contain human remains. After the flesh was removed from the body, the skeletal remains were then placed in the log and inserted into the cave, in place of the common lau´hala wrap.

Besides the ohia logs, I came across another detail that intrigued me. Several skulls, mostly those of children and infants, seemed to have been patched at the top with some sort of plaster. These patches were barely discernible, as the plaster was very close in color to the bone and just as hard. I noticed them only because the rectangular outlines of the patches stood slightly higher than the surfaces of the skulls. I later asked Willy Kani about the patches, and he told me they were repairs made to the skull after it was damaged in the ritual preparation of the remains (*kapa lau,* or "garment of leaves"). The process of removing the flesh from the bone involved wrapping the body in shredded banana stalks and leaves and heating it in a pit about twelve inches underground by lighting a fire on the covering dirt. After a few days the flesh would fall easily from the bones. However, the heat from the fire often damaged the thinnest part of the bone at the top of the skull (especially the less developed bone of young children) and would then be repaired with a plaster made from lime before interment.

Willy Kani answered my questions but always asked me if I had come across any artifacts. One day as we sat talking on his front steps, he got up, went into the house, and brought out his collection of fishhooks. He had fishhooks made of human bone *(makua iwi kanaka)*, dog bone *(makua iwi ilio)*, shark tooth *(niho mano)*, and turtle shell *(makua ea)*. The fishhooks made of shark teeth also contained cartilage from the human nose. The smallest fishhook he had was about half an inch long, and the longest about three inches. The largest fishhooks were made of whalebone *(makua iwi kohala)*, and were of the type known as *kohe,* with one barb pointing inward at the end of the hook. Some of the smaller hooks had the barb on the outside; this type was known as *hulu.* Finally, he had a few sets of composite fishhooks, which were used to catch squid *(he'e)*. These consisted of a stone sinker, or *pohaku luhe'e,* shaped like a cowrie shell and lashed to a pointed piece of bone. A cowrie shell *(leho)* the same size as the stone was also attached to the bone. The idea was that as the squid wrapped itself around the cowrie shell to eat the urchin inside, it would be snagged on the hook.

Along with his collection of hooks, Willy Kani also brought out bundles of fishing line and cord, most of which were made from the inner bark of the *olona* plant or *hua* tree. He then took me to a grove of hibiscus shrubs growing in his yard. Telling me that they were of the same family as the hua tree, he stripped the bark to show me the inner portion of fibers that were used to make cordage after they were cured in salt water. As with kapa, the outer bark would have to be scraped off with a piece of sharpened turtle shell.

Willy Kani told me then that he would have missed finding the hooks, as well other small artifacts, had he not searched the soil on the floor of the cave with his fingers. He said this was important because at the time of burial, the floor was probably swept clean down to bare rock, but as decades passed, dust and dirt would build up on the floor of the cave, burying many of the smaller items. He advised me to sift through the soil with my hands until I reached the rock surface below and feel around for any little objects that may have been covered up. Often, these were the only artifacts that remained after a cave had been looted.

But I knew I couldn't do it. Because the remains had already been disturbed by looters, bits of bone had been scattered on the floor and were embedded in the earth. Sifting through it with my hands just didn't feel right. In any event, the prize was not one to be taken by the finder. The thought of offending my guardian `aumakua kept me from disturbing the remains any more than they already had been.

The day after Willy Kani brought out his collection of fishhooks, he showed me another artifact: a *lei niho palaoa*, which, if you remember from the story of Umi a liloa, is a type of necklace worn only by high chiefs and chieftesses. There were two parts to the necklace: a *lei* (the part that is worn around the neck), which was made of hundreds of strands of human hair, and a hook-shaped pendant about three inches long made from the tooth *(niho)* of a sperm whale *(palaoa)*. Since the ivory remains of sperm whales generally washed ashore only at Kualoa on the eastern coast of the island of Oahu, such a necklace would have been very rare and valuable. Looking at the fine braided strands of black hair one inch in thickness, it felt strange to think that the person or people from whose hair it had been made had been dead for hundreds of years. Even stranger, the hair still seemed be producing its own natural oils.

This was one artifact that Willy Kani did not dwell on. He brought it out, let me examine it for a few minutes, then carefully took it back inside. Upon returning he sat down on the steps and told me its story. He had found it in 1919, wrapped in an ancient *pu`olo* (secured bundle) made from kapa, in the depths of a burial cave below the heights of Pe´e kaua´i, where the western walls of the gorge rejoin Poki´i Ridge. I immediately knew the place he was talking about, for over the last months I had covered every inch of the gorge more than once, exploring Poki´i Ridge almost into town toward the south of the gorge and well past the Menehune Ditch to the north. Willy Kani had already told me that he believed the cave was one entrance to an ancient lava tube that stretched underground from Poki´i Ridge in the Waimea Valley to the Waipao Valley at Kekaha Kauai, where another Poki'i Ridge existed with the other entrance to the traveling cave. I had been looking for it without success myself.

Willy Kani knew from his discovery of the lei niho palaoa that either ali'i were buried in this cave or their life was connected to it in some way. He also found evidence of sorcery. Another pu'olo he discovered in 1919, deeper in the cave, woven of fine sennit, held a kapa cloth–wrapped petrified female head with very long black hair. (I am tempted to say mummified; however, I still can hear him saying petrified). Willy Kani explained how these pu'olo were normally made by a kahuna for use in sorcery. The head he found could have been that of the owner of the lei niho palaoa. Its contents were considered a secret source of power similar to an unihi pili. The pu'olo discovered by Willy Kani contained a human head, but these bundles could also be made with other body parts (hands were common). The bodily remains of Willy Kani's find may have been divided among many chiefs and priests of the time; the higher the rank of the deceased, the greater the power of the pu'olo, it was believed. Akua and 'aumakua stones (stones associated with a god or ancestor) and even sticks carved by a kahuna could be made up into bundles to serve a similar purpose. Once the bundle of the deceased was completed, it would be worshiped as an unihi pili housing the remnants of an 'aumakua inside. This unihi pili could then be used to bring sickness or death to another, especially to close relatives of the dismembered deceased, an art often referred to as *kahuna ana ana aihue* (sorcery used to steal another person's life or property, or even kingdom). Willy Kani's bundle containing the human head was a rare find, for such a prize was usually destroyed by its maker once the pu'olo had accomplished its purpose. Otherwise, the pu'olo could be stolen by another kahuna and turned against its original maker. Willy believed its maker had kept the pu'olo here in this cave because it afforded him ceremonial secrecy and security that made it unlikely to fall in to the hands of a rival kahuna, since the cave was probably accessible only to one particular line of the hereditary priesthood that acted as its keeper, and was kapu (here, off-limits) for all others. He also admitted removing the pu'olo from the cave, though he told me he no longer had it in his possession. It was taken from him without his knowledge by a foreign acquaintance from the island of Oahu, who had probably sold it to a collector. He still seemed to be pondering the color and pattern of the kapa cloth in which the head was wrapped, ending the story by describing it as red sprinkled with tiny white dots.

After telling me all this, Willy Kani went on to describe the interior of the cave. He said that the initial cavern appeared to come to an end after about a hundred feet, but if I felt around the right side of the wall, I would find a concave area in the rock big enough to walk into. In this covelike area, he said, there was a narrow tunnel that ran down about thirty feet into the cave floor at an angle of sixty degrees. After the first fifteen feet or so, the tunnel became so narrow that there was barely room for a man to squeeze through, but at thirty feet the passage grew a little wider, until it opened up into a subterranean cavern even larger than the one above it. He explained that on his first trip he had followed the underground cave to the west for more than an hour before concern about running out of oxygen made him turn back. It was just a little beyond where the tunnel entered the cavern below that Willy Kani found the lei niho palaoa and petrified head. He never said whether it was lying on the ground by itself or in the company of an individual's remains.

On a second visit, he brought candles to test the oxygen supply and claimed to have traveled for about two hours. He said the tunnel grew bigger as he walked deeper into the cavern. Eventually, deep within the ridge, the tunnel leveled off and led into a huge underground room with a large freshwater pool at its center. He said the water appeared to have a greenish tint to it, but that may have been because of the old-style incandescent lights that he used, since the cavern itself took on a strange hue under their illumination. When he started to notice that the air smelled dead, he checked the candles, which were still burning, though much more faintly, and decided to turn back. He said he could tell that the cave continued beyond this large cavern, and that he could see no end in sight. He was sure it was the legendary traveling cave of Pokiʻi.

Willy Kani never ventured into this cave again, although he did spend a lot of time walking Pokiʻi Ridge, trying to find the cave's other entrance. He didn't find it. Even if there had been an opening in the ridge, it might long ago have been sealed; landslides were common enough there. One old Hawaiian man told him that he had heard stories suggesting this was precisely what had happened, except that the landslide was not an act of nature but was instead intentionally created by the ancient priesthood, upon the coming of the white man, to keep the location of the cave a secret. On the many trips that Willy Kani still made to Kokee during this period, he now took me along, and when traveling by the Kekaha Road, he would often point out a large rock on the ridge where he still believed the second entrance existed.

In telling me the story of this deep cavern, Willy gave me the impression that he wanted me to explore the cave myself to try to find what lay beyond the point at which he decided to turn back. This I attempted to do, but with even less success than he had. The cave was as he had described it—a large room eight to ten feet wide at its entrance, with a ceiling five to six feet high. The walls were circular, which suggested it was in fact an ancient lava tube. The one thing Willy Kani hadn't prepared me for was the prodigious number of burials I encountered there. I estimated there were fifty individuals from the entrance of the cave to the back wall. The older burials had been stacked to make room for more recent arrivals, which, by tradition, had been placed at the feet of those interred just before them. Most of these piles reached a height of three feet or more. Oddly enough, there were very few skulls. Most of the bones were from the arm, ribs, and leg. Willy Kani would later tell me this was because skulls had been collector's items in the past, and had probably been removed from the cave and sold.

On my first visit to the cave, I couldn't locate the hole in the floor. Once inside the covelike area where the hole was supposed to be, there was no natural light. The wall curved just enough so that it blocked the entrance. When I peeked out to look back, I could see nothing but the stacks of skeletal remains, dimly lit by the rays that filtered in from the entrance beyond. Thinking about the puʻolo that Willy Kani had found gave me an eerie feeling, and I decided to turn back.

When I told Willy Kani that I had found and entered the cave but was unable to locate the hole in the floor, he seemed to get upset with me— something he had never done before. He insisted that the hole was there and told me to try again. So I returned to the cave and for the first time in all my explorations, despite the fact that Willy Kani had forbidden me to bring guests into Paliuli, I brought help: two of my classmates from school, Junicio and Ishidro Cacal. The Cacal brothers, however, followed me only about halfway into the cave and then turned and ran out, ignoring my shouted entreaties for them to stay. I was unaware that often traditional Filipinos at that time believed in the existence of ghosts.

Though I was uneasy about exploring the cave alone, I decided to return to the covelike chamber and search for the hole in its floor. This time I did locate the hole, but it was not as Willy Kani had described it. Since he had been here, the hole had filled with debris driven in by decades of rain and wind. Bones and sand now covered the rear of the cave and filled the hole. The thought of going back to Willy Kani and telling him I found the hole but didn't make any attempt to explore it brought me such apprehension that I sat down and began to dig with one hand while holding the flashlight in the other. Scooping sandy granules mixed with bone dust out of my way, I began to sink into the circular rock walls of the hole and could tell that the tunnel started to narrow just a little farther below the reach of my feet. Having no one with me, I reluctantly gave up for the day. As I pulled myself out of the hole, I could feel the debris I had removed sliding down my back and refilling the cavity as if I were caught in the draining sands of an hourglass.

On my next attempt, I brought another classmate, Malcolm Azeka, who was of Hawaiian and Japanese ancestry. While Malcolm didn't seem afraid of the burials, he would not enter the hole to help me dig, although I passed him handfuls of bone dust and dirt to toss behind me. I cleared the hole down to where the passage narrowed and then, with Malcolm holding on to my legs to keep me from being swallowed up by the rolling debris, I tried to drop through the passage to the cavern below. As I hung suspended, one hand clinging to a flashlight, the other swimming in the air to keep the rolling debris away from my face, the hole seemed very deep and very narrow indeed. With only a dim view of what seemed to be the beginning of the cavern below, I began to wonder if, once I succeeded in squeezing my way through, it would be possible for me to return to the entrance of the cave and the light of day. Finally, I gave up on the idea and Malcolm pulled me out. For some reason I never returned to this cave again. Maybe it was because of the way I felt when leaving that day: my hair, face, hands, legs, and feet were pure white from digging through the dust, and I felt like gagging from all that I had inhaled. Willy Kani later agreed that going farther would have been dangerous. If the mountain was still settling, he said, the hole might be even smaller now than when he had entered it decades before.

In any event, that was the end of my exploration of the traveling cave on Poki'i Ridge. But from this experience, and from all my other cave explorations, I seemed to have gained a sixth sense, for from that day on, without having any prior knowledge of their existence, I was able to feel the presence of burial places.

The Search for Pohaku kani—the Bell Stones

Every time I took the Paliuli Trail, I passed in front of the gate leading to the old Gay house. Built by Roland Gay's father, Charles Gay, in 1895, the house was a classic example of regional Hawaiian architecture influenced by the architecture of early New England–style homes. One day as I made my way past this gate, I heard Mr. Gay calling me. He told me he had seen me in the area many times, sometimes alone and sometimes with Willy Kani, and was wondering what I was up to. At first I was hesitant to talk to him, for the imposing lanai that surrounded his house reminded me of those at my grandmother's, and I felt I was not to trespass there. However, when I told him of my explorations of the burial caves, he invited me onto the large patio at the rear of his house and shared stories of ghosts, spirits, and curses connected to the caves and Paliuli. Mr. Gay spoke as an authority—he was then in the process of producing the book he would later entitle *Hawaii: Tales of Yesteryear*—but it was clear to me his information came from books and not firsthand experience. No one who had learned Hawaiian folklore from the old men in the region would have spoken interchangeably of ghosts and na 'aumakua in the way Mr. Gay did.

After that first visit, Mr. Gay told me it was not necessary to walk around his place to get to Willy Kani's house, and so I began to take the shortcut through his yard—although it took awhile for his dog, a large German shepherd named Pali, to get used to my presence. Most days when I passed Mr. Gay's patio, he invited me in for a soda and a story. He was always surrounded by books on Hawaiian folklore and legends, which he collected and later compiled to create a radio program called "The Hawaiian Dinner Hour," which aired on Sunday evenings during the late 1960s.

When I told Willy Kani about Mr. Gay's ghost stories and his warnings about curses placed on burial caves, he didn't seem to take them seriously. He just laughed them off with some remark about tall tales. Later that day he called me into his parlor, where I found him holding some kind of wand. It was made of a light-colored wood, probably milo, and consisted of a twelve-inch handle topped with a ball about five inches in diameter. It was hard to distinguish whether the ball and handle had been carved from a single piece of wood or if the ball had been made separately. It was in perfect condition, its finish still glossy. I believed this wand was a ka'aha stick once held by a priest while sacrificing in the temple. It was decorated with leaves, and strands of kapa cloth were secured to the base of the ball. I thought it strange that Willy Kani didn't bring this wand out into the yard, or even to the porch where we normally sat. Instead, he called me inside to view it. I saw it only briefly, and didn't get a chance to touch it. Almost as soon as he showed it to me, he took it back and left the room to return it to the hidden place from which he had retrieved it.

Willy Kani and Mr. Gay, although only one year apart in age, were very different types of men. Sometimes I thought the only thing they had in common was their insistence that I never bring anyone else onto their property or into the gorge. Willy Kani talked about Hawaiian burials and historical sites that he had personally discovered or explored in the company of the elders of his day. Mr. Gay had been removed as a child to attend private schools, and discussed Hawaiian folklore and legends he had read in books or heard from scholars instead of his elders. Willy Kani had heard his folklore from elder Hawaiians in the early 1900s, making him a master of his environment and affording him the opportunity to test these stories against personal experience and observation during his explorations of the burial caves and other sites. When it came to his ancestral connection, Willy Kani felt it straight from the na'au (gut), where the Hawaiians believed the heart and the mind were bound in deep affection. Mr. Gay, on the other hand, depended on his intellect, which sometimes seemed less a blessing than a curse, since he was so well informed that he often had trouble taking sides with any one of the many opinions he had read.

Like Willy Kani, though, Mr. Gay had knowledge of Paliuli and Waimea geography—and the stories to go with it—that he wished to share with me. On one of my visits he told me about a series of stones on the ridges called *pohaku kikeke* or *pohaku kani,* or "bell stones," which were large, hollow boulders that produced a resonant sound when struck with another, harder rock. Like the drums of the god Lono, which reverberated with the earthly sounds of the elements of nature that were connected to him, the pohaku reverberated with the earthly sounds of the elements of nature that were connected to the god Kane, and, it is said, could be heard only from a distance by the trained ear of a priest who is standing beside another such stone. Because of their use in connection with ancient ceremonial announcements and confirmations, missionaries likened the stones to bells. Twenty-four of these pohaku kani sites were said to have provided long-distance announcements in ancient times, reverberating the birth or return of a high chief from the temples of Waimea all the way to Waialua, a distance of well over twenty-five miles, and twelve were said to announce the same message in the opposite direction to the wilderness depths of Waimea Canyon, a distance of well over fifteen miles. Mr. Gay said the first or source stone of reverberations was supposed to be located at the site of an ancient temple above the cliffs of Pohaku lani. The second, or source stone of the northern line of sites, was located across the valley on Mokihana Ridge. The third, or source stone of the eastern line of sites, was located across the valley on Nonopahu Ridge.

Hearing about the legendary bell stones, I decided to explore the plateau that stretches from above the pinnacle of Kikiao la to the cliffs above Pohaku lani and the Menehune Ditch. I found many signs of ancient people having lived there, and one day, while walking close to the edge of the cliff in the area above Pohaku lani, I came across a large area of flat lava rock spotted with blotches of grayish and greenish moss that seemed to resemble scattered clouds on a dark black sky. Stone walls on both sides formed an enclosure about forty feet across. This enclosure, about twenty inches high, was open at the cliff and had collapsed on itself at the end opposite the cliff, where it seemed to disappear into the soil beyond the lava flat. At its center, almost to the edge of the cliff, there was an oval-shaped boulder about five feet long and two to three feet wide, with a thickness of about eighteen inches. Instead of sitting on the lava floor, it was perched about eight inches off the floor on three or four much smaller stones. The boulder's appearance seemed just as mystical as the rock terrace it was perched upon. I struck a solid stone against it, and it did produce a resonant tone, although the sound was much deeper than a bell would have made. The sonorous note seemed to radiate out over the district.

When I returned to Mr. Gay's house and told him of my discovery, he said I had found the first of the bell stones. Upon telling Willy Kani of the bell stone above Pohaku lani, he told me that he had also visited the site, many years ago, and believed the boulder to be a sacrificial stone used for offerings to the gods, although he allowed it might have been used as a bell stone as well. Willy's belief was my first impression, too, but I never mentioned this to Willy Kani or Mr. Gay. What I found interesting was the similarity of the bell stone perched on three or four smaller stones above the lava rock to the stone of Pohaku lani, perched upon three smaller rocks in the Waimea River, which figured in Auntie Maile's version of the story of the two children of King Ola who were turned to stone for their forbidden curiosity.

Ancient Places Have Stories to Tell

My search for the bell stones diverted my attention from the burial caves, and I started to spend more time hiking the ridges above the heights of Paliuli, Pe´e kaua´i, and Pu´u ki´i, looking for other interesting sites. Willy Kani told me that I had evidently stumbled across the old Paliuli Trail that was once used by the ancient Hawaiians on their trips from Paliuli up into Kokee, and later by Hawaiian cowboys *(paniolos)* for their cattle drives. This trail basically followed the southern rim of the Waimea Valley. After the valley turned to the northwest, the trail followed the crest of the ridge on to the southern rim of Waimea Canyon, in the region of Kokee, the same route that Waimea Canyon Drive winds along today.

When I mentioned to Mr. Gay that I had discovered the old Paliuli Trail, he responded by telling me this story: Many years ago he had guests over for the evening. Upon their departure late at night, a few of them noticed a group of Hawaiian cowboys saddling their horses just outside his gate. When later informed of this by these guests, Mr. Gay asked Willy Kani if he had gone hunting that night, and if so, if any of his hunting party had saddled their horses outside of his gate. He then described what his guests had witnessed. Willy Kani laughed and said that the spot where the cowboys had been seen was once the site of a corral; in the old days, cowboys saddled their horses there for cattle-driving trips up the Paliuli Trail. Mr. Gay's guests had seen, in that place, people who no longer walked the earth, doing a job that was no longer performed there.

While I never saw anything as unusual as the cowboys Mr. Gay's guests saw that night, I did come across other places and sights that were inexplicable to me. One day I was walking around the base of Poki'i Ridge from the pinnacle of Kikiao la to Pohaku lani to explore what may have existed below the site of the bell stone above. The area around me was overgrown with tall haole koa smothered by a thick tangle of wood rose and other vines that grew over the trees and formed a canopy dropping all the way to the ground. As I made my way through the brush, I stumbled and almost fell into a hole in the ground. This hole was circular with a diameter of about four feet, and it seemed to lead straight down into the ground. Carefully peeking into it I could see a dimly lit cavern, the ceiling of which was four to six feet below me. From what I could gather, it seemed to be about twelve feet square and about ten feet from the ceiling to the floor. Had I fallen into it, I would not have been able to get out.

On my way back to Willy Kani's house that day, I stopped to talk to Mr. Gay about the hole and the cavern beneath it. He thought it might be an old-fashioned Hawaiian jail known as a *hale pa'ahao*. He said he had heard that there was one located in the area I had been exploring, and although he had never seen it himself, my description matched the one he had been given.

I tried to locate the hole again but was unable to find it, even though I made several visits to the area. When I mentioned my frustrations at being unable to find the hale pa'ahao again, Mr. Gay remarked to me that the na `aumakua were known to sometimes show you something, but only once. This made me think of my great-uncle David Malo Kupihea and the burial cave he had seen on Maui as a boy but was never able to find again. It also made me think of Willy Kani, who showed me many items and artifacts, but each one only once. With all this in mind, I decided to give up trying to locate the hole again and was later told by Willy Kani that he believed the hale pa´ahao had been filled in years ago. I do not know how I had tripped on the hole, just as Mr. Gay could not know how it was that his guests had seen the cowboys. But perhaps it was my `aumakua at work.

On my following visits to Paliuli I began to concentrate on exploring the heights of Pe´e kaua´i, high above the Waimea Valley, which afforded me a panoramic view of Kauai's western shoreline stretching from the town of Numila, eleven miles to the east of Waimea, to Kekaha and Mana, well over seven miles to the west. Here I would wander among ancient stone walls and through stone-walled terraces upon which stood a few remaining parapets. These once surrounded the floors of ancient grass huts to protect their occupants from the driving winds while they slept at night. There were remnants of ancient house sites that Willy Kani told me had dotted the ridge between Waimea and Kekaha, for the lands that bordered the shoreline below were once marsh. Looking out toward the ridges and ravines that connect the heights of Waimea to the heights of Kekaha, my attention again shifted to finding burial caves.

I soon found another cave of significant size, at about the same elevation as the lowest of the terraces. It was just beyond the first ravine in the direction of Kekaha. Today, just below the ravine, there is a small concrete bridge or culvert where the road makes a U-turn before climbing to the summit of Waimea Heights. If you circle around the ridge to the west of the culvert, you will see a large ledge of rock that protrudes from the summit above, forming the first and most prominent of the many cliffs that jut from the ridges between Waimea and Kekaha. About ten feet above the base of this cliff is a tiny cleft and a small two-foot hole leading into a huge cavern that is about ten feet high and twelve to fourteen feet square before it becomes an oval-shaped lava tube that runs deep into the ridge. I explored this cave many times, and each time I sensed that it had been used for burials, though I was never able to find evidence. However, I could tell from the lava rock debris piled on the floor that the height of the inner tunnel, at present only four to five feet, was once the same height as the large cavern. The cave's inner ceilings showed signs of having collapsed, apparently not just once but many times over the years—the ceiling of the inner tunnel displayed the scars from the loss of the debris that now covered the floor. If it had not been for the space left behind by the fallen debris, the inner tunnel might have been completely sealed off at its entrance in the cavern. There were large slabs of sharp lava rock piled in layers on the floor, and although I tried many times to squeeze my way through the spaces in the debris, I was never able to get to the natural floor of the tunnel, and was fortunate that I was somehow able to squeeze my body back out from the beneath the debris after being wedged in securely on a few occasions. With its history of cave-ins and change, I could not tell where the tunnel might have led.

Although I didn't know it at the time, I would be among the last to explore some of these sites. In the early 1960s, under a training and make-work program known as the Civilian Construction Corps (CCC) funded by the U.S. government, construction began on Waimea Canyon Drive, the road that now stretches from the summit of Waimea Heights to Kokee. During construction I'd often climb to the highest point of Poki'i Ridge above Willy Kani's house to watch the progress, along with a Hawaiian boy named Albert Nawai, who lived close by. One day, during the early stages of construction, we sat on the ridge and watched as huge earth-moving machines and bulldozers completely destroyed all traces of the stone terraces directly in their path. As I sat there watching them breaking up, the larger stones being bulldozed into a ravine and the smaller into the soil, I couldn't help thinking about how much I had enjoyed walking through those ruins, wondering about the people who had originally built them. Now, without the stone terraces to catch the attention of the future traveler, the ancient builders would be forgotten. I had experienced the last days of Waimea Heights in a state of wilderness.

A Final Journey with Willy Kani

My last memorable experience with Willy Kani is a trip we took together to the bottom of Waimea Canyon, deep in the Waimea Valley. Just as our trip to the burial caves was my first and Willy's last, this would be my first visit to the bottom of the canyon and the final visit for him. Willy Kani had spent much of his young life hunting with his Hawaiian elders, and later, as an adult, exploring the area in search of the ancient ruins and legendary caves, the discovery of which could serve to verify many of the stories he had heard as a child. Now he was preparing to visit familiar terrain for the last time to introduce me to what had taken him half a lifetime to learn. I watched him saddle his last remaining horse, but it was hard to say what Willy Kani was feeling. Although he was generous in sharing his knowledge, he was much more reserved when it came to his emotions. That morning as we prepared to leave, he concentrated his attention on the young blond palomino stud he would be riding. As he secured the saddle, he told me that this horse was the descendant of other great horses he had ridden to Waimea Canyon in the past.

Willy Kani rode the palomino and I walked behind. We traveled down the dirt lane in front of Mr. Gay's house and turned onto Gay Road, passing between the taro patches that surrounded the old Waimea Poi Mill. Then, turning onto Menehune Road, we headed inland past the Menehune Ditch to the end of the road, where we crossed the river at Waiahole and left civilization behind. We would cross the river seven more times before we reached Camp One, the site of a small hydroelectric plant maintained by Kekaha Sugar Plantation, which was located about eight miles into the valley at the base of Waimea Canyon.

He remained silent as he rode. Though the horse's gait was steady, neither speeding up nor slowing down, it outpaced my own so that by the time we crossed the river for the second time, I had started to lag behind. By the time I made the third crossing, Willy Kani and his horse were out of sight. The trail up the northern slope of Mokihana (also known as Puʻu kii, or Puʻu tii) Ridge ascended well over nine hundred feet. It was steep and riddled with sharp loose rocks, many of them slippery from springs of water that seeped from the ground. At its height the trail began to follow alongside an irrigation ditch for a four-mile winding stretch. The ditch ran out of the plant at Camp One, six miles above, and wound its way down the valley toward Waimea.

It was a long and lonely walk, and to make sure I was heading in the right direction, I constantly searched the ground ahead of me for any tracks left behind by Willy Kani's horse. As the irrigation ditch disappeared into the mountain, the trail again sloped down steeply toward the river. I passed many side trails leading away from the main trail, and since most of these trails showed relatively fresh hoofprints, I was no longer certain which of them Willy Kani had followed. I decided to stick to the main trail, which now zigzagged across the river. Every time the tracks disappeared into the water, I'd begin to worry I had lost them, but they always reappeared on the opposite bank of the river.

After I made my way across the river for the seventh time, the trail gradually sloped up, turned away from the water, and ran through a dark grove of hau trees. Off in the distance I could see an old weatherworn shack perched on stilts behind banana, mango, and mountain apple trees— the home of an old Filipino man who was employed by Kekaha Sugar Plantation to maintain the ditch, which now reappeared next to his shack from beneath the overshadowing ridge. Continuing past the old shack, I reached the top of the hill. There I stopped, filled with awe by the sight of the mouth of the canyon that opened up beyond me. Each of its many ridges caught the light differently, producing a kaleidoscope of blues, pinks, reds, and purples that shifted and blended as the light changed. Vegetation grew only on certain ledges, so that swaths of green climbed the canyon like a stairway. At the top, a brilliant blue sky seemed to stretch out forever, interrupted only by the occasional cloud, which cast its shadow across the canyon's charcoal cliffs as it drifted by.

Looking down across the river, above the glimmer of its silver stones and amber waters, I could see Camp One. There Willy Kani's horse was tied to a kukui nut tree in front of another old shack at the foot of a suspension bridge that spanned the river. The fire was already going, and Willy was hustling back and forth, setting up camp. I had been walking alone for well over four hours by then, and he was a welcome sight to see.

Upon joining Willy Kani at the campsite, I was introduced to the caretakers of Camp One, who lived in the only house that was still maintained there. They were an old Hawaiian couple named Joechin and Rachel Kaʻpepe, and though originally from the Makaweli Valley, they had lived at Camp One for more than twenty-five years. Willy Kani had already begun reminiscing with them, and when I realized they were going to be talking for hours, I decided to explore the area around the camp (spending most of this time sitting on the suspension bridge, gazing into the canyon beyond). Later, after sunset, I rejoined Willy for a dinner of sour poi, salted dried cod, and goat jerky. As we bedded down next to the fire, he began to tell me a story about Camp One.

These days the hydroelectric plant there is powered by vertical turbines built into a cliff that runs above the river. Water is diverted from two major streams about four miles upriver into a series of tunnels that gradually gain in elevation as the riverbed descends toward the camp. Once there, the aqueduct—now about six hundred feet above camp—spills its waters into a large-force main pipe that runs steeply downhill under the river and into the plant where the water it carries turns the turbines. However, from the early 1900s until 1946, when it was destroyed by flood, the original plant used horizontal turbines that were turned directly by the falling waters of the aqueduct's tunnels added to the current of the river. These horizontal turbines and waterways had to be maintained and continuously protected from debris that could hamper both the flow of water in the river and the falling water from the aqueduct. The Kekaha Plantation, which owned the plant, had to employ many laborers to keep the waterways clean. Camp One became home away from home for a few of these laborers and their families. Three of these old Hawaiian families were the Kapahus of the Waimea Valley, the Aʻanas of the Makaweli Valley, and the Akis of the Hanapepe Valley. I mention their names because they are all a part of the camp, the site of the story Willy Kani told me that night.

It happened when Willy was still a young man. As was common for hunters traveling to Waimea Canyon at the time, he stopped off one night at Camp One to talk, play cards, and drink with the workers and other travelers. At some point during the night, conversation turned to stories of a mummified baby that was said to have been left in a nearby burial cave. Its periodic crying had been reported by a number of old-timers traveling through the area at night. One time, a group of travelers and workers—some of them present at the gathering with Willy that evening—had been sitting by the fire playing cards when they heard the cry of a baby and noticed a Hawaiian woman walk off into the darkness. A while later she returned, carrying a baby, and in the light of the campfire the card players could see she was nursing the infant.

When one of the card players asked those from the camp who the woman and the baby were, he was told that the woman, whose name was not disclosed, was a family member of one of the other workers at Camp One, and that the child was not what it appeared to be. The card players then learned about a burial cave located on a rock ledge known as Pohaku pepe, on the left side of the Waimea River just across from the first shack I encountered at the mountain apple tree. The families who had first occupied Camp One in the early years, as well as the many night travelers who passed through, had been hearing the baby's occasional cries for as long as anyone could remember, but this Hawaiian woman was the first one to search out the infant and find it, and had become the kahu (here, caretaker) of the *pepe pohaku* (a stone—*pohaku*—believed to be possessed by a baby—*pepe*). From then on, whenever she heard the baby crying, she would go to the cave and bring it back to comfort and feed it. Then when the crying—which came from the cave, not the baby—ceased, she'd return it to the cave.

After hearing this story, a couple of the old-timers decided to venture over to the Hawaiian woman to get a peek at the baby she was nursing. Through the flickering of the firelight they could clearly see an infant whose mouth was placed at the woman's breast, but when they drew closer, they saw that the infant looked old and withered, as if it had reached the age of six months and then, without developing further, had aged another eighty or ninety years.

I don't know why Willy Kani told me this story, unless it was to serve as a warning against undertaking *kahu malama,* or "the duties of a caretaker," outside of one's genealogical chain. Had anyone else told me the tale, I would have dismissed it as an entertaining ghost story, but Willy Kani was not one to tell ghost stories. What I do know for certain is that the cave at Pohaku pepe does exist, and there are skeletal remains of infants buried inside. As for the mummified baby, only a descendant of the Hawaiian woman who had made herself its kahu would know of its whereabouts today. In addition, there is in this story the play on names so often found in Hawaiian legend: Echoes of Pohaku pepe can be heard in the name of the old people he had just introduced me to—Ka´pepe, meaning "the baby," and in the original home of one of the old families who used to live at Camp One—the Akis from Hanapepe, meaning "caretaker of a baby."

Whether Willy Kani actually believed the story of the mummified baby I cannot say, but there was another legend he told me that night that I know he did believe, for he claimed to have accidentally stumbled across its existence in the days of his youth while hunting goats along the base of Pu´u ka pele, an extinct volcano that towers above the western rim of the canyon. This is the legend of the traveling cave that was said to stretch from Waiahulu, deep inside the Waimea Canyon, all the way to the beach of Polihale at the end of Mana, some seven miles away. Again, as with Poki´i Ridge, it was twin place-names that had led him to the belief, and then he stumbled across the Waiahulu or canyon-side entrance to this cave. Adding to his belief was the existence of yet another pu´olo (bundle) in the cliffs of Pale u´pa that was said to contain a petrified head and the existence of the mummified remains of a woman of status covered with black kapa cloth and deposited in a cave that faces Pale u´pa. Willy Kani believed the mineral waters, high in salt and lime content, deep within these traveling caves played a major role in the mummification and petrification of the human body.

The entrance to the traveling cave was located well above the river, near where the sheer cliffs of Pu´u ka pele meet the bold red slopes of Polihale Ridge. Polihale Ridge, a name associated with a great white-sand beach and sacred spring at the end of Mana, is known today as Polihale State Park. Willy Kani told me the cave had an underground stream running through it, and the water flowed to the west, in the direction of Mana. This matched the stories he had heard from the old-timers that one entrance to the cave was at the site of a freshwater spring near the end of Polihale Beach, at the point where the beach disappears into the cliffs of Ka´aweki. According to their stories, the sacred spring was covered with sand during most of the year, but at certain times the waves swept in far enough to remove the sand and expose the spring—the same spring dug each summer by Maha Leoiki, our friend of the traveling huki lau.

After talking of mummified babies and traveling caves and sacred springs deep into the night, we fell asleep. The next morning we arose early, and with Willy Kani on his horse ahead of me set off for Ka'aha, a deep and narrow gorge in Waialae Gulch. Once at Ka'aha we hunted goats that had descended from the ridge to drink in the stream. By mid-afternoon we had shot all we could carry and were ready to begin the long journey back to Waimea.

Upon reaching the junction of the Waialae and Waimea Rivers, Willy Kani stopped to tell me about an ancient Hawaiian quarry and foundry he had stumbled upon while hunting goats in this same area during his youth. He said it was located on a ledge that runs just below the rim of the plateau known as Ponolu'u, between the gulches of Waialae and Koaie farther up the canyon. He also said that at the time he discovered the quarry, the remnants of an old grass hut, which he assumed was the workers' living quarters, were still visible. Scattered around the site he found many unfinished adzes, as well as some that were broken during the process of being shaped into chisels, wedges, axes, and other stone tools.

After stopping to tell me about the quarry, and again at Camp One to bid the Ka'pepes aloha, we headed home. Once again Willy Kani was silent as we left Waialae and Camp One behind us. The one last echo of the ancient in names and words that I am left with from this trip centers on the gorge called Ka'aha. The *ka'aha* (wand) draped with black kapa cloth was the last implement Willy had shared with me in Paliuli. The deep gorge known as Ka'aha, the last place we had visited on this journey, refers to a "sacred gathering place or assembly." And finally, the word *aha* by itself refers to the umbilical cord of life, a cord the ancients made of coconut fiber or sennit to knot and thereby record their lineage. Willy Kani, on this trip and in all the time I had spent with him, had stretched his aha and had shared its gathering places and thoughts with me as he had shared the ancient kapa-draped ka'aha. The places we talked of and the places where we spent our time had become, like the Ka'aha Gorge, sacred gathering places.

A View from Na mo´o ekolu

After the canyon trip, the tone of my visits to Paliuli appeared to be set by my personal resolve and independence; Willy Kani seemed content for me to wander the uplands of the gorge on my own, and to experience whatever I encountered there in the light of my own reasoning, offering only apt comments to my accounts of new discoveries. He had stretched his aha cord, and now it was time for me to develop my own gathering places and thoughts, to begin stretching my own aha cord, with its knots of memory that bind me to my ancestors and my descendants.

In the months that followed, I wandered the uplands and my knowledge grew, as did my sense of the echoes of Waimea's ancient past in the surrounding areas. I often returned to the site above the heights of Pe´e kaua´i, where I had witnessed the destruction of the stone terraces. From here I was afforded a panoramic view of the western shoreline of Kauai and a panoramic world of thoughts through which I could travel amid my ancestors.

The area where I sat is called Namo´o ekolu, meaning "the third serpent," a name given to the irrigation ditch that runs along the summit there, winding its way to Kekaha like a snake crawling along the side of the ridge. It is the continuation of Namo´o elua, "the second serpent," which is the irrigation ditch that winds its way down from Camp One. The aqueduct beyond Camp One is called Namo´o ekahi, "the first serpent." The word *mo´o* also refers to genealogy, which, the ancients believed, wound its way from ancestor to descendant like a reptile.

Looking out to the ocean from my seat at Namo´o ekolu, I could see the islands of Ni´ihau and Lehua beyond *komohana hema*, or the "southwestern" shore of Waimea town, which was built on a narrow strip of ancient sand dune between the southern base of Poki´i Ridge and the ocean. Looking to the northwest *(hikimoe akua),* I could see as far as Kekaha and Mana, and to the east I could see the little villages of Kapalawai, sites of priestly fishponds and springs. I could see Kekupua, ancient home of those thought of as demigods; Makaweli, also called Pakala, the ancient boundary of the priestly lands of a ka la; Kaumakani, ancient place of the winds; the plains of Hanapepe above the salt ponds;

and Numila above the plains of Wahiawa, site of the last recorded case of mummification in the Hawaiian Islands: In the 1950s a Hawaiian man named Paul Kawai was discovered to have preserved the corpses of both his mother and grandson in a cave at Kukuiula.

My seat can easily be found today. The Java plum tree I sat beneath is still there next to a small wooden bridge that crosses the irrigation ditch as you make the first major climb when traveling up Waimea Canyon Drive.

Looking southeast *(hikina hema)* from my seat, I could see Po'o Point at the tip of the tiny peninsula that forms the western side of Makaweli Bay. This is the birthplace of the legendary chief Lu'anu'u of the tenth century A.D. Lu'anu'u was the son of the ancient king Laka (or Laka a Waheiloa), chiefly ancestor of the people of Maui and Hawaii, and of Hikawaelene, high chieftess from the ancient village of Pe'e kaua'i at Waimea, Kauai. Lu'anu'u was thirty-fifth in the hereditary succession of ancient kings that began in the first century A.D. with Wakea, father of Haloa, who is often called the procreator of the Hawaiian people, and ending in the fifteenth century A.D. with Liloa, father of Umi, whose story I have already told. The story of the birth of Lu'anu'u can be found in the *Traditions of Laka*, translated from genealogical chants and handed down by the nineteenth-century scholar Kamakau.

The story tells us that shortly before Hikawaelene's pregnancy came to term, she decided to return from the island of Maui, where she had been living, to Waimea, the place of her origin. As the double-hulled canoe she was traveling in attempted to make a landing at Po'o Point, her child was born, and in the confusion the baby fell through a space in the platform (pola) of the canoe and *lu'u* (plunged) into the water. From this incident the child was called Lu'u, and because the child was laid in the *anu'u*, or oracle tower of the heiau of Pohaku ha'ule, he was called by the name Lu'anu'u, and he became the ancestor of the chiefs of Kauai.

On the shoreline just a half mile west of Po'o Point, I could see where the Waimea River enters the ocean. Here today on another tiny peninsula that forms the southeastern tip of Waimea Bay stand the ruins of a Russian fort. This tiny peninsula was known as Laau o a ka la (wand of the sun) and was the location of the Pu'uhonua, or "terrace of refuge," of Hikina a ka la, a terrace constructed of earth and stones and termed a platform heiau because it had no walls. Willy Kani believed it to be a place of asylum and healing for people who had arrived from distant lands and a place of orientation for people who departed to find asylum in distant lands. The high chieftess Hikawaelene, upon leaving Maui, was probably on her way to the Pu'uhonua, but was forced to shore when she unexpectedly gave birth in the canoe.

From the southeastern end of the present Waimea Bridge, just inland of the Russian fort, I could look a little farther upriver and still see the concrete footings of the old Waimea Bridge. Here on the hill known as Akia was the site of Pohaku ha'ule Heiau and the platform of Kapale. Willy Kani believed this was a heiau for the consecration of a newborn or an arrived chief. The name Pohaku ha'ule was the same as that of the stone called *pohaku kahe ule* (stone-split-penis) used for sub-incision, the Hawaiian practice comparable to Judaism's circumcision.

After the fall of the kapu system in 1819, when the old religion was abolished and the destruction of the heiau was ordered, many heiau were simply converted to pig or goat pens, and later, upon their introduction, to cattle and horse corrals. Willy Kani believed the walls of the Russian fort, built in 1816, were constructed by simply relocating or rearranging the stones from the core of the terrace that once made up the platform of Pu'uhonua Hikina a ka la.

Inland from Akia lie the flat farmlands of Mahaihai that run farther inland until they adjoin Waikai'a. The name Mahaihai comes from an ancient clan that was konohiki (landlord) over this land, and their corpses are lying in the cliffs of Mahaihai in a series of caves just beyond Akia. In the days of old, this area was famous for its akala plants, *akala* meaning "reddish" or "pink"; the kapa cloth made from the akala bark of Mahaihai was known for its pink color achieved from the berries of this plant.

I could look to the black sands of Waimea across the mouth of the river at the point of Laau o a ka la and see the ancient tip of the beach of Luhi, where today a large boulder sits bearing a bronze plaque that marks the site of Cook's arrival in 1778. The boulder sits in front of what is now Lucy Wright Park, named for the first public school principal of the district, who donated the land for the park's establishment. This area, known as Pana'ewa, adjoined our old home. Long ago, ancient fishponds stretched from Pana´ewa, at the mouth of the Waimea River, to the present location of the Waimea Honpa Hongwanji Mission and the Valley Estates subdivision on Menehune Road. The area from the end of the fishponds to the gorge of Paliuli where Willy Kani lived was once occupied by the ancient village of Pe´e kaua´i, and the stretch of black sand that ran from the mouth of the river to the shores that fronted this ancient village was called Luhi Beach, where the children of this village once played. In the time of my visits to Paliuli, this area was occupied by the Waimea Sugar Plantation. Willy Kani would walk it every year, just after the sugarcane was harvested and the fields were plowed, to examine the soil for artifacts. He found so many of them year after year, buried in different layers, that he believed the area had been populated for hundreds of years.

The ancient fishponds were long gone by the time C. B. Hofgaard built his general store in the 1890s. In the center of Waimea town today, the Cook monument is located in Hofgaard Park, named after Hofgaard, who in the 1890s noted many remnants of stone walls while he was building his store. He believed the area was the original site of the Pu´uhonua Hikina a ka la, though the name once used for the area that now stretches from the park to the Waimea Big Save was not a *pu´uhonua*, or "place of refuge," but a place where fishing nets were made and stored. Willy Kani recalled the name of this place to be Ke kilika a mauna, and it was here, he believed, that sheds once stood on an ancient platform that adjoined the fishponds. In these sheds twine was produced for the making of fish nets. (This land adjoined Papalekoa, where I lived as a child, which in turn adjoined Namahana, the site of my grandmother's house.) Such ponds, constructed only at the mouths of rivers or streams, were of the type known as *loko i´a kalo* because it was a Kauai custom to grow kalo (taro) in (*loko* means "inside") the ponds along with the fish.

Hofgaard, having heard of another pu´uhonua called Laau Hikina a ka la at Waialua, Kauai, and it being of the walled-enclosure type, assumed that the pu´uhonua at Waimea was also of this type and believed that he, in fact, had uncovered it. By Hofgaard's time, the last remnants of the ponds had been destroyed in the floods that devastated Waimea Valley in May 1826. Another destructive flood hit the town in 1862. (Floods seemed to occur every fifty years up to the time of my grandmother's day.

Willy Kani told me that in 1900, when he was eleven, much of the town was covered in sand dunes.) The remnants of the ponds were inhabited by Chinese immigrants, who grew rice there.

Besides what I learned about the ponds from Willy Kani and family members who had been living on Papalekoa and Namahana since 1902, I learned the boundaries of the fishponds from my mother, who received this knowledge from Maha Leoiki's father, Andrew. He was even older than Willy Kani and had first heard from his grandparents the stories he told. According to these stories, the Leoiki ancestors—who were Ni'ihau people—were skilled in the tradition of net making and came to the ponds to trade for *anae* (mallet fish) to bring home to Ni'ihau because these freshwater fish raised in the ponds were considered a delicacy there where no ponds were found and fresh water was scarce.

In May of 1820 Waimea witnessed the arrival of the first missionaries, Samuel Whitney and Samuel Ruggles, who first settled on the lands of Laau o a ka la, near the Russian fort. They planted vineyards in Mahaihai and expanded their influence beyond the western banks of the Waimea River. In 1828 they moved across the river and settled on lands in and around the Keali'i Heiau, where they built their own residence and a church of stone. In their determination to turn Hawaii's hallowed places into holy places for their own religion, these two used the sacred stones of local heiau for their churches and consecrated the burial grounds of Hawaii's ancient priests in the name of their own God.

Looking down from my seat at Namo'o ekolu, I found that the lands of Papalekoa and Namahana were hidden from view—they sit below the lower cliffs at the southern base of Poki'i Ridge; however, I can clearly see the place of my birth on the low plateau that shadowed the lands below. The site of Keali'i Heiau (dedicated to Lono nui akea), the temple in the famous sketch made by John Webber during Cook's 1778 expedition, was located along the ledge of this plateau overlooking the fishponds. The area known as Ka na'a na'a, which the temple complex once occupied, stretched from the site of the old Waimea hospital, through the grounds now occupied by the parsonage of the Waimea Foreign Church, to the end of the Crowell estate adjoining the parsonage.

A few hundred feet to the west of the temple site stands the Waimea

Foreign Church, designed and constructed by the missionary George Rowell and originally known as the Great Stone Church of Waimea. The walls of the church were built of stone blocks quarried and cut from the limestone ledges of Kekaha and Mana; its foundation and roof were constructed of heavy timbers cut and hauled from the upland forest of Kokee. Although work on the church began in 1848, it was not completed until 1859, when it replaced Samuel Whitney's earlier church.

The area that the church and surrounding cemetery (and Waimea High School) now occupy was known as Papa ena ena (glowing red earth) because of its stretch of rich red soil that slopes from the oceanside face of Poki'i Ridge until it joins the black sands of the beach at the site of the old Waimea Landing.

My great-uncle Alex Blackstad believed the church and cemetery stood on an ancient burial ground for priests, and he said that even in the days of his youth, when new grave sites were prepared there, burial cists were often found. All of our early ancestors who had emigrated from Norway are buried there in the red earth.

When I looked in the direction of Kekaha, I could see the roof of the old Mission Home, peaking through the giant monkeypod trees that surround its grounds. The home is a two-story residence originally built by Peter Gulick in 1829 and later renovated to its present design by George Rowell during his stay there between 1846 and 1865. The house and grounds stand on the western boundary of the lands of Papa ena ena, and were part of the lands taken from Haakulou (baptized Deborah Kapule), the last queen of Kauai, who was the favorite wife of Kaumualii, the last king of Kauai. My grandmother's niece Ruth Blackstad Nordmier and her husband, Otto Wramp, were the last family to live in the Gulick-Rowell house, moving there in the late 1930s and remaining until their deaths in the early 1980s. My grandmother often told the story of the untimely death of her niece's grandson. The child died on the staircase that leads from the parlor to the bedrooms upstairs. His spirit or ghost, she said, was still often seen by family members as it stood on the staircase or in the parlor.

Looking farther in the direction of Kekaha, I could envision only ancient marshland and the early sugar plantations that followed. The owners of these plantations, Willy Kani once said, in their quest to cultivate every inch of land in cane, destroyed more historical sites in Hawaii than Father Time had taken in the thousand years that preceded the coming of Cook.

Beyond Kekaha I could see the white sands that stretched along the shoreline in front of the ancient marshland of Mana and faced the islands of Niʻihau and Lehua. I think every family that had resided in the Waimea or Kekaha district for more than three generations had a story of an encounter with ghosts or spirits while traveling through the lands of Mana at night—and some even had stories of visitations during the day. This was where Maha Leoiki claimed to have seen the spirit of Old Lady Makuaole, whom, months earlier, he had carried in the back of his weapons carrier to her eternal rest on Kanikula. The lands of Mana are mentioned by the people of old as *ao ʻauwana*, or a "place of wandering spirits"—where the homeless souls, those not claimed by a friendly or family na ʻaumakua after death, entered the *ao kuewa*, or "realm of homeless souls."

Wandering among the Ancients

Upon leaving my seat at Namoʻo ekolu, I would often return to Willy Kani's house by walking inland along the irrigation ditch until it disappeared in a tunnel at the base of Puʻu kii, a solitary hill I often climbed at the northern end of Pokiʻi Ridge. The hill of Puʻu kii, high above the bend in the river at Pohaku lani, is like an observatory that has lookouts in every direction. To the northwest from atop Puʻu kii I could see the mouth of Waimea Canyon far off in the distance.

I wandered about the irrigation ditch near the stretches of the water that the old Hawaiians called Namoʻo elua and Namoʻo ekahi. Were these the legendary lands that once belonged to the priesthood of Kane, before the rise of the line of ancient kings who stripped the ancient priests of their land? Legends say that in the hidden lands of Kane lived the Ke na wa, Ke na mu, and the Menehune. The Wa were a people who possessed large mouths and were known as shouting people, the Mu were a people who possessed small mouths and were known as silent people, and the Menehune were the dwarf people who built upon stone.

These three were said to be the original peoples of Hawaii nei.

Looking to the north, in the direction of Mokihana Ridge across the upper Waimea Valley, I could see the remnants of Kane he´e nalu (Kane of the fleeing or vanishing surf) Heiau, perched beyond the ledge. On the black cliffs that fall beneath these ruins into the lands of Waiahole below there are large petroglyphs, visible only in the early morning hours, depicting the arrival of a sailing canoe. Jerry Arruda, a descendant of the Naumu family, which has lived in the area since ancient times, worked the lands of Waiahole during the plantation era, and because of the many stone anchors he found there when plowing the fields, he believed Waiahole to be an ancient mooring site for canoes. In looking down at the gorge of Ka ho´o manu (pathway of birds) above the cliffs of Pili a mo´o, it seemed as though I was immersed in Kane hune moku, or the "hidden lands of Kane," a land that, according to legend, was covered with birds.

I could see the old Paliuli Trail down to the east, winding along the northern edge of Poki´i to the flatlands of Paliuli that stretch from the cliffs above the Menehune Ditch to the pinnacle of Kikiao la above the gorge where Mr. Gay and Willy Kani lived. In descending the old trail to the flatlands I would often stop at the remnants of a grass hut, just to enter its doorway, the opening of which was still visible in the stone wall that had once enclosed the floor of the hut. Willy Kani believed this place to be an ancient rest stop used by the people who traveled the trail.

Once on the flatlands I walked above the cliffs of the Menehune Ditch to a site called leina a ka`uhane, above the stone of Pohaku lani in the river below. Leina a ka`uhane, or "leaping place of the spirit, or soul," was a site of jutting rocks that point to the north, known as the black road of Kane, where the spirit of the deceased was caught or reclaimed. Any site chosen for this reclamation was always in close proximity to the ocean because the valley was seen as a continuation of the deepest floors of the sea and because it was believed that from here the spirits could cleanse themselves in the salt water of the sea. Such sites once existed in every district, on every island in Hawaii nei.

Here at leina a ka`uhane a person near death was placed upon the jutting rock, and in passing into death, his spirit or soul was apportioned in time (mahele ana) to seek the realm of wandering spirits, the ao kuewa or ao `auwana. However, if the spirit could find or be claimed by a family member, the living `aumakua, it could enter or return to the ao (light), into the realm of a o `aumakua. If the spirit lost its way or memory, it then fell into the realm of endless night, the *po pau ole*. The leina a ka`uhane adjoined another rock that was slightly lower and jutted out even farther. This was called Leilono or the "garland of voices," because it had a circle about two feet in diameter carved, like a petroglyph, on its surface. Here the person who came to claim the spirit or soul of the dead would stand and travel into the `aumakua realm to retrieve the spirit and guide it to a sacred place where it could be fetched by a family member and enter the realm of ao `aumakua before it fell into the realm of endless darkness.

From the top of the jutting rock ledge of leina a ka`uhane and Leilono, I had a bird's-eye view of the mouth of the Makaweli Valley and the bluffs of Mokihana and Nonopahu Ridges that form the northwestern and eastern walls of the Makaweli Valley. Looking out at the bluffs of Mokihana, beyond the burial mound of Kanikula, I could see the ledge of rock called Pe´e a moa that stands above the site of the ancient village of Pe´e a moa, ancient home of the people of Naulii. There below the ledge once stood the terrace heiau of Pe´e a moa, the remnants of which could still be seen when I was child. Willy Kani told me the word *moa* in Hawaiian refers to a red jungle chicken or rooster, and was used to describe chiefs because they wore cloaks and helmets that were decorated with feathers taken from sacred birds. Members of the Makuaole-Apo family used to repeat legends passed down from their ancestors about an order of the ancient Hawaiian priests who gathered at the temple periodically and who practiced the art of *kahuna ana ana* (praying to death). To determine which of them was most powerful, these kahuna would sit in a circle on the stone terrace and take turns trying to will a moa to death, using only the power of their minds.

Across the Makaweli River, to the east of Pe´e a moa and below the bluffs of Nonopahu, lay the remnants of Nana ika lani Heiau. Nana ika lani, or "seer of the heavens," was a heiau where priests of the order of heavenly seers studied and interpreted the omens in cloud formations. Because of this the heiau had a very tall anu´u (oracle tower). Its steeple-like frame, exceeding fifty feet in height and supporting three evenly spaced platforms, was wrapped completely in white kapa cloth. The anu´u, built upon two elevated stone platforms, stood high above the river and was said to have competed with the heights of Nonopahu at that time. The kupuna named Ohu Hookano often spoke of a pure white rainbow that was said to have appeared periodically over the Makaweli Valley in the days of old, stretching like an arch of clouds from the bluffs of Mokihana, over Nana ika lani, to the bluffs of Nonopahu above.

When Cook first saw the anuʻu of Nana ika lani from afar, he mistook it for a pyramid. His expedition attempted to reach Nana ika lani Heiau, but was forced to turn back because the backwaters of the Waimea and Makaweli Rivers were then quite deep. Deciding instead to visit the Kealiʻi Heiau, Cook followed his guide along a trail, much like the trail below the ledge of Pokiʻi, from the Menehune Ditch to the site of Willy Kani's house today, from where the trail connected the ancient village of Peʻe kauaʻi to the heiau complex on the ocean end of Pokiʻi Ridge. The trail up the ridge started at a location just behind what is now the Honpa Hongwanji Mission in the Waimea Valley and climbed to where the Crowell estate is now located. Remnants of the trail, which was still used by schoolchildren in the 1930s, can be seen along the cliffs to the rear of the mission today.

Leaving leina a kaʻuhane, I would head off to what had become my favorite stop, the sacred terrace of Kopahu, the site of the sacrificial bell stone I had discovered above the cliffs of Pokiʻi, that point to the east that overlooks the Waimea River's final run to the ocean. Kopahu, or "the rising or fluttering terrace of spirits," was a sacred place where the spirits or souls who were sought or lost at leina a kaʻuhane gathered to be snatched by family members. The large stone perched upon the smooth lava rock floor served as an altar, or *ku pahu*, in ancient times and was known as a pohaku o Kane or "stone of the god Kane." This place was believed to be a *puʻuhonua*, or "place of spiritual refuge," and a gateway to the spirit world.

When ceremonies were conducted at Kopahu, the stone was covered with fine white kapa cloth, and sacrifices of fish, animals, and possibly even humans were offered to the hereditary gods of the family line, the akua ʻaumakua. The stone of Kane was said to have been pointed out by the god himself, not merely set up by men. The god guided people to the stone through their dreams or visions. Once there, the arriving family member or members (not more than three) as well as the returning spirit were freed from defilement and wrongdoing because both must be consecrated upon unification. The stone than resounded in confirmation of the rebirth of the `aumakua in the new birth of the family line, indicating that the aha cord was secured. An old Hawaiian woman named Julia Naumu Akana, the only sister of the Naumu brothers (the expert ha builders), related a story of the terrace of Kopahu that was handed down by her ancestors: The spirits or souls of many ancient ancestors still frequented the terrace to be fetched every other month, during the night of the full moon, starting from Hili o holo, or January. In fact, Hili o holo means "to appear and disappear" like mist or fog.

The last stretch of land above the eastern cliffs of Poki`i was known as Kikiao la, "the flowing spirit light *la*." The *papa* (surface) of the sacred grounds of Kikiao la was an extension of the same papa or flat lava surface of Kopahu, and was separated from it only by Kopahu's stone enclosure. Kikiao la was the place of sacred births *(ka papa o laka)*. Here the cycle of the `aumakua descending into po (darkness) and ascending into ao (light) was attained through the sacred births and rebirths of the sacred line of hereditary chiefs in the ancient land of gods known as Paliuli.

In the traditions handed down from the Menehune people, Ola (200 A.D.), eighth in the line of succession of ancient kings and called Kikiao la or "of the flow of life" in legend, was chief of Waimea and desired to bring the waters of Kane to the flatlands of Waimea. The priest Hulukuamauna heard from Kane that only through Kane huna moku (Kane's hidden land) could the mano (watercourse) of Waimea be constructed. Kikiao la offered himself as the sacrifice upon its completion, if he could have the sacred chieftess Nama o ka hai for his wife, but this offering was refused. The Menehune people were requested to do the work and Kane huna moku (Kane himself) was given a branch of red fruit as compensation. After the completion of the work, Kane departed with Nama o ka hai and the Menehune and the Mu from Laau o a ka la to the floating land of Kueihelani and never returned. And so, in the story of Kikiao la and Kane huna moku, the arrival or rise of one caused the fall or departure of the other and the demise of the sacred lands of Paliuli, since it was during this time that the hereditary line of Ola turned to image worship. Hence Ola is called Ole, meaning "without," in the genealogy of ancient kings.

In the traditions of Kane handed to us by the scholar Kamakau, the god Kane said upon his arrival to Hawaii nei, "Hiki au, e ola"—"I have come; live." Ku and Lono responded, "Ola. Hiki au, e ola. Ola."

Gather as in a great and lengthy net, in the inner recess of the ear, a resounding verse from memory, the ancient Polynesian prayer of knowledge. I have traveled full circle within the ancient lands of Paliuli, and the sounds of one called Kani still reverberate upon my return. Willy Kani did not inform me of the sacred places of the spirits I have just described until a later time in my life. He had sent me off to wander, I believe, to fetch for myself the offerings that the ancient lands of Paliuli still possessed and to judge by my attractions if I had been touched by an `aumakua, so that I could echo, someday, the sounds he made and instilled in me.

The past does not disappear; it is merely silenced. Rediscovering the heiau, for example, sometimes required little more than listening closely enough to the old place-names to hear the secrets they still utter. Such is the sound of the `aumakua, which I was slowly beginning to recognize. When I first began hearing it, I was still a boy. Those years between the ages of nine and eleven that were spent exploring the area of my birth were a time of discovery for me, as they are for every boy—preadolescence is a time in which the boy begins to find out just who he will be as a man. It is a time of breaking away and delighting in the things that truly inspire and amuse us. Because of my fascination with the past—and the encouragement it evoked from my mother, Willy Kani, and Mr. Gay—my initial taste of independence led me not away from my family and its heritage but instead even closer to it. Unearthing the legends and artifacts of my homeland became a sort of quest for me—not for its own sake, but because these reminders of the past stirred in me something that was old enough to remember them.

Although I was only nine years old, in the descending voices of the kupuna I had access to sixty or seventy years of knowledge prior to my existence, and when this is considered against the time span of life for all our kupuna, such knowledge, in reality, stretches back thousands of years.

Old stories stir even older memories. The voices of the past are always whispering in our ears. Today, whenever I shut my eyes and grow very still, I can hear the sounds of Willy Kani and Mr. Gay. What they say may be only memory, but those who speak this memory live on in the world of ao `aumakua.

CHAPTER FIVE

THE VOICE OF THE 'AUMAKUA

WHATEVER THE CULTURE EACH OF US HAS COME FROM, we all have oral traditions—tales told around wooden tables in quiet rooms in the dark evening hours; a reminiscence shared over a drink or two; stories recounted by adults that the young, sprawled comfortably on the floor nearby, are welcome to overhear. While history read from the page can teach in its way, it is this history told by the human voice that can best give us our sense of place, of who we were and who we are.

Although I spent most of my youthful days with Willy Kani—either at his home in Paliuli, listening to him tell the old legends and beliefs of our ancestors, or hiking with him to nearby sites of ancestral importance—and the rest of my days exploring the burial caves and other places he so often mentioned, I headed home with first sight of the evening sky to spend my nights with my mother in our old dining room. These nights, surrounded by the aura of our house's past, became a reflection of my days with Willy. My mother was always eager to hear about the day's activities, and was always willing to discuss them at length. As we sat at our wooden dining table, built by Willy Kani himself, his presence seemed to linger in the chair beside us.

On one of these quiet evenings, my mother left the table and returned with a book I had often seen her bring out when she and Willy conversed about Hawaiian traditions and needed to solve some point of argument. The book was *Mo'olelo Hawaii (Hawaiian Antiquities)*, a collection of papers on Hawaiian history written by David Malo in the 1830s and 1840s. My mother seemed very proud of this book, and the night she first brought it out and showed it to me, she shared what she knew about our ancestor David Malo and the written accounts of pre-contact Hawaii he had left behind for the coming generations so that the vanishing traditions of his people might be preserved.

My mother received her copy of the book from her uncle Charles Ke ola Kupihea Johnson, who was the son of David Malo Kupihea's sister Kahili lukahi mo'i Kupihea. The book's publisher, the Bernice P. Bishop Museum, had presented it to Charles and other family members when the museum published a special English edition in 1951, which was only the second time the book had been printed since the museum's first publication in 1903, after Dr. Nathaniel B. Emerson purchased the original manuscript from a collector for a thousand dollars in 1898 and translated it.

Not only was *Mo'olelo Hawaii* one of the first histories of the traditions of the Hawaiian people in pre-contact Hawaii, but it was also one of the first books to be written in Hawaiian. Although the language had survived for thousands of years as an oral tradition, it had never been put to paper until the early missionaries codified grammar and spelling in order to translate the Bible. When missionaries decided to open one of Hawaii's first mission schools at Lahainaluna, Maui, to teach this new written Hawaiian language, David Malo was one of only a handful of native Hawaiians selected by the ruling monarchs to attend. Because the selection process of these early students was based upon hereditary lines and political loyalties to the monarchy's Kamehameha line, the traditions Malo recorded were mainly those of the chiefs and priests of Hawaii Island and their descendants; he does not truly speak of the traditions of Maui, Molokai, Oahu, and Kauai. My mother, a descendant of the hereditary line of chiefs and priests of Hawaii Island, would not question the book's content, although she did question Malo's motives for his presentations. The Hawaiians who had adopted Catholicism had been, in the eyes of the Boston missionaries, still participating in ceremonies that could be seen as resembling Hawaiian traditional ceremonies. It was in the missionaries' interests, then, to suppress Hawaiian history, including the Hawaiians' historical relationship to Catholicism, and to see that others did not present this connection. Perhaps this was in Malo's mind when he wrote. Willy Kani, who was a descendant of Kauai Island chiefs and priests, took issue with many of Malo's descriptions of traditions, especially those that addressed religious practices.

Opening the book to the frontispiece, my mother showed me the portrait of David Malo and noted the striking resemblance he bore to her older cousin John Tremane Sr., the eldest grandson of David Malo Kupihea. It was this relative, she reminded me, who gave me the name by which I am known—Moke. She also told me how John Tremane Sr. had been influenced by what she believed to be the descending spirit, or `aumakua, of David Malo. The connection, she said, began in 1957, when John Tremane Sr. was involved in a near-fatal accident while working construction on Queens Hospital in Honolulu. At first the doctors didn't expect him to live. Even after he pulled through, they said he would never walk again. During John's stay at the hospital, he was regularly visited by the Reverend Abraham K. Akaka, who would later become well known as the pastor of Kawaiahao Church (the church of Hawaii's first queen regent, Kaahumanu) on the island of Oahu. Although John was not really a religious man, he allowed Reverend Akaka to pray for his recovery, and after a while he even joined in prayer himself. Before long, John completely recovered the use of his legs, and believing that the Reverend's prayers were responsible, he joined the church and offered his services to the man who had convinced God to spare his life. The mission he was assigned by Reverend Akaka was to go to Maui to help restore the Lahaina Mission. John became the pastor of the Waiola (waters of life) Congregational Church in Lahaina. Built in 1827, it was known at the time as the greatest stone building in all Hawaii.

The Lahaina Mission and school were established by the Reverend William Richards of the American Board of Missions. It is said that he had barely stepped off the boat from Boston in 1823 when he was invited by Queen Keopuolani to begin a mission and school in Lahaina. (Queen Keopuolani was the first wife of Kamehameha the Great and mother of Liholiho—who would become Kamehameha II—and Kauikeaouli—who would become Kamehameha III.) In 1831 Reverend Richards went on to establish a high school called Lahainaluna on the heights *(luna)* above Lahaina. One of his first students was a not-so-young man, already thirty-six years of age, placed there by the most powerful person in all of Hawaii nei, the Queen Regent Kaahumanu, the second and favorite wife of Kamehameha the Great.

Malo, as he was then called, was converted by Reverend Richards, who gave him the name Davida, or David, at his baptism in the Wainee (or Waiola) Church, and gave Malo's wife, Pahi`a, the name of Batesepa (Bathsheba), who was the biblical wife of King David. While Reverend Richards taught Malo to read and write in his native Hawaiian, Malo aided Richards in his translation of the Gospel of Matthew into Hawaiian; in this way each seemed to serve as friend and mentor to the other. Soon after completing his four years of study at the school, between the years 1835 and 1836 he wrote the first draft of what would someday become known as *Mo'olelo Hawaii.* He was ordained a minister in Reverend Richards's missionary church, but politics and a changing culture would come to govern his life. In the years that followed, Malo was appointed general school agent for the island of Maui, then superintendent of schools for the kingdom, a position he held until 1841. After this he became a legislator, representing Maui in the first House of Representatives of the kingdom, before finally returning to his calling as a minister. He was assigned to the district of Kula, Maui, and was pastor there until his death in 1853.

By the 1950s, the Lahaina Mission was no longer a part of the school founded by David Malo's mentor and had been stripped of much of its land, first by the Territory of Hawaii and later by the State of Hawaii, and the school was made a public institution. It was Reverend Akaka's hope to recover and restore the remaining mission lands, and he chose as his agent John Tremane Sr., a descendant of David Malo, the man who had put the mission on the map by writing the first history of Hawaii under its pastor's tutelage. John's task involved not only negotiating with the State of Hawaii but also gaining support from the dwindling congregation of church members in this district. My mother always believed that John had been chosen primarily because his family connection to David Malo gave him a better chance for success than other ministers of the church, who at that time were mostly Caucasian. However, my mother strongly believed it was the `aumakua of David Malo that brought John to the church, to serve such a purpose. John spent two years accomplishing his mission, and then, once the lands had been restored, he left the church because he felt that funds raised by the congregation were being misused by the upper echelon in Honolulu. My mother always asserted that it was the `aumakua of David Malo, not God, that gave John the will to recover from his accident and to walk again, because once David Malo's beloved church had been restored, John felt relieved of his obligation and returned to his old way of life.

After telling me all of this, my mother handed me her copy of *Mo`olelo Hawaii*, and said it was mine to keep. She told me it was a sign of the `aumakua of David Malo, and that having passed through the hands of her uncle, the publication was even more special. She told me I should always take care of it. I treasured the book, even if I didn't actually read it until many years later. Instead, I'd flip idly through the pages or reread the passage that appeared on the frontispiece below David Malo's portrait:

> I do not suppose the following history to be free from mistakes, in that the material for it has come from oral traditions; consequently it is marred by errors of human judgment and does not approach the accuracy of the word of God.

Such serious text was not exactly compelling to my ten-year-old intellect. Most of the time I just opened the book and stared at the portrait of its author, as if by doing so I could somehow absorb the knowledge contained in the pages and feel his presence in the room with me.

Katie Koani and the Russian Fort Tunnel

I remember many nights lying stretched out on the floor, glancing through *Mo`olelo Hawaii* while my parents entertained a succession of regular guests who offered accounts of Hawaii's past. Sitting in our home—a former mission house—was, I suppose, a reminder that Westernization had distanced the descendants of David Malo from their traditions and relationship to spiritualism. I thought of my days spent with Willy Kani at Paliuli, and in the caves, and how strong my sense of tradition and my relationship to our spiritualism were there. Our guests, who like Willy Kani were part of the Westernized Hawaii, were also, through, their stories, living links to the traditions and spiritualism of long ago.

One of the many voices that accompanied my nightly leafing through Malo's works belonged to Katie Kamai Koani. She was in her seventies and exemplified the true meaning of a *tutu*, or "granny," with her happy-go-lucky personality; she was like a gourd full of song and folklore, a vibrant animation of what life was like in Waimea in the 1920s and 1930s, when she was young. My mother enjoyed every minute of her visits to our house.

Katie Koani lived on the land called Pana´ewa. She was the oldest of the Kamai siblings—the others were her sisters Margaret, Willy Kani's wife, and Eunice (Mamala), and her brother, Tole—and all were natives of the Makaweli Valley, where they were also raised. She was married to a native of Kalihiwai, Kauai, named Nick Waiwaiole Koani, although by my time she was a widower and lived alone in an old Hawaiian-style house surrounded by native plants. Katie usually stopped by in the evening, clutching her collection of twenty-year-old recordings of the Kamehameha School Choir. These records were produced from the late 1930s through the early 1950s, when Katie's sons and other family members sang in the choir, and whenever Katie was feeling sentimental, she'd stop by our house to listen to them, since my mother owned the only working phonograph in the area. They would put on the records, pour themselves a glass of whiskey, and before long would be reminiscing about old times.

Unable to focus on my book, I usually ended up listening in on the ladies' conversations. I remember one time in particular when Katie Koani was talking about playing near the Russian fort at Waimea during her youth at the turn of the century. She said that at that time there were still many Hawaiian families living in the area she also called Laau o a ka la. One of the houses once belonged to Willy Kani, who lived there on the beach during fishing season, and it was known as the Laau o a ka la beach house. Gradually, however, the houses were abandoned, and the properties came into the possession of the Robinsons, who grew sugarcane right up to the walls of the fort.

My interest was piqued when Katie mentioned a cannon she had seen below the old boat landing at the riverside entrance to the fort. She said it was covered with sand and silt during most of the year, but when the river flooded between late August and early November, the silt washed into the ocean, and if you stood on the remnants of the stone wall that marks the site of the boat landing, you could look down and see a section of the gun's barrel. She said she was told that this old cannon was originally from the Russian expedition that occupied the fort site from 1816 to 1818, after which Kamehameha I ordered the Russians to leave Hawaii. Thereafter the fort's armory fell into the possession of Kaumualii, the last king of Kauai, who ceded the island to Kamehameha I. In 1824, after the death of Kaumualii, the Kauai chiefs were stripped of their lands; rebelling against the Kamehameha monarchy, they raided the fort's armory. In the confusion, one of the cannons was lost, and Katie Koani believed the riverside cannon to be the lost gun, which perhaps had been covered with boulders in an attempt to conceal its location.

She also said that there existed a tunnel connecting the old boat landing site to the fort. The entrance near the boat landing site now lies buried beneath a large flat boulder that slopes to the water's edge, which can be seen from Lucy Wright Park across the river. The tunnel's exit lies along the south wall of the fort, near the first set of stone steps. Today, from inside the fort, it looks like a depression at the base of the wall, as if the rocks there had settled into a hole.

After listening to Katie Koani talk about the Russian fort, I spent the next several days exploring the area. There were still remnants of the houses that Katie said had once peppered the area between the entrance to the fort and the highway at the foot of Waimea Bridge, where concrete steps mark the old tourist path to the fort. Apart from one lonely shack that stood leaning toward the ground, the rest were just scattered ruins. The only sign of current activity I saw was a large private beehive the

Robinsons had set up just beyond the entrance to the fort. Once inside the fort's walls, I quickly found the access to the tunnel leading to the river. It was small, only about three feet high, with a ceiling that was supported with log bracing like the kind used in old mine shafts. I followed it until I had traveled beyond the reach of light and then turned back. (Later the tunnel was filled in to prevent curious kids like myself from getting hurt.) I also discovered a bell stone in my explorations, at the site of what was once the fort's armory. It was a flat stone, only about six inches thick and two or three feet high. When I pounded it with a solid piece of bluestone, it rang loudly. This bell stone would later disappear, apparently taken by some collector.

Moving on to explore the site of the old stone landing, I was shown the tunnel's river entrance by Carmen Leoiki, the son of Maha who ran the huki lau. After diving into the river, we swam through a short passageway beneath the boulder; when we surfaced we were in a fairly large underground cavern that Carmen had used as a secret hideout.

I marveled at how easy it had been to find those places that Katie had remembered. None of it may have looked as it looked in her youth, but the traces and evidence were there. The voice of Katie Koani in our dining room, talking and laughing above the sounds of the Kamehameha School Choir, led me to places and signs of the past just as surely as the voice of Willy Kani did in the Paliuli Gorge.

The Hand in Balance Is the Hand of God

Another of my parents' friends who often dropped by was George Cliff. George was a small, hunchbacked man with snow white hair who bore a strong resemblance to the elderly Walter Cronkite. George's high-pitched voice and jerky laugh, always working through a chew of tobacco, were constant sounds in our dining room, especially during the holidays, bringing to our house a knowledge and perception of the natural history of Kauai that seemed foreign to many of my mother's guests.

He was born in 1896 in Oswego, New York, near Lake Ontario and the Adirondack Mountains, and came to Hawaii in 1922 as a member of the

U.S. Army, after having served in France and England during the First World War. George's first impression of Hawaii was vividly marked by the participation of his unit in the funeral parade and services for Prince Jonah Kuhio, the only person to have been both a member of Hawaii's royal family under the kingdom and a U.S. delegate to Congress from Hawaii as a territory. George said the color, pageantry, and wailing of women mourners had impressed him greatly, and he never forgot that day.

Upon leaving the military in 1927, George found a job working aboard an interisland steamer. He first saw Kauai during a trip from Oahu after he grew ill and was forced to go ashore at Waimea for medical treatment. He immediately fell in love with the island and decided to make it his home. He worked with the U.S. Army Corps of Engineers building the first good road into the Kokee area, and when the road was finished, George remained. At first he lived with the MacDonald family in the mountains of Kokee. Later on he moved into a shack in the area known as Hale Manu (house of birds), which he rented from Hannah Knudsen. On his trips to Waimea for supplies he stayed at my grandmother Lena K. B. Wilson's house at Namahana, but Kokee would be his home for the next forty years.

George became an expert in the geography and history of the region by combining what he learned from Willy Kani and from my great-uncle Alex Blackstad (who had been in the Kokee area since the turn of the century, raising cattle with his father, Martin O. Blackstad) with what he learned from reading Hawaiian scholars such as Malo, Kamakau, and Hale´ole, whose texts he found among the Knudsen family's treasure chest of Hawaiian literature. It was interesting to note the difference between George's and Willy Kani's styles. George studied the region from the viewpoint of a naturalist, whether reading about it or hiking through it. Willy Kani, on the other hand, was a master whose understanding of nature extended from the ancient peoples and gods who once populated the land. Willy was born on Kauai and had the instinct of a native son. He, like Katie Koani and all natives in their place of origin, possessed the `aumakua. It connected him spiritually, not scientifically, to the history of the land. For Willy Kani, books were a way of testing and refining his own ideas and conclusions against those of other native and nonnative scholars of his era. For George, they were a source to shed light on what was still foreign to him.

If George wasn't exactly a *kamaaina* (native-born person), he was a perceptive student, and as his knowledge of the mountains grew, he found he could make a living acting as a guide to hunters, Boy Scouts on expeditions, and other travelers who wanted accurate explanations of the areas they were visiting. His expertise included the region that stretched from Hale Manu above the Waipo'o Valley to Hale Manu beyond Pili i kaha and the forests crowning the mountaintops of what is known today as Kokee State Park, where he worked for more than twenty-five years as the curator for the Kokee Museum.

George was a dedicated conservationist who had a keen interest in how plants and animals had evolved on Kauai, how they were being used (or abused) in the present, and how they might be threatened in the future. He was a self-proclaimed atheist, seeing the hand of God only in the hand of nature, and believed entirely in Charles Darwin's theory of evolution. Whenever George told the story of one of his travels through the wilderness regions of Kauai, he incorporated his view of the two hands at work in the world—the hand of nature (which he termed "natural selection") and the hand of man (which he termed "unnatural selection"). He believed in the balance of man preserving the life of nature and nature preserving the life of man; if one—either man or nature—tipped the scale, the other would be destroyed.

I remember George sitting at our dining room table talking about the different trails that crisscrossed at Pu'u Hinahina, the pinnacle of Hale Manu at Kokee, where he made his home. Atop Pu'u Hinahina, George said, he found the stone remnants of a rest stop used by the ancient people who once occupied the stretch of tiny villages from Haeleele to the Kalalau Valley along the northern coastline of Kauai—today known as the Na Pali coast—on their journeys to the inner gorges, valleys, and crowning forests of the Waimea Canyon, and used in return by the villagers of these inner gorges and valleys as they traveled the trails to the Na Pali coast. Over the years George explored many of these ancient trails. One ran between the two Hale Manus—a trail of well over sixteen miles that wound through tropical fern forests and swamps and above sheer waterfalls and cliffs that dropped to form the inner walls of the deep gorges of Waimea Canyon below.

From his travels between Hale Manu at Kokee and Hale Manu at Pili i kaha, George came to think of the geography of Waimea Canyon, if viewed from the perspective of a bird flying from one "house of birds" to the other, as a giant hand of nature that left its imprint on the side of the massive single cone that forms Kauai's central mountain mass. Eager to share his geographical knowledge and his findings, he would often use his hands and arms as a three-dimensional map to help his listeners visualize the overall view of large geographical areas. He would stretch out his right arm, turning his hand outward, fingers spread apart; align his extended thumb with his chin; and then describe the area that encompassed the top of his hand as the main trough of Waimea Canyon. Each finger became one of the five major gorges that make up the canyon as a whole, while the spaces between each of his fingers became the major ridges that create the walls of each gorge. Through these five major gorges fall five major water-falls that, in turn, make up five major streams, which, upon entering the main canyon, combine to make up the carving hand of the Waimea River.

His thumb, George said, was the Waipo´o Gorge or Valley, crowned by Pu´u Hinahina above Hale Manu at Kokee. His index finger stretched out to the right was Po´omau Gorge or Canyon, separated from Waipo´o by the Kumuwela Ridge. The middle finger was the Koaie Valley or Gorge, sepa-rated from Po´omau by the Mohihi Ridge. His ring finger, which had become the Waialae Gorge or Valley, was separated from Koaie by the Kalu-aha´ula Ridge. Finally, his little finger, which had become the Ka´aha Gorge or Valley, was separated from Waialae by the Pili i kaha Ridge. George then bent his elbow until his arm was parallel to his chest, using it to illustrate a picture of the Waimea Valley in relation to the canyon, with the Waimea River winding through the valley on its way to the ocean (his torso).

When I arranged my arm and hand the same way George's were set and looked at my wrist, I could see the location of Camp One, where Willy Kani and I had stayed, and, at my elbow, the irrigation ditch where I had followed behind Willy. My shoulder, I thought, must be the final bend in the river, with the flatlands of Paliuli above. My left arm, I then thought, must represent the dark or spirit coast along the lands of Mana and beyond. . . . But George had not yet finished his story.

He balanced this giant hand of nature with the hand of man by using the Hawaiian names given to each digit, with the prefix *mana mana* (to impart *mana*, or divine power, to idols or objects) before each name. Hence the thumb, called *mana mana lima nui*, represented the aggressive spirit of nature in man; the index finger, called *mana mana miki*, represented the active spirit of nature in man; the middle finger, called *mana mana loa*, represented the distant spirit of nature in man; the ring finger, or *mana mana pili*, stood for the clinging spirit of nature in man; and last, the little finger, called *mana mana iki*, stood for the lesser spirit of nature in man. George saw the entire hand of man, called *lima mana mana*, as the collective power of these five forms of nature's spirit in man, which imparted their mana, individually or collectively, to everything they touched in nature. When these five sources of nature were neatly interwoven, George claimed that the hand became a spiritual limb of balance, something that many see and feel as the hand of God.

Hands of Light and Dark: Pu´u Hinahina to the Na Pali Coast

Of all the places that George traversed through the years, the parts of "the hand" that he found most interesting and recalled most often were the highlands of Po´omau Canyon and Mohihi Ridge, which separated it from the Valley of Koaie. It was here that George claimed to have discovered the ruins of ancient villages he believed were of Menehune origin. There were two reasons George felt the Menehune had settled the area. The first was altitude. Hawaiians traditionally settled in the lower valleys and coastal areas; the ruins he discovered were in the mountains. George figured that the Menehune, like other ancient dwarf tribes such as the Pigmy of Africa and the Ilongot of the Philippines, would have kept as much distance between themselves and the larger Hawaiians as possible, and when he discovered caves located on inaccessible cliffs high above the gorges and valleys of the canyon, he was sure they were Menehune burial caves. Another piece of evidence that led him to suspect that Menehune had inhabited the area was the presence of the small dark opae (the shrimp said to be favored by the ancient tribe) in the streams above Po´omau and Mohihi. Because the opae found in the lowland streams and rivers were much larger and lighter in color, George suggested the Menehune had actually stocked the shrimp in the creeks and streams of their highland stronghold.

Besides the trails that led into the canyon, George also described a maze of trails that led out from the canyon, crisscrossing in the area of the ancient rest stop atop Pu´u Hinahina. These trails, George believed, were once used by the villagers of the inner gorges and valleys of Waimea Canyon to journey to the precipice gorges and valleys of the Na Pali coast, and by the villagers living along the Na Pali coast to access the inner canyon.

Once again George used his hands and arms as a three-dimensional map—this time depicting the precipice ridges and valleys of the Na Pali coast in relation to the pinnacle of Pu´u Hinahina and Hale Manu above the canyon. He extended his arms while crisscrossing his hands at the wrist, right under left, fingers spread apart and bent like claws. The triangular void between his crossing wrists and his chest represented the area of Waimea Canyon. The top of his upper wrist represented Pu´u Hinahina; the surface of his hands represented the crowning forest of Kokee sloping toward Na Pali, with the spaces between the fingers and between the outside of the thumbs and the forearms illustrating the ten major valleys beginning at the inner gorges. The ten clawing fingers represented the ten major ridges of Na Pali plunging precipitously to the blue Pacific Ocean from two thousand feet in the southwest and four thousand feet in the northeast.

The five major ridges and valleys of the southwestern coast of Na Pali (illustrated by the fingers on George's right hand) are called Haeleele, Polihale, Ka´aweki, Kauhao, and Makaha. The trails to and from these southwestern ridges and valleys were once safe and provided easy access to and from the crowning forest of Kokee. In noting that these safe and easy trails could be seen on the map of George's right hand, it is interesting to consider that the Hawaiians referred to the right hand as *akua mana mana* (source of the spirits or gods of light).

The five major ridges and valleys of the northeastern coast of Na Pali (illustrated by the fingers on George's left hand) are called Miloli´i,

Nualolo, Awa awapuhi, Honopu, and Kalalau. The trails to and from these ridges and valleys were dangerous and difficult to access from the forest of Kokee. Interestingly, the Hawaiians referred to the left hand as *hema mana mana* (the hand of the destitute, a source of the spirits of darkness).

As a final illustration, this one of more than just geography, George would place his right hand beneath his left—this was light's constant burden of lifting darkness in the survival of the natural and spiritual worlds.

Ancient Trails and Plum Trees

George's fondest memory was of descending Miloli´i Ridge with Willy Kani. To hike down the old Miloli´i Trail, the traveler had to follow a ledge from the point where the vegetation of Kokee ceased and the dry, barren terrain of Miloli´i began, near the two gorges that merge to become the Miloli´i Valley, not far from its entrance to the ocean at Keawenui Point. Getting into the valley required climbing from shelf to shelf down steep cliffs. In the days of old it was accessible by a trail that led down from the point of the ridge at the ocean's edge. Following this trail, however, involved climbing down an ancient rope ladder to descend the final three hundred feet.

Willy Kani often brought George along when he took the Po´opo´oiki Trail to Miloli´i to catch the turtles that frequented the beach there during the winter months. While Willy Kani caught turtles, George explored the valley floor. He followed both branches of the Miloli´i stream and came across the stone foundations of homes and pigpens, and terraces used to grow taro. In the stream he saw the same black opae and opu´u fish that lived deep in the Waimea Canyon. He also explored the ruins of Keawenui Heiau at Keawanui Point, and recalled the remnants of the ancient ladder of rope and wood treads that still hung on the cliff at Keawanui, at the mouth of the valley. By the time George returned to the beach, Willy Kani would usually have caught as many turtles as he could carry. Then they'd strip the meat and pack it back up to Kokee.

As for the trails that led from the crowning forest of Kokee via Makaha Ridge to Kauhao, Kaaweki, and Polihale—those that were easiest and safest long ago—I made this trip at age thirteen, following an older

Hawaiian by the name of Abraham Reis of Numila while we were hunting goats at Polihale. We climbed to pursue a herd of goats from the rock-laden coastline of Polihale up and across the ocean cliffs of Kaaweki and Kauhao, ascending from there the face of Makaha Ridge to its summit. We stopped along the way to fill our canteens with fresh springwater from a crevice between Kauhao and Makaha Ridge. Although many of the ledges were less than three feet wide, altogether it was a very passable trail, if one had no fear of heights. As I walked where the ancients walked, I thought that surely they navigated these trails easily, and no doubt many times. I thought, too, that it was easy to see why George Cliff was so drawn to walking them.

Next to his love of the ancient trails of Kauai, George was especially fond of plum trees—and they can be seen all over the mountains of Kokee State Park, part of the legacy he left behind. (He also planted avocados so that, in the words of George himself, "the wild pigs would have more on their menu.") His fascination with plum trees began when he and Willy Kani traveled from Hale Manu at Kokee to Hale Manu at Pili i kaha, where they took slips and seedlings from plum trees that had been planted by the Robinson family, who had built a ranch house there along the rim of Alaka´i Swamp. Upon returning to Hale Manu at Kokee, George experimented with grafting and eventually planted about five thousand trees in the Hale Manu area alone. Today, every year, families from all over the islands rush to the mountains during plum season to harvest George's crop.

Seeing the Menehune

Yet another of the guests who often showed up in our dining room was Roland Gay Sr., Willy Kani's neighbor from Paliuli. Mr. Gay was a sociable man who liked his gin, and after he and my parents had enjoyed a few highballs, their conversations became very lively, often focusing on the existence of legendary or mythical Hawaiian figures based on their personal accounts.

My father, for instance, told of once seeing a Menehune at the minister's house at Ka na´a na´a, back in 1917 or 1918, when he was five or six years old. Instead of attending Sunday school, as he was supposed to, he was out playing hooky. At such times, his favorite place to hide was an area about one hundred feet from the old parsonage, near the edge of the cliff on an outcropping of rock that overlooked the Waimea Valley and his grandfather's house at Namahana to the south. Here, on one of the rocks, the image of a ship's anchor had been carved. The carving, my father believed, was a marker left by the Cook expedition in 1778 during a visit to Keali'i Heiau, which had previously occupied the site. Others say it was the image of an arrow left behind by another English expedition that took place in 1874, when the English returned to Waimea, Kauai, to observe the rare phenomenon of the transit of Venus.

My father claimed to have seen three Menehune that day: one standing by the carved image on the outcropping of rocks and the other two nearby. He said they were stocky little brown men with curly black hair, and they wore nothing but malo (loincloths). They were all about my father's height, even though he was only five or six years old and they appeared to be fully grown men. He also said that they seemed just as startled by the encounter as he was. My father immediately ran back to the minister's house to tell him what he had seen. Far from being surprised, the minister admitted to having seen a group of Menehune in his yard more than once over the past few weeks, though every time he had tried to approach them, they ran off in the direction of the Crowell house and disappeared. Since the only time the Menehune ever seemed to be visible was when they gathered under a large mango tree located between the parsonage and the Crowell house, the minister suspected it was the mangoes that attracted them. My father and the minister ran back to the outcropping of rocks at the ledge, but the Menehune were already gone. However, upon returning to the parsonage, they once again found the Menehune gathered under the mango tree. The minister, my father, and a group of kids from the Sunday school gave chase, but the Menehune again disappeared in the direction of the Crowell house. My father said that this account was written down by the minister in the church records. It was my grandfather's suggestion that the Menehune probably used a tunnel for access and escape that stretched from the Crowell house to the parsonage.

Mr. Gay, who had been listening to the tale with keen interest, said that he, too, had heard stories of Menehune sightings in the Waimea Valley. The source of these stories was Moke Kua, an old-time Hawaiian cowboy who was killed during the Filipino revolt of 1924. Moke Kua was an expert hunter who traveled as far as Kokee, Hale Manu, and Mohihi above Po´omau Canyon. All of these places were true wilderness areas back then, accessible only by foot or horseback. Few people knew of the trails that Moke Kua followed up the southern and northern ridges of the Waimea Valley on his way to Kokee and the Alaka´i Swamp, which covers the plateau that surrounds the summits of Mt. Waialeale. Most of Moke's sightings occurred above the Kukui Trail in the vicinity of Pu´u Opae and Papa alai Ridge. It was Moke Kua's opinion that the Menehune probably made their homes in secret caves within the walls of Waimea Canyon, traveling surreptitiously from place to place through underground lava tubes.

The Spoken Word Is the Mother Stone

After hearing all of this, I started flipping through Malo's book, looking for references to the Menehune. There were none. Other than his own experience and the stories he had heard from his kupuna, Malo's primary sources of information for the whole of *Mo´olelo Hawaii* were the genealogies of ancient kings, which he learned from the members of Kamehameha's royal court, and which had been passed down through chants like the Kumulipo. Since the whole purpose of these chants was to preserve the claim of the ali´i to their royal and godly bloodlines, nothing was mentioned of lesser-ranking individuals, other than their purpose to serve, let alone other clans that may have existed alongside them. Comparing the rich conversations I overheard in our dining room from the voices of those like Katie Kamai Koani and George Cliff with the sparse facts of Malo's book, I couldn't help but believe that most of our history was still out there among the dwindling number of elderly kupuna.

It might be said that Malo's book shows the influence of the missionaries at Lahainaluna, of those who directed his education, of the Kamehameha line who placed him there, and of the Bishop Museum, which published his work. Both the missionaries and the burgeoning monarchy wouldn't have minded the recording of a few Hawaiian traditions and genealogies that served to inflate their own hold over the people, which is what *Moʻolelo Hawaii* turned out to do, but it was not in the churches' best interest, or the museum's best interest as a beneficiary of the Kamehameha line, to create a history book capable of breathing life into Hawaii's pre-missionary, pre-monarchy past. If works such as Malo's book become standard references over latter works of Hawaiiana, they could very well cut off the fragile lifeline of knowledge that still flows among many of our people who sit in the aged rooms of memory.

The value of *Moʻolelo Hawaii* lies in the detail and accuracy of Malo's descriptions of the technical aspects of Hawaiian life. It's a fine reference for explaining how either a house or a canoe was built and blessed, but it reveals little more than a glimpse of the life of those who lived in the houses or sailed the canoes. You must look and listen elsewhere to learn how life was lived and felt by the Hawaiian people.

Nevertheless, there is something about Malo's book, something he shares with other Hawaiian scholars like Kamakau and Haleole, that is noteworthy. Remember that Hawaii had an oral culture whose information was passed down by memorization. Since so much had to be memorized, what one learned depended upon the role and position to which one was born. This essentially meant that knowledge was held on a need-to-know basis. The written language changed that forever and allowed Malo and other scholars to pull together various strands of Hawaiian culture into one tapestry in a way that had never been done before.

To illustrate both the strengths and weaknesses of *Moʻolelo Hawaii*, consider the following excerpt from the chapter entitled "Agriculture," which describes a typical taro patch:

> On the irrigated lands, wet patches were planted with kalo [taro]. Banks of earth were first raised about the patch and beaten hard after which water was left in, and when this had become nearly dry, the four banks were reinforced with stones, coconut leaves, and sugar cane tops until they were water tight. Then the soil in the patch was broken up, water let in again and the earth was well mixed and trampled with the feet.
>
> A line was then stretched to mark the rows, after which the huli or taro tops were planted in rows. Sometimes the planting

was done without the rows being lined in. Water was then constantly kept running into the patch. The first two leaves which appeared were called laupai. The taro attained full size but it was not until after twelve months that the tubers were ripe and ready to be made into food.

Although the instructional tone of these paragraphs does not lend them much in the way of dramatic interest, they do reveal that much less has changed between then and now than one might think. When I was a child visiting the Makaweli Valley in the 1950s, taro was still grown the way that Malo described some one hundred and twenty years earlier. The making of poi also remained much the same, as it does even today, except that the imu has been replaced with gas or electric steamers in some applications and the poi board and stone pounders have been replaced with the meat grinder. While many talk about Hawaii's lost traditions, the true value of Malo's book is its demonstration that some of these traditions have not so much been lost as they have evolved.

The same thing is true of Hawaii's spiritual past. Perhaps the ancient religion can still evolve, even through the existence of Western religious thought. Perhaps the elaborate rituals of times past are no longer needed to make contact with one's 'aumakua. Just as many Christians and Jews no longer consider it necessary to attend a church or temple service in order to worship God, I believe that our ancestors' rituals are no longer necessary. Simply by thinking of our na 'aumakua, we automatically acknowledge them. In his book *The Kahuna: Sorcerers of Hawaii, Past and Present* Julius Rodman states:

> The failure of the Hawaiian arts of healing at present is due to the loss of subtleties in the language when used in prayer today. One must remember that no missionary to Hawaii in the past, nor any clergyman present today in Hawaii, can speak the dialect of Aramaic, the language of Jesus Christ, but they continue to pray. The 'aumakua, like the God of the Hebrews, dwells inside one's self, and one's inner thoughts are the only language one's inner self needs to know.

As for those who dismiss too easily the folktales of other cultures and other times, such as the stories of the Menehune that I've related here, it might be wise to reconsider modern prejudices. Certain stories in the chapters ahead contain information that simply doesn't fit the modern Western paradigm. Does that mean they are fiction? Not necessarily. For example, when I was growing up I saw my mother carefully watering certain stones scattered around the yard. One day she called me over and pointed one out to me. It was about twelve inches long and was shaped like a human kidney. It had a blue-gray color, and its surface was smooth. She told me her grandmother Lukahi had said that watering this particular type of stone would cause it to give birth. Then she lifted up the stone, and there beneath it were many tiny stones of exactly the same shape, color, and texture, most of them not more than an eighth of an inch in size. My father, who was of Caucasian descent, always complained about her teaching me such nonsense. However, as the years passed my mother would occasionally take me to this stone and show me how the little pebbles had doubled and later tripled in size. Whether the mother stone had given birth or not, I cannot say, but I don't know of any better explanation for what I saw.

The ancients lived in a world saturated with myth and legend. In such a world, truth did not always reside on the surface as it does today, but often lived at the heart of teaching stories passed around campfires. This is the world that inspired the stories that have preceded this chapter and that are to follow. That is not to say they are free of error. . . . Is it odd that after all these years the few sentences from *Mo'olelo Hawaii* that I read and reread as a child should find a place here in my own story? David Malo writes, "I do not suppose the following . . . to be free from mistakes, in that the material for it has come from oral traditions. . . ." I believe that the traditions of my ancestors most certainly have their own form of wisdom, and I have invited you to hear their voices in the oral tradition they have passed on to me. Even though they may not be free from mistakes, whatever the earth your family comes from, these traditions can be the water for your roots and the answer to your questions, whether historical or spiritual. Hear the voices of your ancestors as they gather around a wooden table in the quiet of your room.

CHAPTER SIX

THE TOUCH OF THE ʻAUMAKUA

EACH OF US, AT SOME TIME OR OTHER DURING OUR LIVES, has at least one moment that is profound, even miraculous—a moment of seeming divine intervention, when the thread of connection to life or our world as we know it seems frayed to the point of breaking, but instead some mercy is shown, some unseen hand of rescue is offered. A child almost twelve years old is both old enough to understand the depth of the darkness before rescue and young enough in spirit to be awed and changed by the touch of mercy leading him out of the dark. A child of twelve remembers such a moment forever.

At Kilohana Crater in the early 1960s, when I was between eleven and twelve years old and halfway through the sixth grade, I experienced the touch of the ʻaumakua—the touch of the spiritual being that gave me another chance to live at the moment when I might have lost my life. For months after, I told no one—and even then, I shared my experience with only my mother. I think I understood that such a moment as I had at the crater was intensely personal and could truly be believed only by the one who had experienced it. Why I was chosen for mercy when there were so many in need remains a mystery to me. But it was a moment I will never forget.

The Kilohana Crater is an extinct volcano located approximately four miles due west from the town of Lihue, Kauai. Traveling west from Lihue in the direction of Waimea along Kaumualii, look toward the north and you will see the rolling hills of Kilohana along the stretch between the Kipu turnoff and the bridge that spans the Hule´ia Valley and stream. This stretch of highway is commonly called the Kipu stretch by the local people. The rolling hills that you see toward the north form an ancient volcanic cone that stands out by itself against Mt. Waialeale in the background toward the northwest. These rolling hills are actually the southern rim of Kilohana Crater, which is visibly marked today on its eastern side by a radio transmission tower that can be seen from as far away as the towns of Puhi and Lihue.

Kauai in the 1960s

There was a specific chain of events that led me, not quite twelve, to a situation in which I was left stranded, alone, starving, and lost twenty-five miles away from home, in the then wilderness mountains between Lihue and Waialeale. While there is no excuse for my actions that played a role in these events, perhaps some insight can be gained by understanding what life was like for a Caucasian-Hawaiian boy being raised in the mid-twentieth century in Kauai, in what could be classified as a family that, though rich in love and caring relationships, was financially poor.

Kauai in the year 1960 was still a sleepy little island paradise floating on the Pacific Ocean (a picture the tourist industry still tries to project today, though this characterization has long since lost its truth). Its people, numbering 27,922, were accustomed to living in open spaces. Outside of the Filipino immigrants, it was rare to meet someone who was not born and raised on the island. Only 9,325 automobiles traveled our narrow highways from Haena to Kekaha. After ten o'clock at night you might not see another car pass through the town of Waimea until six o'clock the next morning; you could drive from Waimea to Lihue and pass fewer than ten cars heading in either direction. A trip to Lihue was looked upon much as we would look upon a trip to Honolulu today, and was a journey made fewer than three or four times a year. There was no reason to travel to Lihue, other than to pick up family at the airport or to register a vehicle once a year at the county building.

In 1960 the hillsides on both sides of the highway approaching Kalaheo, Lawai, and Omao were covered with the blue-green color of acres and acres of pineapple fields, with no houses in sight except for a few dark green dwellings that had been inhabited by the Portuguese immigrants who settled this area in the 1920s. The road to Lihue from Omao on was lined with giant shell gingers on both sides, their branches hanging over the pavement in spots along the way.

In 1960 tourism absorbed less than 4 percent of Kauai's workforce; the average number of tourists to visit the island on any given day was less than 2,235. It was still a novelty to see tourists wandering around town; it was something that did not occur often except for, perhaps, a few stopping off now and then at the Russian fort in Waimea. Most, however, would pass through town and head directly up to the canyon.

There were only four major hotels on Kauai: the largest was the Coco Palms Resort Hotel with 110 rooms; the newest was the Kauai Surf at Kalapaki Beach, with 104 rooms; Hanalei Plantation had 70 rooms; and the oldest, the Kauai Inn in Lihue, had 78 rooms. In the town of Kapaa there was a little hotel known as the Coral Reef, which had 10 rooms. Up in Waialua there was another little hotel, the Waialua Ranch, with 12 rooms. Over in Lihue there were a few motels that catered mainly to inter-island travelers—the Hale Pumehana, which had 20 rooms, and the Motel Lani and the Palm Haven, each with 8 rooms. In Koloa and the Poipu area the Prince Kuhio Apartments were the closest thing to a hotel. And last of all there were six cabins available in the new Kokee State Park.

If you visited Lihue Airport in 1960, you would find a tiny terminal built alongside a single runway that resembled a small strip of two-lane highway about five thousand feet long. On each side of the terminal was a small fenced-in area where you could sit and wait for your incoming or departing flight. Employing the old propeller planes, Hawaiian Airlines made an average of five flights per day to Kauai, with Aloha making six; there were no jet aircraft or helicopters. The average price for a one-way trip to Oahu was sixteen dollars. Across from the terminal were a few rental car stands. There were no vans or foreign cars on the island at this time; rental cars were mainly full-size Chevys and Fords or two-wheel-drive Jeeps with green and white or pink canopies attached. For carrying larger numbers of passengers, stretch-outs were used instead of buses. These were six- or eight-door sedans that carried nine to twelve passengers including the driver. We would rarely see tourists in rental cars where we lived on the west side of the island. During this time tourists mainly used the tour companies for these trips around Kauai; we often saw stretch-outs passing through town on their route to Waimea Canyon lookout.

The slow rate of change on the island, which could be seen in both the minor role that tourism played in our economy and the fact that less than 3 percent of the total workforce was employed in the construction industry, belied the total destruction of our lifestyle and environment that was about to take place within the next ten years.

In 1960, however, the plantations ruled the land. If you sat around the dinner table and with a family member who had just graduated from high school, the conversation would center on mainly two options: joining the military or working for the plantation. *College* was a word seldom mentioned, although there was a trade school located in Lihue known as Kauai Technical School.

For over 50 percent of Kauai's workforce, the plantations were both the place of employment and, through the camp system, the landlords. More than 50 percent of Kauai's population dwelled in plantation camps provided by the sugar and pineapple industry. There were Filipino camps, Portuguese camps, Japanese camps, and *haole* camps (more commonly known as supervisor housing). The Hawaiians were still living more or less on *kuleana*, family lands that came down from the Great Mahele, and were still scattered in the back valleys and gorges of the island. Because the largest part of the population dwelled in camps concentrated in areas that were within walking distance of mills and plantation fields, Kauai was truly the "Garden Island," with most of its land either under cane or pineapple or still virgin forest.

The second largest employer on the island was the government—the federal government, the new state government, and the county government, for which my father worked as a laborer earning a salary of two hundred and sixteen dollars a month. The minimum wage for the State of Hawaii at this time was set at one dollar per hour, an amount that, while not generous, was reasonable considering that most rents were less than twenty dollars per month and gasoline prices averaged about forty-two cents per gallon. Mortgages were unheard of for the majority of island residents.

For most people on Kauai it was accomplishment enough to have the basic human needs of shelter and food. Regarding shelter, ownership didn't seem to matter; the word *home* meant more than the word *house*. Food was simple, was often caught or harvested by individual family members, and was something to enjoy and share together. The concept of balanced nutrition that we who shop in supermarkets are so used to today was not a primary concern. If your family could provide a meal that night, you ate. If not, you waited for the next day. Similarly, health and welfare did not come from the care of doctors or hospitals; they were simply provided by the laughter and support of friends and family—these were enough to overcome hardship, sickness, and death.

The people of Kauai lived on their island in their own world. Out of all the households, less than 50 percent of them subscribed to the *Honolulu Star Bulletin*, and the *Honolulu Advertiser* had a circulation of only about 20 percent. The *Garden Island* newspaper, however, had a circulation of well over 80 percent, though forces conspired to keep the islanders insular even when they wanted to connect with the world. Because the one radio station on the island—KTOH, located in Lihue—had only a 250-watt transmitter, we could never listen to it on the west side of the island. Though television had arrived on the island in the late fifties with two stations available (KGMB and KHVH-TV), most people still didn't have a set.

In the town of Waimea there was a shop called Slim's Appliance, and it was the first appliance store in Waimea to venture into the television business. In the front of Slim's store there was a large display window in which was placed a television set. At night Slim would leave it on, facing the street, to advertise this new product. We gathered in the dark—along with about half of the town—and sat on the sidewalk and in the road to watch television until the station went off at eleven or midnight. If it started to get windy or it rained, people would take empty appliance boxes to the road and sit inside them, and then continue watching the screen through the store window.

And such was life in 1960 on Kauai, our own private little world floating on the Pacific.

The Tin Boat

The road that led me to Kilohana Crater began on the banks of the Waimea River. In the early 1960s the popular activity for kids of Hawaiian or part-Hawaiian ancestry who lived in or near Waimea was to build and sail tin boats on the river. These boats resembled the original Hawaiian canoe with its outrigger, but instead of being made from hollow logs, the canoes were made out of an old piece of corrugated metal roofing. The first step was to scout the neighborhood for this metal piece—and with all the old shacks in Waimea, it wasn't hard to find. The length of the boat was determined by the length of roofing found. If it was too long, it could be shortened by using a hammer to pound the blade of a cane knife through it. A good length for a canoe was seven to nine feet.

Once the metal was found, the next step was to lay it on the ground and proceed to pound the ridges with a hammer until the metal was a flat sheet. Then the bow of the canoe could be formed by centering a two-by-four on the sheet about four inches from its forward edge, folding the metal up to the two-by-four, and nailing it to the sides of the wood. It was important that the two-by-four be long enough to allow six inches to stick out above the metal edge of the canoe, to serve as a post to tie it to shore. The stern was fashioned in much the same way, only with a one-by-twelve board.

Next, to help shape the canoe, two pieces of two-by-four cut to the same width as the stern were fastened crosswise in the boat, one a quarter of the length down from the bow and one the same distance from the stern. These also served as supports for the outrigger. One last piece of two-by-four was fastened between these, in the center, to serve as the seat.

The final work for the hull was to patch all the old nail holes in the metal. Once again the neighborhood was searched, this time for tar, which was heated to boiling in an old coffee can over a fire. With a stick dipped in the tar, the holes as well as the bow and the stern could be sealed.

After the hull of the canoe was finished, it was time to search for the outrigger *(iako)*. The wood that was used for this came from the hau tree, which grows in groves along rivers and streams or in swampy areas. It is a wood similar to balsa, light in weight when dried but not as porous. In addition, the bark of the hau made very good cord for lashing. Two arched pieces of hau were cut to construct the outriggers, each about two inches in diameter and five to six feet long, and one piece about four inches in diameter and slightly shorter than the length of the canoe was cut to use as the float *(ama)*. Next, the bark was stripped from these pieces and they were left to dry in the sun. In the meantime, the bark was soaked in seawater and left to dry in the shade. The outrigger pieces were then lashed with the bark to the two crosswise pieces in the canoe. Finally, after rounding its ends with a knife, the float was lashed to the outrigger. This, then, was a tin boat, a modern-day version of a *waa'kau'kahi* (single-hull or one-passenger canoe). A *hoe* (oar) could easily be carved from a short piece of one-by-six or one-by-eight.

The tin boat that I constructed at the time was eight feet long. After finding a gallon of old, dark blue-green house paint, I painted the hull. In honor of my Norwegian ancestry I made the tying post in the bow an extra two feet tall and carved on it the head of a serpent, such as those seen on Viking ships. From a movie I had seen at the Waimea Theater about German U-boats during World War II, I painted the name SEA WOLF on each side of the bow.

These were the days of the tin boat wars. The kids who lived close to the mouth of the river would gather together all their tin boats into a fleet, and the kids who lived up in the valley would do the same. They filled their boats with as many stones as they could carry, and with one fleet sailing up the river and the other sailing down, they would clash at the halfway point and stone each other until one side would either flee or abandon its boats to swim to shore. The final blow of victory entailed breaking the outriggers and sinking the boats of the enemy.

Because I had spent so much time at Willy Kani's, or exploring Paliuli and the burial caves, I was used to doing my own things and was neither a follower of anyone nor a leader. I constructed my tin boat alone, and sailed alone.

The Riverside Camp

I spent a great deal of time exploring the uninhabited banks of the river, paddling my canoe into the small canals that flowed from the swamp area of Mahi´ai, remnants of the irrigation system from the days of taro and rice fields. Along these canals I could see the ancient coconut trees and giant ferns that grew in the swamps, and old trails and stone walls. Sailing down to the banks of Laau o a ka la, I recalled my father telling me that when he was young the mouth of the river was much narrower and deeper, and the original breakwater of boulders stood there. I convinced my older brother Butch to come with me to explore this breakwater (located in the area that is, at present, between the Waimea Bridge and the ocean).

We paddled out to the center of the river, where I tied an old piece of communication cable around my waist and held on to a large rock so that I would sink to the bottom of the river while Butch lowered me. In this way I could measure the depth as I went down, and he could pull me up. The river was still quite deep in many areas back then—more than twenty feet in parts. Because the water was dark green in color, most of the light was lost only five feet below the surface and the water turned very cold. I tried my best to trace the original breakwater, or just to feel what existed on the bottom of the river. We did find segments of the wall, but the river bottom was mostly thick mud, which was quite unpleasant in total darkness—especially with the possibility of large Samoan crabs lurking in the muddy depths. These were known to grow to ten pounds, with claws larger than a man's hand.

As time went by, those of us who always seemed to be on the river with our boats banded together and built a camp on the Makaweli side of the river where we could hide out and spend our weekends. Our camp was located just above the spot where the old Waimea Bridge met the Makaweli side. Here were large hau trees, with their branches hanging twenty feet over the river, and an ancient irrigation canal that led into the swamps of Mahi'ai. This was a perfect location, for it was away from town, and with no trails leading in or out, it was accessible only by boat.

We cut an anchorage under the hau branches so that when we tied our boats they could not be seen from across the river. We also cleared an area on the bank and made a camp, secluded under the hau bushes. Here we gathered every day to sail our boats and *pulehu* (barbecued) fish and Samoan crabs that we caught in the river. As soon as the weekends approached, we camped out the whole time, not returning home until Sunday evening.

We were a mixed group of diverse backgrounds and talents. From up in the valley came Malcolm Azeka, who was of Hawaiian and Japanese ancestry, and whom I renamed Manny. There were the Cacal brothers, Filipinos of Ilocano ancestry: Junicio could run like a bullet and spear fish in waters so dark that you could not see your hand in front of your face, and Ishidro was as strong as a bull. From Waimea Beach toward the landing were the Vea brothers, who were of Hawaiian and Filipino ancestry, and whose names were Feleciano (renamed Flash) and Hanohano (called simply Hano). Flash, even at this young age, was a very good guitar player, while Hano was a skilled surfer. From the area around the mouth of the river, besides myself, came Isaac Hookano, who was of Hawaiian and Japanese ancestry and whose Hawaiian name was Liko Boy. He was a very good surfer and also played the guitar. Finally, Lynn Dela Cruz, whom we called Linko, was of Filipino and Japanese ancestry and surfed as well as Hano.

What began as a simple weekend of camping and enjoying the river slowly became an invasion of Waimea town at night, as it grew necessary to gather supplies for our camp. It is important to know that in those days there were incandescent streetlights rather than the mercury vapor lights that we have today, so the town was very dim at night, with plenty of shadows in which to hide. But the greatest difference in comparison to today is that at midnight all the streetlights would shut off—not just in Waimea, but on the entire island—and it would remain pitch dark until morning.

On this particular weekend at camp I recalled that when I was younger I would spend the night with my oldest brother, Leslie, camping and catching *ko ono* (white crabs) on the old Waimea pier. To make some extra money he would do this often and sell the crabs for pupu to the old Hawaiians drinking in the bars at night—a five-gallon pail of crabs could fetch up to fifteen dollars.

One night he was so bent on making this cash that when the crabs were not entering the nets, he proceeded to stuff the five-gallon pail with newspaper and cover the top with just enough crabs to make the pail look as though it was full, and sold it at the Lucky-U Bar, which was located next to the present-day Waimea Big Save market in the old Ho Min Hee building. He would normally wait until midnight to sell his crabs, when the Hawaiians were drunk and paid more. After, we would return to the pier and then, at 4 A.M., go to the Waimea Bakery to buy fresh-made pastries.

The Waimea Bakery, once located next to the present-day Waimea Hawaiian Church, just across from the police station, was the largest supplier of bread, pies, cakes, and pastries on the island. (It relocated to Lihue in the late 1960s and became the Tip Top Bakery.) It was during these 4 A.M. visits with my brother that I noticed that at this time all the delivery trucks were loaded for island-wide distribution, after which the bakery would close up. From 4:30 in the morning until 6:00 there was no one there until the drivers came in to make their deliveries. What's more, none of the trucks was locked or secured; they were simply loaded and the doors closed.

After a moment or two spent recalling all of this, I asked my camping friends if they'd like to eat pastries—all they could carry. Those who wanted to came along, and we launched our boats at three in the morning and paddled down to the mouth of the river. We left the canoes on the sandbar and walked along the beach in total darkness; the streetlights were already off. We hid in the bushes across from the bakery, waiting for the bakers to load the trucks and leave. It was a kid's dream—all the goodies you could possibly eat. My favorite was the lemon chiffon pie; I carried at least ten of them back to camp. During these days when we went camping there was no excess food at home to bring along. Sometimes we could sneak canned goods from our houses to share, but most of the time we had to catch fish and forage for ourselves. This was likely the reason we were so anxious to get our hands on these pastries. After a while, the raiding trips became routine; we would sit around the camp waiting for the streetlights to go out.

Before long we had moved from simple pastry raids to infiltrating the entire town at night. There wasn't a store or warehouse that I could not find a way into. All of this was done without disturbing or breaking any entrances, so that the crime would go unnoticed. Thus we were provided with a steady supply of food and drinks. Items taken from the shelves were kept to a minimum, to avoid discovery. I would initially explore all the stores alone. Only after I mentioned my findings to the others as we camped would they ask me to come along into town with them as they carried out the raid. I was never a follower of anyone, nor a leader.

Where Are the Police?

One day, while paddling my boat under the Waimea Bridge, I looked up and stared at the high concrete girders that spanned its length from column to column, supporting the road above it. These girders started at about eight feet in height as they left each column and formed an arch in the center of each span. On the inside of each girder there was a lip on the bottom about twelve inches wide. If you could scale the columns and get to the girders high above the river, you could walk on this lip or ledge. There were four girders per span spaced about eight feet apart. I decided to build a hideout inside of them by laying boards from one girder to the other, with the ends of the boards resting on the ledge. It took awhile to gather all the old boards, haul them to the river, and float them out under the bridge between the second and third columns, away from the bank on the Waimea side, but within a few weeks I had my hideout between the girders with the road above for a roof, and it could not be seen except from directly below.

In the hideout I had kerosene lanterns, mattresses to sleep on, even a two-burner kerosene stove. In a few months it was stocked with canned goods, candy, and cigarettes (by now we were smoking whatever brand we chose). Before long Liko Boy had built a hideout between the next two girders, and an older cousin of his named Kaleo Hookano built one in the space next to him, but theirs were not as elaborate as mine; I had floored half of the span of the girder. Altogether it seemed at the time that we had created a life that even Tom Sawyer and Huckleberry Finn would envy.

If you are wondering where the police were while all of this was taking place, you must bear in mind that in the early 1960s there were only four police officers on duty at any particular time at the Waimea substation, known then as the Waimea District Courthouse. These four officers were responsible for the area from the little town of Kekaha all the way to Koloa, roughly one third of the island. This usually meant that there was only one officer free to patrol the Kekaha-to-Waimea area at night, and he was seldom seen.

The Waimea courthouse was a wooden structure built in the late 1800s. It stood about five feet from the ground, high enough to save it from the potential flooding of the Waimea River; it had a double-pitched Hawaiian-style roof of shingles; and it was wrapped all the way around with a lanai. Surrounding this dilapidated building were large *keawe* trees. It was here in this old courthouse that Koolau the Leper was ordered to go to the bleak leper colony of Kaluapapa on the island of Molokai in the 1890s. He refused to be separated from his family, however, and escaped with his wife and son to the remote valley of Kalalau, and there he fought it out and killed the sheriff of Kauai along with some members of the U.S. Army who had accompanied him. An unmentioned piece of history is that the judge at the time was having an affair with Koolau's wife and was in love with her. It is speculated that this is the main reason he refused Koolau's request to bring his family along with him to Molokai, since it was a wish granted to others, and that it was this that made Koolau flee. This story was passed on to me by the old-timer Kala Kapahu, who had heard it from his grandmother, who had been alive at the time and knew of the affair between Koolau's wife and the judge.

In the rear of the courthouse were the old stable buildings, a reminder of when the police were still on horseback. I believe if proper historical societies existed on the island in the 1960s, this building never would have been torn down and the grounds destroyed to make way for the new Waimea substation and fire station. The old Waimea fire station was located at the present-day site of the tennis courts that serve Waimea High School. Here the same mango tree stands that stood next to the old station. The fire department back then was known as Only Ashes Remain because firefighters never reached a fire in time to save the structure.

During these days the police still used their personal cars for patrol. These were marked with the installation of a single large loudspeaker; a siren resembling a large horn on the front passenger side fender; a single red light in the middle of the roof; and a very tall radio antenna mounted on the rear fender. The officers' uniforms were an olive drab color, as if they had been made from old army blankets. In the early 1960s there were many tidal wave alerts, and we would be forced to evacuate to high ground, usually to the top of Waimea Heights. The officer who was in charge of the Waimea police station suffered from the speech disorder of stuttering. During these tidal wave alerts his job was to drive through town and the entire valley and announce the potential wave on his loudspeaker. "Ti—ti—ti—tidal wave alert; ti—ti—tidal wave alert," he announced, and our laughter, though not kind, did ease the tension of the evacuation. This, then, was the status of law enforcement on the west side of the island at the time of our raids.

Imaginary Consequences

Soon, because we were kids, we began to brag about our nighttime activities. Those who went on the raids started going out on their own and bringing their own friends with them until it came to a point when half the kids in town were "shopping" at night. I once went shopping at 1 A.M., in Waimea's largest store at the time, and counted nineteen kids already there. Eventually the police became aware of these robberies and assigned a detective by the name of William Ching to the town of Waimea. He was of Hawaiian-Chinese ancestry, overweight, and always dressed in baggy gabardine pants and an oversized aloha shirt. Overall, he resembled an Asian Jackie Gleason. William Ching would get his information by plying kids with soda, ice cream, and candy. After being questioned by him many times in the Waimea courthouse, I and a few others of our original camp were arrested, although we never confessed to committing any crime.

We were then scheduled to appear in juvenile court at the Lihue courthouse. I was about to encounter for the first time the world that existed outside of the boundary of my family and the surroundings of Waimea. Despite my weekend activities, in many ways my life was sheltered. I had spent much time with people who were born in the nineteenth century and who, although raised in the twentieth century, retained the ideas and understanding of an earlier time. Both of my parents, although children of the twentieth century, were raised by their grandparents, whose minds and ways were of the century before.

All of this accounted for the freedom we enjoyed. When my parents and grandparents were raised, the rivers, ocean, valleys, and mountains were home. Genealogies did not merely account for family bloodline but were connected to the land; although immigrants could pass down the history of family, they could not pass down the history of their present environment as it related to ancestors who dwelled there before them, as far back as ancient times. While many immigrants were taught to look to the future and create an environment that would raise them to the level of the haole who then governed Hawaii, and to someday surpass them, we were taught to recall the folkways and environment of our ancestors. Thus there were no restrictions as to how much time we could spend outside the house; even outside, you were still home. Our parents were not unfit or negligent; they were simply used to this free way of life—a way that was fast disappearing. I know now that I did take advantage of this generous view of home and living by breaking the law.

I did not at the time, however, view our break-ins as stealing or as a major crime. In part this was because of my ignorance of the law and its role in the rule and government of an orderly society. Nor was I aware of the consequences one must face after breaking the law. I looked upon the owners of the stores in Waimea, who were largely Japanese, as people who seemed to have a great deal. They had beautiful cars and beautiful houses; their kids were never allowed to associate with us, and they themselves would never associate with our parents—except to collect their money at the cash register. Since they had so much, I thought that it would not harm anyone to take a little. After all, it was common knowledge that most of these stores would carry their Japanese customers on account and bill them at special rates that were often less than the shelf prices charged at the register. I didn't break any doors or windows, or commit any type of vandalism. I took a little to eat because, in my mind, I thought these people had plenty to share.

In all of my adventures—exploring burial caves and climbing the steep walls of the Waimea Valley—I used my belief in the `aumakua to eliminate fear. Fear exists only if the thought of consequences exists. If you truly believe in your `aumakua, then you eliminate the thought of consequences. The thought of doing something wrong can exist only if it can be compared to or weighed against the thought of right. At twelve years old, raised as I was with a belief in the `aumakua, I did not have the perspective to weigh right against wrong. There is no logical excuse, however, for breaking the law. In the early 1960s in Kauai there were no sociological studies or drugs that could be pointed to as an excuse for our actions. The system was simple: If you broke the law, you suffered the consequences.

The only way out was influence—if your parents knew someone influential or had a family member on the police force, the crime could somehow be buried before it reached the courts. None of us was this fortunate. I received a year's probation—which had no impact on me at all. I was never sentenced by anyone. We went to court and waited in the lobby while our parents faced the judge in a private room. Then a Japanese man came out and said he was our probation officer and would be checking up on us once a month for a period of one year, and that if we got into trouble again we would be brought back to court, which meant nothing to me but more waiting in the lobby.

We went home with our parents and life never changed in any way. My father's thoughts centered on the injustice of the process; the judge and the probation officer were, as far as he was concerned, crooks themselves and had no right to be judging others. Both became suspect for having secretly participated in real estate *hui* (partnerships) that were required to hold development permits from governmental organizations in which the two men wielded political power—a conflict of interest at the least. But for them, being unethical was not being unlawful.

Within a week we returned to shopping at night and found that the stores had taken no precautions. We soon ended up in court again, and this time our probation was increased to three years, but it still seemed like an imaginary or invisible punishment. The probation officer would show up and ask me how I was doing. I would say, "Fine." He would then ask me if I was staying out of trouble. I would say yes. He would write something in his folder and leave. There was no exchange of philosophy or any attempt made to sway my actions in any way or to show if he really gave a damn. But soon this imaginary punishment would become very real.

Real Consequences

I had given up camping on the river for the time being and had lost my tin boat in an attempt to paddle from Waimea to Ni'ihau, the neighboring island across the channel. This was a ridiculous idea—a tin boat sits heavy in the water and can sink like a beer can full of water. Besides, Ni'ihau, although it can be seen very clearly, is actually seventeen miles from the nearest point on Kauai. With only an empty Vienna sausage can to bail with, the *Sea Wolf* sank about three hundred yards from Waimea landing in fairly large swells, and I had a real battle fighting the current in my swim back to shore as a crowd of people gathered on the beach, all waving their arms at me.

I was now back at Paliuli, spending time with Willy Kani again. He had loaned me an old .22 caliber bolt-action rifle, and my attention turned to hunting birds in the hills at the back of Paliuli, where I would climb up to what is now called Waimea Canyon Drive but was then a dirt road only halfway completed, ending at the top of the ridge called Huluhulunui. It was at this time that I would think about my earlier life spent with Willy Kani and my first trip to Waimea Canyon, how beautiful the colors of the canyon were upon first sight, and how remote and undisturbed nature seemed to be in the depths of the canyon, far away from civilization below.

But my dreams of becoming a mountain man in this wilderness would have to wait for one night, and we once again infiltrated the stores in town. I began talking to two of my companions who always accompanied me on these shopping trips and who also were serving probation since they were the only ones besides me who had been caught. They, too, were interested in hunting, and one of them mentioned an appliance store in Waimea that sold firearms. Little did I know then that I was about to make a serious mistake by breaking into this store. I was unaware of the gravity of the crime of stealing firearms and I was unaware that such a full-scale investigation would be launched in search of these missing guns.

At the time I could see no difference between a few canned goods and a few firearms. If we hadn't been so eager to shoot these guns on the outskirts of town to see how much havoc they could play on such targets as trees, cactuses, and rocks, we might not have been caught. For one thing, we had no idea how far the sound of these fired guns would carry, and how frightened people would become upon hearing hundreds of rounds being fired not far from town. The police investigation was concentrated on adults; no one even considered that any eleven- or twelve-year-olds would take possession of such powerful weapons. The owner didn't discover the break-in until after our third visit; when a customer asked to see some guns, he discovered they were missing, along with cases of ammunition. Because it was a very secure building and there were no signs of a break-in, the police had no idea how the shop had been entered. In our possession at the time were a .300 Special Edition Savage level-action rifle with gold-plated engravings and trigger; a .270 Winchester Model 70 bolt-action rifle; a 12-gauge chrome-plated Remington semiautomatic shotgun; a 16-gauge Winchester pump; and a .22-caliber semiautomatic Winchester rifle, along with cases of ammunition for each gun.

This time, while I waited in the lobby of the Lihue courthouse, the mood seemed different. One of the Cacal brothers turned to me and said that his probation officer asked him if he'd packed his clothes prior to coming. The decision reached in that private room down the hall was that I alone would be removed from my home and Waimea, from family and friends, and sent to a home for troubled youths that was located on the opposite side of the island in the little town of Anahola, some forty-two miles away by car.

It was determined that it would be best for me to be separated from the rest of the youths in Waimea for my own benefit and for their benefit, since I was considered the leader of these raiding parties. That I was the leader was untrue, an excuse used to spare nearly twenty kids in Waimea and their parents the agony of going to juvenile court and having their names recorded in a police file. Outside of five or six kids in our group, I never brought anyone to any of these stores. I felt I was being punished for the actions of others based on a false and inaccurate reputation. Like some legendary outlaw of the past, I was placed in what seemed like one hundred different crime sites at the same time. To me, taking some canned food to eat and some guns to shoot at trees and rocks had taken on the proportions of the Great Train Robbery, and for my decisions, however construed, I was going to pay the consequences.

Anahola

Anahola, which could be translated as "a measurement or span of time," was a sleepy little village in comparison to Waimea. I cannot speak historically of Anahola, for I spent such a short period of my life there that I never really came to know any of the local kupuna well enough to share their knowledge of the area. My first impression upon arriving there was how prehistoric the mountain range to the west of Anahola appeared. It seemed to overshadow the entire town below. The jagged peak and ridgeline viewed from the Anahola Valley gave me the feeling of being lost in time. When I was a boy the mountain seemed to be a good deal more wet than it is today, and much greener, with low, foglike clouds appearing regularly at the peak in the mornings and evenings.

The house I was sent to was located in the Anahola Valley, one of the last houses just before the narrow dirt road that led to Anahola Beach Park and about three or four houses before the area where a family named Valpoon lived in a group of old shacks with rows of fishnets laid out in the front yard. The people I lived with were the Lemms, who were of Hawaiian and Caucasian ancestry. The husband, whose name was William, was a patrolman on the Kauai police force, and his wife, Annie, ran a luau catering business as well as a chicken farm and piggery. There were three other boys who were living there: Edwin Rita was a senior at Kapaa High School, as was David Kaneholani, and Antony Jaramillo was the same age as I and was in the sixth grade at Anahola Elementary School, as I would be.

My first week in Anahola was spent learning what was to be expected of me during my stay, however long that would be. Days began at 4:30 in the morning with some chores: collecting and washing eggs and feeding chickens and pigs; then we ate breakfast; and then I walked to the elementary school, which was located across the highway at the top of the valley. After school there was more work to be done on the chicken farm and for the catering business. Our food consisted of eggs from the farm and leftovers accumulated from catering jobs. The day ended at seven or eight in the evening. On weekends it was strictly work from sunup to sundown, with no school to act as a break in between.

On Sundays we would have to attend the Anahola Hawaiian Church, and this afforded me my first look at Anahola Village, which consisted of a small wooden building that was a store and post office run by a man named Ben Williams. Across the street was a small Shell service station run by a Japanese family, and on the Kilauea side of this service station was the Anahola Hawaiian Church, which also seemed to be run by Mr. Williams.

During my first week I thought of escaping and returning to Waimea, and in the weeks to follow I began to plan it more seriously. The other three juveniles seemed to be quite proud of the events that led them to this place and were always trying to get me to disclose what I had done to earn my sentence. I was not interested in portraying myself as a little Al Capone or as a tough kid on the block because I was neither. These three, however, seemed all that I was not. At that time in my boyhood, much like today, rivalries existed among the island school districts. Because my fellow boarders were originally from the Kapaa district, Waimea was their sworn enemy. Often when no adults were present they would try to interrogate me about different school gangs in Waimea, even though I was only in the sixth grade and really had no idea what went on at the high school. I was threatened with physical violence—even with knives—but none of it worried me because I could sense how much fear they had of the Lemms, and I knew they could never carry out such threats. They could only attempt to intimidate me, and my laughter at their efforts enraged them.

The idea of belonging to a gang was foreign to me—the necessity of being accepted, of having to adjust oneself to fit in. The thought of becoming something else to accommodate someone else never crossed my mind. My younger days spent with people like Willy Kani and Mr. Gay and George Cliff had given me the ability to see people and ideas with a perception that did not exist in this place in Anahola.

For the next two months I would live here, the place that the court referred to as a better environment for the benefit of the child. It was a very lucrative business for the Lemms, who undoubtedly could turn quite a profit from their chicken farm and catering business with the use of our unlimited free labor, and the fee paid by the State of Hawaii for our room and board could be largely pocketed by feeding us catering leftovers.

Mr. Lemm seemed to be a nice man, though he was very quiet and rarely spoke to me. He was a big man physically but was dominated by his wife. Although he did have a temper if pushed too far, perhaps his wife's domination contributed to his silence. She was a very aggressive woman, always giving orders and keeping strict discipline among us. They had two sons of their own, Bobby and Billy, who were both married and had their own homes elsewhere but showed up to help with the catering business and seemed also to enjoy giving us orders. It was easy to see that they were still involved in a sibling rivalry for their parents' attention, with Bobby, who resembled his father, being a very hard worker, and Billy, who resembled his mother, being quite spoiled.

The one valuable thing I learned during my stay in Anahola was how to prepare different dishes for luaus. Both Mr. and Mrs. Lemm were experts at preparing Hawaiian food from scratch, and they used no shortcuts. The majority of their cooking was done on outside fires. If we made chicken luau, all the ingredients were gathered, not bought—from the chickens that were killed and the coconut meat that was cleaned and crushed for its milk, to the taro leaves and stems that were picked and cleaned. And it was the same for everything else, from lau lau (which, back then, always contained beef, butterfish, and salted salmon as well as the pork that they have as their sole ingredient today), to the imu in which, besides the pig, kulolo (coconut and taro pudding) and sweet potatoes were cooked. If I enjoyed any part of my stay there, this was it.

Flight

After two and a half months had passed, I finally decided to escape and make my way back to Waimea. And with this decision I began the journey that would lead me to Kilohana Crater.

While in school I had made a list of items to collect, such as canned goods, blankets, a flashlight, and matches. About a week prior to my escape I asked Antony if he wanted to come along. My plan was to go on the evening when the Lemms were scheduled to attend a meeting at Kapaa High School, leaving us home alone with Edwin in charge.

By the time this night finally arrived, Antony had disclosed my plans to the two older boys and they decided to come along. Despite my intentions, I hadn't collected any of the items on my list and left the house at nine dressed only in shorts, a T-shirt, rubber slippers, and a thin khaki jacket. The three boys were following me, and to avoid being seen by the neighbors we sneaked across the road into a cattle pasture, walking among the cows until we reached the top of the valley where the road joins the highway. Here we waited until there were no headlights approaching from either direction, and then we ran up the road, crossing the highway onto the elementary school grounds.

Climbing the steep hill on the east side of the school, we could look over the Anahola Hawaiian homes, which were mainly on the west side of the highway with a pineapple field stretching in back of them. I decided that to avoid being discovered by anyone, I would circle around the homes in the direction of this field. It was at this point that Edwin changed his mind and turned back toward the Lemms'.

After successfully making our way around the homes, we headed toward Kapaa town, walking in an irrigation ditch on the side of the highway. This time it was David who changed his mind and decided to return to the Lemms'. So now it was just Antony and me, and the thought that the two older boys would certainly tell on us to save their own skins drove us to move as fast as we could to get as far away as possible from Anahola before the Lemms returned from their meeting and heard word of our escape.

We crossed the highway again just before the steep hill that leads to Kealia town below and climbed down through huge plum trees toward the present-day rodeo arena. Then we followed the haul cane road past the old Kealia store, crossed the highway yet again, and followed the beach and coastline to just outside of Kapaa. Here we waited awhile for the streetlights to go out before trying to get through town, for by now we knew the Lemms, together with the police, were probably out looking for us.

As soon as Kapaa became dark we proceeded along the beach at the rear of Otsuka's furniture store and followed the coastline to Waipouli. At this time Waipouli was mainly made up of coconut groves and pastures, with none of the hotels or town centers that it has today. Climbing down the rocks where the Sea Shell Restaurant is now located, we followed the beach fronting the old Coco Palms Resort, crossed the Waialua River on the iron bridge, and entered the cane fields where today the Kauai Resort Hotel is located. From this cane field we again headed for the coast, passing through Lydgate Park, following the beach at the rear of the Waialua Golf Course, and walking through the old Marine Corps camp into the pasturelands of Nukolii, where the present Nukolii Resort stands. From here we followed a haul cane road back to the highway, crossed it, then continued on toward Hanamaula Camp. Here, below the ridge known as Kalepa, we hid in the pine trees as the sun slowly began to light the island. Antony decided that he was going to hide out at his grandfather's house in Hanamaula Camp. He tried to persuade me to come along with him, but I wouldn't. We shook hands and I told him that I was going on to Waimea, still over thirty miles away.

After Antony left, I decided to climb Kalepa Ridge to avoid Hanamaula, sensing that they would surely check Antony's grandfather's house. I headed up to where a telephone relay station sits today, visible above Hanamaula from as far away as Lihue. I kept in the pine trees, then circled Kalepa Ridge toward the west where today there is a water tank. From here I had a good view of the surrounding area, and started to plan a route that would avoid Lihue and be the shortest path to Knudsen Gap across the rolling hills surrounding the tallest hill, which was Kilohana Crater.

Far off to the north on the Waialeale side of the Kalepa Ridge as it makes its way back toward Waialua, I could see the hill known as Aahoaka because of its solid *aa* (rough, textured volcanic rock) peak that stands out in the sun, devoid of vegetation. This hill lies between the two streams that make up the Waialua River. The south fork, plunging over the cliffs at Waialua Falls, runs down to the fern grotto below; and the north fork, which plunges over the cliffs at Kohola lele Falls, enters the Waialua River below the fern grotto. These rivers and deep valleys form the northern perimeter of Kilohana Crater.

Looking just below me toward the west I could see the Hanamaula stream bending into the Kapaia Valley to the south, on its way to the ocean at Hanamaulu Bay. In the east this stream forged the valley that separates Hanamaula from the flatlands of Lihue above.

Toward the south, the Hule´ia Valley acts as the southern and western boundaries of the Kilohana Crater. Beyond it and its river runs the Hoary Head or Ha´upu mountain range. Ha´upu is the highest peak of this range, which is also commonly referred to as Queen Victoria's Finger, the shape of the ridgeline giving it the appearance of a crowned queen lying on her back with her finger pointing to the sky.

Mr. Gay once told me a story about Mt. Ha´upu when I was younger: it was here that the high chiefs of Kauai gathered to gaze out over the ocean toward Oahu for first sight of Kamehameha's invasion fleet in 1804. At that time the slopes of Kilohana contained an ancient lehua forest. The chiefs' warriors pulled up these trees by their roots, leaving the red soil attached, and hauled them up to the top of Mt. Ha´upu. Upon first sight of Kamehameha's invasion fleet approaching Kauai, they threw these trees down the slopes of Kipu Kai on the ocean side of Mt. Ha´upu, thus creating a great dust cloud that could be seen from far out at sea—which caused Kamehameha and his warriors to believe that thousands of soldiers were descending toward the beach to be ready to battle his fleet as soon as it attempted to land. And this is why Kamehameha decided to turn back to Oahu, and why no lehua forest exists today on the slopes of Kilohana.

The Ha´upu range turns toward the north, separating Koloa from the flatlands of Lihue, and runs to the southwestern foot of Kilohana Crater. Here the Hule´ia Valley stretches between it and the Mt. Kahili range, which sweeps down from Mt. Waialeale, forming a notch between the two mountain ranges known as Knudsen Gap.

In the late 1800s a man by the name of Knudsen cut a corridor for a road through the ridge to make the trip shorter from Koloa to Lihue. The corridor, just west of Hule´ia, connected the Lihue and Kipu flatlands with the Koloa and Omao flatlands. This gap was my destination, and once through it I would be much closer to the west side of the island, where I was more familiar with the backroads I would need to travel to avoid being caught. What stood between me and this gap was the high hill that was

Kilohana Crater, surrounded at its base by cane fields, narrow valleys, and thick giant ferns.

I decided to descend Kalepa Ridge and cross Hanamaula stream above the present-day site of the Kauai Memorial Gardens. From here I could make my way through the cane fields and head directly for the crater. Because it was the highest hill in the area, it made for a landmark that I could use to target Knudsen Gap, knowing that it would be directly on its opposite side. I had no idea how thick the fern forest was that covered Kilohana, nor did I know that a large crater dropping down into the earth existed in the middle of this fern forest. After crossing Hanamaula stream and entering the haul cane roads, I became disoriented—the cane, being full grown, obscured my view of Kilohana in the distance. I decided to use Mt. Waialeale as a landmark instead, thinking that as long as I headed toward the mountains, I would be avoiding Lihue.

As I walked, I began to feel the effects of hunger and lack of sleep; I had neither eaten nor slept since leaving Anahola the night before and had already walked well over fifteen miles. This added to my disorientation as the day went on. To sate my hunger I broke sugarcane stalks and, since I had no knife, smashed them with rocks to remove the thick skin in order to chew the sweet meat inside. When away from the clear streams, I looked for the cleaner irrigation ditches to get a drink of water. It took me nearly the entire day from the time I crossed the old Waialua bridge in the dark of early morning to the time I finally found my way to the north-eastern rim of Kilohana Crater, overgrown with giant ferns. Upon climbing a hill above a small nearby plantation reservoir, I could see that the top of the crater was flat, and that a ridgeline with depressions on either side ran through the center of what seemed to be a forest there. Although it was late and the sun was already in the western sky, it was still not behind Mt. Kahili, which towers to the west of the Ha´upu mountains. I stood on a small mound of red dirt to face this forest of ferns before me.

The ancients called these giant ferns *hapu´u,* or "tree ferns," and believed them to be *kino lau,* or earthly bodies of the god Lono in nature. Hapu´u can grow to well over twenty feet in height, towering from a trunk that can grow as large as three feet in diameter. I looked in awe at the giants standing in my path. Their blackish yellow roots reached down into the moist black volcanic soil through the layers of loose lava rock above it. Nature's survivors from a more primitive earth, these towering trees concealed the eroded slopes upon which they grew. Their thick growth absorbed all light and space and the younger ferns fought for survival in the darkness of their shadows. Their massive leaves were dark green on the side facing the sun and a lighter, almost silver, color underneath. On this silver side there were hairs to which spore cases clung, waiting for some element of nature to release them into the air. Finally, I saw, beneath the ferns' trunks layered with stiff reddish brown bristles, tiny black thorns that protected the giants from trespassers. This was the forest that stood between me and my way home.

I decided to climb a nearby hill to get a better view of any existing trail that might have led across the crater, only to find there was none, or, if there had been, it had long since disappeared. From this higher vantage point the crater, with its tall ferns, seemed to be a series of lush rolling hills, although I could barely see a hint of a ridgeline running through the center of the forest, and the slightest dip of two huge depressions on either side of this line.

I returned to my former place with no more certainty of how thick the fern forest was, and no real knowledge that the depressions I could barely discern in that mass of green were, in reality, two large craters dropping deep into the earth. The sun was still visible in the western sky, but I knew that soon it would begin to disappear over Mt. Waialeale. I decided to cross Kilohana before dusk truly set in.

Miracle

When I first entered the fern forest it didn't appear very thick, though as time passed and I walked on, it began to close in on me. Although I seemed to be traveling downhill, I thought that this was because I was walking on the side of the ridge I had viewed from the hill, and kept going.

I continued on, weaving my way through the plants. It was not until well over an hour had passed that I began to realize that I was actually descending into the crater. I was no longer walking on soil and my feet began to get caught in the tangle of roots anchored to the lava rock. The ferns became so thick that I could not move an inch without having to smash my way through. I tried to backtrack, but this was no use—everywhere I looked, everything looked the same. I knew that my only hope was to travel uphill. At least, I thought, I would not be plunging deeper into the crater.

Hundreds of spores drifted into the air each time I pushed a fern frond out of my path, making it difficult to breathe. The fluffy spores clung to my clothes and to my sweating face, and the tiny thorns on the ferns' trunks cut at my jacket and skin. I began to slug my way up the slope. The darkness told me the sun had dipped behind Mt. Waialeale and had begun its descent into the Pacific. I thought that if I were now standing on the shore, I would be watching it disappear into the waters beyond Ni'ihau. As night set in, my body and mind were exhausted, and I was starving and so thirsty that I licked the sweat from my face to wet my lips.

Desperate thoughts came to my mind: I would never get out of the forest alive; I would never be found. I envisioned myself becoming like the skeletal remains I had seen in the burial caves in the upper Waimea Valley. I was lost and losing strength. Every move now became a great chore. As total darkness set in, I felt completely hopeless. I sank to the forest floor amid the roots and rocks and curled up in desperation.

It was at this time that I knelt on the ground, bowed my head, and clasped my hands together. I began to pray to my 'aumakua, and to the Christian God, and to Jesus Christ, with my head bowed to the earth and my eyes closed: Oh, 'aumakua, give me strength and knowledge and the will to continue to search. Show me the path, 'aumakua, that will lead me out of this darkness.

As I finished praying and slowly lifted my head and opened my eyes, I witnessed the strangest sight I had ever seen, and would ever see, at least to the point of this writing, after the passing of thirty years since that day. There was a light shining through the fern forest—not an ordinary light, for it had no source and was confined to a limited area. It was like the rays from a car's headlight or a flashlight, but with no visible source or end of the beam. It was simply rays, like the light shining through salt air on the beach at night—not bright, but shining enough to illuminate a corridor that had opened in the ferns, as if those giant ferns had all bowed their heads to the ground.

I stood and walked through this corridor in the mist of glowing light, following the rays and noticing, in looking back, that there was no light behind me—the corridor there disappeared as the ferns stood tall again. It shone only in front of me, just enough to light the path a little way beyond me. As I walked forward, it seemed the rays moved along with me and the ferns continued to bow down until I finally found myself back on the red dirt where I had stood before entering the forest.

The rays of light disappeared the instant I stepped into the clearing, and I was once again surrounded by the darkness of night. I looked up into the clear sky and found myself gazing into a crystal-clear heaven sparkling with the light of millions of bright stars.

The Journey Home

I curled up on the ground and fell into a deep sleep, feeling neither the wind nor the cold of night, and I didn't awake until the next morning when I felt the sun on my skin. I washed my face at the reservoir and then tried to find the corridor in the ferns through which I had walked the night before—but I could find no sign of any trail or any trace of anyone having walked there. I decided then to travel the haul cane roads, and tried to find one that would lead around the crater in the direction of the gap.

As I began to walk, I had no idea that by the end of the day I would be back in Waimea. After a time I came across a ditchman's house; its resident, an old Filipino man assigned to maintain the irrigation ditches and water the nearby fields, was preparing to go into Lihue to shop. He saw me and asked what I was doing way out here alone and so far from town. I told him that I was a Boy Scout who had been separated from my troop, and asked directions to the road that would take me around Kilohana Crater toward Knudsen Gap. I don't think he believed me; I was in bad condition—quite dirty, with my jacket torn from fighting the underbrush. He tried to convince me to go to town with him, and although I didn't want to go, I ended up climbing into his old Jeep and traveling with him back to Lihue.

His first stop was the Tip Top Cafe, which was located at the present-day site of the New County Annex on Rice Street. He offered to buy me breakfast and I gladly accepted. After we ate he told me to go home, wherever home was, and not attempt to go back into the mountains. I thanked him and headed for the highway to try to hitch a ride back to Waimea.

No sooner had I reached the highway just past the Lihue Plantation Mill than a large white convertible with red upholstery pulled up alongside me. The driver was a young Portuguese man dressed all in white with a red sash around his waist. He asked me where I was going and offered me a ride, explaining to me that an actor by the name of Dick Van Dyke was on the island shooting scenes for a movie, and that he was Mr. Van Dyke's chauffeur. In fact, he was on his way to pick up the actor in Koloa town and could bring me that far. This was the first time I had ridden in such a beautiful car. We passed Kilohana Crater and I finally passed through Knudsen Gap—driven by a chauffeur.

No sooner had he dropped me off outside Koloa town than another car pulled up, driven by an old Hawaiian woman whose name, I recall, was Iwaʻlani, which refers to "a bird from the heavens." She told me she was on her way to Kalaheo, but upon mentioning to her that I was from Waimea she said that she would bring me there, fourteen miles past her destination. I spent the whole time convincing her to drop me off before the bridge at the Russian fort rather than in town, and this she finally agreed to do, leaving me just above the bridge before Waimea.

I then started to walk up the Makaweli side of the Waimea River toward the Makaweli Valley, passing through the ancient farmlands of Mahiʻai and the junction of the Waimea and Makaweli Rivers. I crossed the Makaweli River in the vicinity of Old Man Kalei's house and Old Man Kualu's house and ended up on the trail at the base of Kanikula, walking toward Puʻu lima and the old suspension bridge that spans the Waimea River at Pohaku lani and the Menehune Ditch. Here I crossed the Waimea River, climbed to the top of Pokiʻi Ridge by the old cliff trail just inland of the Menehune Ditch, and stayed at the site of the heiau known as Kopahu and Kaleinakauhane until late in the evening. Finally I took the old Pali-uli Trail that led to Willy Kani's house and fell asleep in his yard.

The next morning, when Willy Kani found me and awakened me, he arranged for me to go home, where I stayed for a week before being picked up by the police and returned to Anahola. Once at the Lemms' I was told that I would be released in three days to return home, and neither the courts nor the police bothered me again.

Openings

I believe what I encountered at Kilohana Crater was something like a spirit that would come to me throughout my life even to today, a being that entered me when it chose or when it was called upon and left when it decided to go elsewhere or its energy was no longer needed. Whatever this energy is, I do know that it exists and, as you shall see, I have called upon it many times. I believe anyone can call upon it, this energy, this `aumakua—especially if one works to retrain a mind that has not yet been programmed by the modern world, and works to reclaim roots that have been transplanted. Knowledge of one's ancient genealogy and a relationship to one's native soil make the connection to this `aumakua even stronger.

I have talked to an old-time Hawaiian named Gabriel I (pronounced "E") who is well known as a kupuna on the island of Kauai. He was born in the Nawiliwili Valley, and was raised in and around Niumalu and the Hule´ia Valley. I believe that at the time of this writing he is still alive and in his nineties. I told him of my experience in Kilohana Crater, and he shared with me this story of the past that had come from his grandmother.

The Hawaiians in the days of old believed that there were certain areas on each island where were openings from the dimension of the living world to the dimension of the spirit world. It was believed that only in these areas could the spirits, or na `aumakua, enter into this world and return to their own or could we enter their world and come back to our own. These openings were much like the leaping points, or *leina a ka`uhane*, from which, upon death, the spirits would leap into their world. Some of these places were Polihale at Mana, Kauai and Poki´i at Waimea, Kauai or Kahoihomawakea and Keawaula on Oahu. Often in the night skies in the days of old, observers would notice small fireballs heading out from the Hule´ia Valley and the Kilohana area in different directions around the island or out to sea in the direction of Oahu. These fireballs, which would rise in series or intervals spaced apart by minutes, were called *akua lele*—*akua* referring to a god and *lele* meaning "to fly." It was believed that the fireballs, visible energy in the night sky, originated from a kahuna practicing sorcery and were on their way to the kahuna's victim. If the fireballs were followed to their source, the kahuna's location would be discovered close to one of the spirit openings and marked by a large flat rock or a terrace similar to Kopahu at Waimea. The word *kilohana* in the days of old referred to astrology and the art of reading omens and signs from the heavens—and, as Gabriel's grandmother believed and Gabriel himself felt, Kilohana was a place used by kahuna as a known spirit opening.

The concept of these spirit openings has not been solely a Hawaiian belief. Many such openings appear in both the Old Testament and the New Testament of the Bible. Moses used Mt. Sinai as an opening to gather spiritual powers and knowledge from his akua. And when forced to flee from the pharaoh, he headed directly to the mountain, to the source of his power, in order to gain control and establish laws for his people. Jesus, in the New Testament, searched forty days in the wilderness for his opening and source of spiritual power, and again in the garden of Gethsemane on the Mount of Olives the night before his death.

All those years ago, when I was not quite twelve and was lost at night and hopeless, Kilohana was my opening, the place where I first saw, in full, the light of my ʻaumakua. On my knees in the green ferns I had reached out to touch a spirit and a power, and in return I was touched.

CHAPTER SEVEN

THE PEOPLE OF THE `AUMAKUA

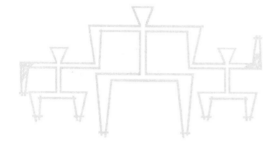

IN WHAT SEEMS LIKE THE TWILIGHT OF A CULTURE there are always those who, in holding tenaciously to the old ways, come to embody all that may be lost. To a young man of fifteen or sixteen, older men of this group who adhere to all that has remained the same for generations rather than bend to the force of change become something more than men. To a young man following them they are the strong who, in walking ahead, throw aside the stones blocking the road; they are the shepherds guiding through the maze of late youth those who will watch and listen; they are the lords of a land, familiar with the mana´o of every rock, every tree, every gift to be found there. A young man's time spent with them means that when these old men pass away, leaving their world in a kind of darkness, their light, however small, is left behind in him, a piece of dawn that he can carry and share, the mana´o of the land.

Upon my return from Anahola I seemed to have lost all aspirations for being part of the community of Waimea or of society as a whole. It is the nature of people never to let you forget your past actions, and to believe that you will behave similarly in the future. Thus from mid-1963, when I entered the seventh grade, through 1969, when I finally graduated from high school, I removed myself from this atmosphere of assumption, suspicion, and rejection. During these years I spent the time when school was out of session wandering the valleys that lead to Waimea Canyon and the Alaka'i Swamp above. This turned out to be a blessing in disguise, for these became the years when the world of Kauai would be introduced to the mainland surfer, hippies, drugs, and rock music, along with the rising social difficulties that were the result of the Vietnam War. My withdrawal meant that I inadvertently avoided this flood of psychedelic culture that would ultimately take its toll on many of our youth—and would, sad to say, be most destructive to those of us who were of Hawaiian ancestry.

Instead I spent my time with the last true surviving mountain men of our era, sharing their expert skills, knowledge of the mountains, and spiritual ties to a land that they still referred to as being theirs.

Many of them were descendants of the original people who occupied these same mountains, rather than the ocean, before the arrival of Captain Cook in 1778. At this time there were very few of them left living their lives in the old way. Many of their generation had moved to other islands, becoming, in the process, part of the modern world, but the few who remained to continue with the only life they knew were living treasures of the past.

Willy Kani, the sole survivor of his time, was one generation ahead of these men who were born between 1900 and the 1920s. Their names are with me to this day. There were the Naumu brothers, John (Nahuka) and Samuel (Ka'ili); Joaquin Arruda; Robert (Holi) Kaialau; William (Kanaka nui) Kualu; Philip (One Leg) Fortardo; Eugene (Capri) Makaaila; the Kapahu brothers, Ashford (Kala), Edward (Bahuk), and Masa; Mitsu Kajiwara; Manny Naholoholo; Lahaina and Abraham (Bull) Kahalekomo; and the Taniguchi brothers, Eddie Sr. and Sonny Hulu. Two other old-timers of this group, although not of Hawaiian ancestry, were Masao Okamoto and Carl Dusenberry Sr., who was married to a Taniguchi. These were the last true mountain men of Waimea Canyon. The Kapahus, Taniguchis, and Kajiwaras were all descendants of the Naumus. Others whom you have heard me mention—Pipito Makuaole, Barney and Ernest Char, and the Kuapahis and Hookanos—were natives of the Makaweli Valley, Mokihana Ridge, and the forest above.

Hunting and Horses

The Waimea Canyon up to this time was an isolated, insular world, and the destination of few outsiders. These men were well aware that the game they hunted—not for sport, but for food—was just as much a part of their heritage as was the land itself. The pigs were originally brought here by their Polynesian ancestors during their original migration, although the animals had since mixed with other breeds that had been brought to Hawaii by early explorers such as Cook and Vancouver between 1778 and 1794 and given to the Hawaiian people as gifts or payment in the trade for food and water. The goats were also gifts given to the Hawaiian people; the first billy goat and two nanny goats were left on the island of Ni´ihau by Cook in 1778, and more were given by Captain Vancouver in 1794, after which the ruling chiefs placed on the goats a ten-year kapu (meaning "ban" as used here) forbidding any consumption of them so that they could multiply.

In the 1960s these old-timers still made the laws of the mountains, and everyone respected their words or stayed out of the canyon. To them the edicts of the new state Fish and Game Department meant nothing, and the older wardens respected their right to the land and did not enforce new hunting regulations until the late 1960s and early 1970s. Fortunately for most of these mountain men, they did not have to live to see this change and watch as their once sacred hunting grounds became an amusement park for tourists and seasonal sportsmen (often called Hollywood hunters).

These people were only the fourth and fifth generation of descendants from those who saw the first goats introduced to Hawaii, and only the third to populate the mountains and to hunt with firearms. They still possessed many old octagon-barreled 45–70, 25–35, and 25–20 Winchesters, but their favorite hunting rifle was the later Model 94. Other firearms were mainly military surplus that they collected between World Wars I and II and the Korean War. Next to the Model 94 they preferred as a hunting rifle the M1 .30-caliber semiautomatic carbine made famous during

World War II and the Korean War. They removed the original peep sight from the carbine and replaced it with an open sight like that found on the 94 Winchester because it was their habit to aim with both eyes open—a habit that could not be adjusted to accommodate the peep sights that were standard on military rifles. Aiming with both eyes open allowed them to watch the impact of the bullet if the target was missed. In this way they could compensate for any misalignment by altering the way they looked down the barrel instead of adjusting the sight itself. This habit might have come about in the old days when the only firearms they could get were worn to the point where each bullet would leave the barrel on a slightly different trajectory, meaning the sight could not really be fixed on a setting. These firearms were mastered by feel and by the two-eyed aim.

While their firearms were certainly valued by these men, their horses were most prized; to each man his horse was a close friend and companion, not merely an animal whose sole mission was to carry his burdens. A horse was usually broken by the owner when it had reached three to four years of age, and once it was determined that it would become a hunting horse, it would remain with this same owner for its entire life. A good hunting horse would give the owner sixteen to twenty years of service and would come to know the mountains just as well as the men knew them. Billy Boy, the mule of One Leg Fortardo, was still hunting at thirty-six years of age and Molasses, a mule I often rode, was thirty-five. Willy Kani had a horse named Daisy that lived to well over forty. During their years of service there would be many times when the old-timers would get quite drunk prior to leaving the Waimea Valley for the canyon, and would nonetheless head out during the night, whether or not there was a moon. At such times they could rely on their horses' knowledge of the mountains and trails to get them safely to their destination.

All of the old-timers were territorial; each hunted in the same area of the canyon, generation after generation, as though there were established districts for each family, so that they would not scare away game or interfere with each other in any way. Each man kept to his family's territory—this was the unwritten law by which everyone abided. Territory was so familiar that even horses and dogs knew their destinations; all an old-timer had to do was to saddle up, mount his horse, and give it a little kick to start it going. From that point on he could relax in the saddle, either drink or fall asleep, and his horse would take him to his ancestral campsite, usually a four- to five-hour ride in the dark, often through steep valleys and ravines.

Horses, like the firearms these men used, were introduced only a few generations prior to their time. But in this relatively short period, mountain men had become experts in the art of breeding, raising, and training these animals. If asked how they had become so adept at traveling through the mountains on horseback, these old-timers would say that the knowledge came down from their grandfathers, but that the generations who preceded their grandfathers were not, it seemed, fully familiar with using horses.

We know from the recorded history of Hawaii that horses first arrived here in 1803, when they were given as gifts to Kamehameha I by Richard Cleveland and William Shaler on the island of Hawaii. We also know that some time between 1803 and 1820, King Kaumualii of Kauai acquired horses but did not actually use them for quite a while. These animals ran wild in the backcountry of Kauai, living and breeding without anyone possessing the knowledge to put them to any use. The Russians, upon their short stay here in 1816, probably introduced the Hawaiians to the usefulness of the horse, and they were likely used in a limited way during the sandalwood trade. The missionaries who arrived in the 1820s obviously knew the value of horses for travel, and familiarized the Hawaiians even more with this aspect of their use, but were not experts in training them. These old-timers' ancestors did not gain full knowledge of the use of these animals until the establishment of the cattle and sheep ranches on Kauai. The men I knew and their forebears credited their knowledge to one ranch in particular, known today as the Gay and Robinson Plantation and Ni'ihau Ranch, owned and operated by the same family since its creation in the 1860s.

Certainly Gay and Robinson's was not the first such operation on Kauai. The Knudsen Ranch, owned by Valdemar Knudsen, located between Kekaha and Mana, Kauai, had its start long before the Robinson family arrived on the island, beginning operation around 1854. This was the ranch that my great-grandfather worked on upon his arrival from

Norway in 1880. The old-timers would say, however, that Knudsen was very unkind to the Hawaiians who lived in the area, which resulted in many of them fleeing to the towns of Waimea and Hanapepe to separate themselves from his wrath.

In 1863 the Sinclair family arrived here from New Zealand, the forebears of the family we know today as Robinson. Upon their arrival they purchased the island of Ni´ihau from Kamehameha V for ten thousand dollars as a place to settle their family and start a sheep and cattle ranch. Two years later, on June 29, 1865, they purchased, for fifteen thousand dollars, a large section of land on Kauai known as the ahupua´a of Makaweli through a man named Charles C. Harris, acting trustee for Victoria Kamamalu, a granddaughter of Kamehameha I. This ahupua´a contained 21,844 acres, accounting for the majority of the lands that exist today between the Waimea and Hanapepe Rivers, from the ocean to the mountain. Here they raised cattle and later started a sugar plantation.

The ahupua´a of Makaweli began on the east bank of the Waimea River, crossed the flatlands of Mahi´ai, and climbed the hill called Akia just inland of Laau o a ka la to the Russian fort at the base of Nonopahu Ridge. From there it crossed over Nonopahu Ridge into the shallow valley known as Mahaikona, and covered the flat sloping lands beyond that bore place-names such as Kalaeloa, Po´o pueo, Mo´o muku, and the little village of Kapalawai, which is on the edge of the ocean below. Then it traversed another valley known as Kekupua, below A´a kukui and beyond, with place-names such as Ka´a wanui, Puna ka´awe, Mahinauli, Waikoloi, A´aka, and the village of Pakala, on the ocean below. Passing through two valleys known as Maku and Kalaakoi, separated by Papua`a Ridge, it finally stretched onward to Kaumakani above Kaluakoi Valley.

It was here in these valleys and hills of the ahupua´a of Makaweli that the ancestors of these men would become Hawaiian cowboys who were proficient in the use of horses, exchanging with the Sinclairs their knowledge of this land for a new way of life introduced by the New Zealand family. The Olekele Valley became part of this ahupua´a and is known as part of the Makaweli Valley today; only one canyon, deep within the Makaweli Valley, remains known by the name of Olekele. Later the Robinsons leased the entire ridge of Mokihana, the Mokihana Valley, and

Pu'u ki'i Ridge all the way to the eastern rim of the valley known as Waialae in Waimea Canyon. In this way the majority of the Hawaiian families that I have mentioned throughout this book came to live on or be surrounded by Robinson land, and were eventually absorbed into the Robinson operation.

The Hawaiians called the horse *lio*, which is taken from their word for "fright" or "frighten," no doubt due to how easily horses startle or spook. The saddle was called *noho lio*, *noho* meaning "seat." The pommel or knob at the front of the saddle was called *maku'u*, referring to something standing up, such as a pedestal. The stirrups together with the supporting straps were called *pali wawae*: *pali* meaning "something steep," such as a cliff, and *wawae* meaning "feet." The Hawaiian saddle always had a covering boot in front of the metal stirrup to prevent branches from wedging into the ring when the rider traveled through heavy brush; this they called *o'oma*, referring to something concave. The girt that secured the saddle to the horse they called *opu lio*: *opu* meaning "stomach" or "belly," and the bridle they called *kaula waha*: *kaula* meaning "rope" and *waha* meaning "mouth." The horse blanket was *hulu lio*: *hulu* referring to anything fuzzy. The horsewhip was simply called *uwepa*. It was necessary to coin these words because there were no words in the Hawaiian language for such things that were, up until that time, unknown. The same was true for goats, called *kao*, which actually refers to a spike or javelin in Hawaiian. Many of the old-timers, however, called the goat *kunana*, meaning "to stand and stare," which goats are in the habit of doing.

By the time these mountain men were born and being raised—between 1900 and the 1920s—there was a breed of horse on the island that had come to be known as the Hawaiian horse, and this is what they most often rode, though none of them quite seemed to know the original bloodline of this animal, only that it was mainly owned and ridden by Hawaiians. During their upbringing in the Waimea Valley, the only horses any could recall, other than the Hawaiian horses, were the draft horses, which were used mainly for drawing loads on the plantations, or for pulling the family wagon or buggy. Horses with clear bloodlines, such as the thoroughbred or Arabian and others, were seen only in the private pastures of the plantation owners and were never allowed outside to roam, for fear that they might breed with what their owners classified as inferior horses with no clear bloodlines. The Hawaiians who lived on or around the large plantations such as Gay and Robinson's were not allowed to raise any studs, and would be fined if caught doing so—all to protect the bloodlines of the plantation owners' horses from the "poor man's horse" of the Hawaiian.

The Hawaiian horse is a descendant of the horses that were brought here from many different places and allowed to roam free and breed in the mountains of Kauai for years. This animal could be compared to the *poi* dog, which is a product of many years of interbreeding between the original dogs of the Hawaiians prior to the arrival of the white man and the many different breeds introduced here after the white man's arrival, to the degree that these dogs bear no clear resemblance to any particular strain. The same holds true for wild chickens, pigs, and goats—they have interbred to the point that all, perhaps, can be classified as Hawaiian by this time.

Kala Kapahu, one of the old mountain men, told me that the Hawaiian horse originally came from Japan in the late 1800s. In his youth it was referred to as the Mokuleia breed, and he laughed after telling me this, as if he were telling a joke. But in checking back in history we know that William Hyde Rice, founder of the Kipu Ranch in the 1880s, raised thoroughbred horses and exported some of these to Japan, including a prize stud given to the emperor as a gift. It may be possible that the Japanese sent their own breed of horse in exchange or in gratitude to Mr. Rice. The ranch eventually became well known for its breed of Hawaiian horse.

These horses were particularly well suited to ranch work. Having been raised in the wild, they were very well adjusted to the rocky terrain of Waimea Canyon and could outdo any other breed of horse when it came to driving cattle through a landscape so difficult that it took its toll on any horse whose hooves were not accustomed to walking on loose rocks. In addition, because of their short stature they could maneuver easily under the low trees and branches in the narrow valleys of Kauai.

Besides becoming proficient in horsemanship, the Hawaiian cowboys also became expert in the art of making saddles; over the years they developed a saddle to suit their smaller horses, which became known as the Hawaiian saddle. Again, the old-timers did not quite know how the original style of this saddle came to be. Kala Kapahu told me that he believed it came from the English, mainly the Robinson family, who taught the art to the Hawaiians on Ni´ihau, who, after generations, developed their own style. In Kala's youth, most of the Hawaiian saddle makers were on the island of Ni´ihau. One famous for this art was a man named Willy Kaohilaulii. Others were Makawelo Kuapahi and his son Kale, and Kapepe, an old man who lived in the Makaweli Valley.

Constructing the *pahu* (stick), the wooden frame inside the saddle, was an art in and of itself. Kala said that the experts in making this, too, were all on the island of Ni´ihau, with Willy Kaohilaulii being one of the best. It is said that patterns were given to these experts by a Portuguese immigrant named Mac Andrade, who was an early rancher in Kalaheo, Kauai, where today there are still descendants who carry his name. The Hawaiians used the wood from the *inia* tree to carve the frame and the wood from the hau tree (the species having an orange flower and growing low to the ground like a vine, not the ordinary yellow-flowered hau that grows close to the rivers) to form the pommel, or maku´u. This art of constructing the pahu—in fact, the art and skill of fashioning the entire saddle—was taught to many others by the saddle makers of Ni´ihau, who, in turn, passed it down to the men of Kala's generation.

All of these old-time hunters and mountain men, along with their animals, were a link between the past and my present as a youth. They were history itself riding into these mountains. To them every trip into Waimea Canyon was a trip home, and when it was time to leave, they had that feeling of leaving home, not of heading home. There may have been others like the men whom I have noted here, but these are the ones I remember best. Some of them stand especially tall in my memory and remain with me even today. I hunted with only a few of them, and shared tales with some on my hunting trips; others I saw in passing on the trails into or out of the canyon.

Over the span of years through high school I found my own hunting ground in Waimea Canyon. But more than this, in the time that I spent with them and in what they shared with me, I found connections to the past and more ways to reach and recognize within me the `aumakua, the descending spirit of our ancestors.

Eugene Makaaila (Scorch Eyes)

A man who was known, in my early youth, as the greatest mountain man alive died before I could have the chance to hunt with him, although I did hunt with Carl Dusenberry Jr., who had been taught by him. Eugene Makaaila—nicknamed Capri—was a close friend of my parents and at least a generation older than they were. He was known as an expert in the cures and doctoring of horses, making his medicine from different herbs that he gathered, and claimed that besides his Hawaiian descent, he had some American Indian in his blood from an ancestor who had emigrated here from America in the 1800s. Many of his remedies contained tobacco, as did the medicine of many American Indians, so his assertion might have been true. Eugene wore his hair very long, past his shoulders most of the time, while everyone else wore theirs short, often in crew cuts. His long hair and his medicines made him a unique Hawaiian in the Waimea Valley.

Eugene lived in a very old house partly fallen to the ground at the corner of Menehune Road and Ola Road, about three quarters of the way into the Waimea Valley. Willy Kani told me that as a boy at the turn of the century he would often walk past this house and notice Eugene's grandmother, who was still living in a *pili*-grass hut of the type that the ancient Hawaiians used, refusing to live in a modern house with her children. When a crowd gathered to drink at Eugene's there was always a cow's head roasting on the open fire, and this seemed to be his favorite dish, as were the heads and intestines (na´au) of cattle that he cooked for his guests. It seemed as though everyone gathered at places like Eugene's to eat those foods that were no longer proper to serve in their own homes.

As it was for many old Hawaiians, Eugene's horse and dogs were his constant companions and probably his best friends. His horse, a beautiful light brown and blond palomino stud named Golden West, was quite tame; while adults drank and sang songs at Eugene's gatherings, the horse entertained the kids by allowing them to hang on his legs and neck and climb up his tail and swing on it between his hind legs. It was not uncommon to see six kids sitting on Golden West's back while he stood still without twitching a bit.

I often stopped at Eugene's house to sit and talk story with him on his old front porch, and many times I watched him make *pa'a kai ula ula* (also called Hawaiian salt; *pa'a kai* is "salt" and *ula* means "red"). When salt is first harvested from ponds such as Salt Pond at Hanapepe, Kauai (where Hawaiian salt is still being made today), it contains a slight tint of red from the red clay in the pond itself. Upon bringing the salt home, Eugene spread it out on a table and let it dry completely in the sun. Then he washed it with water, rubbing it to remove its coating of dirt a little at a time so the salt would not melt away. For three or four weeks it was wash, then dry, wash, then dry, until the salt was as clean as possible, which, for Eugene, was quite clean. In fact, his salt would be almost as white as the kind you see in the grocery store. His next step was to pound the salt to reduce the size of the crystals.

When the cleanliness of the salt and the size of the grain met his approval, he would color it red with *alae* (or *alaea*) from the mountains above Mokihana Ridge. Alae is a brick red mineral that is very hard, almost like stone, and contains hematite. With a knife he would scrape the alae into a powder, then mix this with water to create a dye. Finally, he would dip his hands into the dye, then into the salt, and *lomi* (meaning "to massage with the hand") the crystals again and again until he was satisfied with the color.

Eugene's salt was medicinal, based on the Hawaiian beliefs pertaining to the use of alae. It was believed that there were two types of alae, one male and the other female. Just as in the animal kingdom, where the male is often more beautiful in color than the female (the cardinal is a good example of this—the male is bright red, the female brown), so it was for alae. The male alae was a very bright red-orange with streaks of blond, while the dull female was really more brown than red. In addition to color, texture, too, was said to differ from male to female. The male alae was very hard and smooth, while female stones, such as those used in the imu, were covered with pores. The male alae, which was the one said to have medicinal value, was quite rare and not easily found. This was the alae used by Eugene, and was what made his salt so special.

It was about the time when I began visiting Eugene that my mother suffered a stroke, which left her partially paralyzed on her left side, mainly affecting her leg. I watched Maraea Kaialau Cox, my auntie Maraea, come to our house every day with a bottle containing egg-sized rocks of alae colored a rich red-orange. She scraped some of this alae into a glass of warm water, along with a sprinkling of Hawaiian salt. While my mother drank this, Maraea said a silent prayer every day for three weeks—and after the third week the effects of the stroke had completely disappeared. My mother felt as though it had never happened, and does so to this very day. Such is the value of alae.

Sometimes when I camped on the side of the river, I would wake up at about midnight and walk down to Eugene's house. He was usually just coming home from the bars in Waimea. His old living room had no furniture except for a wicker table and chair and a mattress on the floor. Golden West often slept with him in the parlor—I have been at his house at one in the morning and found him passed out on the floor with his horse lying on the mattress next to him. But when he was awake, I would sit with him in his kitchen as he prepared his coffee and food. Because he had no refrigerator he kept his mountain meat in the wooden barrels in which it had been salted with Hawaiian salt and cured. He would fry some of this pork on his kerosene stove in an old cast-iron skillet, and this made for the best meal we could ever eat.

One day Eugene told me that on his next trip to Mokihana Ridge to gather alae, he would take me along so that I could see his source of this clay. This trip, though, would never occur; three weeks later he died after a fight while drinking in Waimea. Before he died, however, he gave me a large bottle of his salt—and there is still some remaining today, over thirty years later. In the beginning I used it only medicinally, for gargling whenever I had a sore throat from a cold, for instance. Over the years I have used it on all of my children when they had colds. But as time went by, I began to see Eugene as an ʻaumakua and used his salt to make charms— as an unihi pili—for purposes that I will not disclose in this book. Suffice it to say that when modern remedies no longer work, sometimes the ancient ones provide solutions.

Besides the salt, Eugene gave me an old hunting backpack of his, and this I used all through my years of hunting during high school; it, too, became an unihi pili. I treasured his gifts and valued all that he shared with me. The short time I spent with Eugene instilled in me a sort of spirit that, after his death, became an ʻaumakua in my life.

Kanaka nui (Big Man)

Another old-timer during these years was William Kualu, known by his Hawaiian name, Kanaka nui, which means "big man." Although he was no taller than five feet five inches, he was built like a pit bull, and had the strength of a man well beyond his size. In the depths of the Makaweli Valley there is a stream that enters the Makaweli River from the first major valley you encounter on the left side of Makaweli, heading inland. This is Mokuone stream, and the valley is the Mokuone Valley. The trail here, as in the Waimea Valley, zigzags from one side of the river to the other, depending upon which side has a bank wide enough to accommodate a path, making for many river crossings. Just prior to the Mokuone Valley and the junction of Mokuone stream and the Makaweli River, this trail seems to pass through the center of a very large island. Although the river is on the left of this strip of land during the dry season, during the rainy season the river rises and overflows on the opposite side, making a temporary island of the sandy earth here. At the end of this piece of land there is one final crossing before the trail reaches Mokuone. On this islandlike land there stands a lone large mango tree. This is where Kanaka nui was born, in a house with a front porch that once stood next to this tree.

I already knew Kanaka nui from my childhood, but only by sight. As I started to venture regularly into the upper Waimea Valley, I befriended a boy by the name of Hiriam Kimo Kaʻili, or Kimo, who was a nephew of Kanaka nui. His father, Abraham Kualu—known as Waitata, or Waikaka—was Kanaka nui's brother. You will notice that in the Makaweli Valley there are many Hawaiian names that use a *t* instead of a *k* in their spelling and pronunciation (such as Waitata), a linguistic heritage from the Hawaiian cowboys of Niʻihau, who, in the days of the Robinson family, were relocated to Kauai to work the portion of the Robinson ranch on this island. The cowboys' pronunciation of *t* for *k* lives on in Makaweli place-names such as Waitolu (or Waikolu) and Puʻu tii (which is Puʻu kii).

After befriending Hiriam I hunted regularly in Waimea Canyon, mainly in the valley of Waialae at first, where I had once traveled with Willy Kani. Because Hiriam's uncle had taught him about the canyon, I learned a great deal from my friend about Waialae and the valley and ridge called Ka´aha and Pue pue, respectively. Ka´aha is the first major valley on the right heading into Waialae; there Ka´aha stream enters the Waialae River from a deep and narrow gorge. Pue pue is the ridge that runs on the right side of the valley of Waialae. I learned, too, of the ancient trail that ascended Ka´aha Ridge to its peak high above the Waialae Valley and just below the slopes of Pili i kaha, which looms over the top of Waialae Falls.

When we were out hunting, I traveled with Hiriam to his uncle Kanaka nui's house, which was once the house of the old man Kale Kuapahi, in the Makaweli Valley. Here I discovered that Kanaka nui was a master of Hawaiian place-names from both the Makaweli and Waimea Valleys. He could recite the names of every single ridge, valley, and crossing on both sides of the river, from Keiki pueo and the valley of Mahele to Camp One. Sadly, when we were young we did not pay enough attention to kupuna like Kanaka nui when they were in the mood to talk, and now these place-names, recorded on no maps, are lost forever. Waiahole, Niuli´i, Pepe kanaka, and Keiki pueo are the only names of river crossings I can recall for this area.

After we hunted in Waialae for a time, Hiriam brought me to the valleys of Waiahulu, Waipo´o, and Poomau, deep within the canyon, and here, too, I shared Kanaka nui's knowledge through his nephew, whom he had taught well. Hiriam traveled with his `aumakua always, walking these valleys and ridges by pure instinct. He did not know the meaning of rest; hunting with him was shoot, kill, skin, pack, all day long, ridge after ridge, until physically we could not carry anymore meat, and then it was time to head home. Waiahulu, in time, would become my hunting ground, the portion of the canyon of which I would be master.

After a time, when there was no partner available, I took my learning with me, along with Eugene's backpack and a little of his Hawaiian salt in a Bull Durham bag in my pocket, and I hunted and camped alone in the canyon. At night I felt no fear of the dark; your `aumakua dwells in the same world as all spirits that wander the night, and it will protect you. During the day there are signs that, if attended to, can also protect. The

Hawaiians believed that if you smell something very fragrant—especially the scent of the *awa ʾpuhi,* which is white or yellow ginger—and there is nothing fragrant to be seen, then this is a warning of danger. When you are climbing a steep cliff with your route already set in your mind, and this fragrance comes to you with no visual cue, stop and reevaluate what you are doing, then take a different route. This warning can occur anywhere—even at home. The Hawaiians also believed that if the name of a deceased relative—an ʾaumakua—comes to your mind, this, too, is a sign of danger nearby.

On some occasions, while hunting in Waialae alone, I would run into Kanaka nui himself, camping under a large guava tree beside the river, just below Ponoluʾu where the trail crosses the river near Pue pue. There is a banana grove there to this day, just before the junction of Kaʾaha stream. At these times he invited me to eat and camp with him. One such time he pointed out to me a large boulder resting in the riverbed just downriver from his camp. Ten to twelve feet in diameter, this stone was referred to as Pohaku uila, or "lightning stone." He went on to tell me that whenever there was a streak of lightning in the skies over the canyon, it would strike this same boulder upon reaching earth. The top of the stone is crystallized, with the surface resembling chips of glass that could cut were you to run your hand over it. Over the years it has crystallized still more, apparently from being struck by more lightning as time has passed. If you wish to see this boulder today, the State of Hawaii now maintains a campsite nearby in Waialae. When you walk the riverbed from the campsite, look toward the left side of the river, about halfway between the camp and where Kaʾaha stream enters Waialae, and there you will see the boulder with its crystal surface.

In the evenings I watched Kanaka nui make tea from a plant known as Spanish needle—since it is not a native weed but was introduced by early Spanish immigrants, it has no Hawaiian name. It is, however, quite common and is found in most yards and alongside the highways. Its seeds are black and resemble bundles of tiny needles that stick to your clothing whenever you come in contact with them. Its blossoms are small and yellow and the plant itself grows to about two feet in height. Kanaka nui pulled them out of the ground, broke off the roots, flowers, and seeds, then stuffed the entire plant into his kettle filled with water and let it boil until the water became dark, though it could be brewed lighter as well. The taste was similar to that of tea, but with a little sweetness to it. The brew also had medicinal value; when used during times of cold or flu, it could perk you up and settle your stomach. The plant could also be dried and stored just as loose tea was stored.

Besides using Spanish needle for tea, Kanaka nui told me that when he was a child the Hawaiians made tea from the hau leaf of the common hau tree, which grows alongside rivers. They would collect the dry leaves from the tree, never from the ground, for once these leaves lie on the ground for a while, they grow a fungus. This tea was one of his favorites, more so than the familiar ko ʻko ʻlau tea.

Another plant Kanaka nui gathered was *honohono* grass, which he used in cooking in place of watercress. Honohono grass grows in wet areas, such as on riverbanks and in swamps where there is a little water trickling from the ground, and resembles watercress but grows upright like bladed grass. It is known as feed for wild pigs, but is delicious when cooked with pork or goat in a soup. It cannot be eaten every day, however; its richness can cause diarrhea. The purple stem of the dry land taro—called *haha*—was another of Kanaka nui's edible plants. It grows close to the river in many spots in the canyon, specifically at a place called Keoki Crossing, on the way to Koaie and Waiahulu. This, too, is tasty when cooked with wild pork or goat.

At night, as we bedded down close to the fire, he told me about the winds in the canyon. These become a major factor when stalking game; it is important to travel against the wind so that the scent of your body will be blown away from the game as you hunt. Goats, especially, and pigs have a keen sense of smell and can pick up the scent of a man from great distances. You can hide or travel out of sight, and you can walk quietly to avoid making noise, but you cannot hide your odor, and the more you sweat, the stronger it becomes. Over the years Kanaka nui had memorized the directions of the different winds within the canyon, as well as the times during the day when they changed direction. If you are hunting in Waialae, you must begin early in the morning, when the wind blows down the valley, because at nine or ten in the morning it will shift to the opposite direction, up the valley. By the time this shift occurs, you should be at the base of the ridge on which you will hunt or on the ridge itself, to be able to surprise game at a low elevation. Hunting in Koaie and Waiahulu and many other ravines and gorges was timed by Kanaka nui in this way, according to the wind.

It was also important to know on which ridges water could be found, even in small quantities; it was best to hunt the ridges that contained no water so that the game would be forced to descend to the streams below to drink. Memorizing the time they came to drink was essential, and it was important to be patient rather than to rush to the game. The hunter should arrive a half hour prior to the animals' arrival and wait—unless the direction of the wind changes, which would require arriving even earlier and waiting above the wind. Kanaka nui did not believe it was necessary to climb the cliffs to stalk goats, but that it was more important to learn their habits and wait below at the rivers or streambeds. After hunting with him in Waialae, it was clear he had the mountains down to a science. He could look up a steep ridge at the possible escape routes the goats would take, then shoot at certain rocks along the cliffs so that the sound of the bullets' impact would turn the herd in the direction he chose, which was often down toward the river where I had been posted to wait.

Kanaka nui's senses were alive on the land. Through my time with him I learned to read rock and wind, water and grass. Through him I learned that the land can tell you everything you need to know.

Kala (the Free)

An old-timer whom I spent a great deal of time with, although I never did hunt with him, was Ashford Kapahu, known by his Hawaiian name, Kala. He was always in the canyon on weekends, or whenever he had a day off from work. For Kala it was not the hunting that was important; what mattered most was being there, on his ancestral ground in the canyon where, as a child, he was raised in the valley of Waiahulu. At that time the plantation maintained a house there for the ditchman and his family so that the tunnel running from Waiahulu under part of the mountain of Paleapa and into the valley of Koaie could be maintained. This tunnel diverted water from Koaie stream into Waiahulu stream, which itself was diverted into another tunnel above the Waiahulu dam. This formed the aqueduct that brought water directly to the powerhouse at Camp One via a whole series of tunnels that ran from Waiahulu, under the Kukui Trail, and through most of the cliffs below, including Pe´e kaua´i. It was in this ditchman's house, known as Waiahulu house, that Kala once lived. Today the plantation still keeps a one-room cabin there for its maintenance crews, but the old Waiahulu house has long since disappeared.

Living there as children, Kala and his siblings awoke at 4:00 in the morning and left at 4:30 to start their long walk to school, to the town of Waimea below—a three- to four-hour journey. After school they started their walk all the way back to Waiahulu, often reaching home in the dark. As a result, most of them chose to hide out in the valley of Mahele during the day and return home in the evening, as though they had attended school.

The Mahele Valley, like the Makaweli Valley, was once the home of many Hawaiians, and taro patches covered the valley floor from Keiki pueo to the Omao Valley to Camp One. With the arrival of the Chinese immigrants they were converted into rice fields, and by the 1930s, with rice no longer a profitable business and the Hawaiian population long displaced, it returned to its natural state.

On the way to Kokee along Waimea Canyon Drive, just beyond the three-mile marker, there is a lookout where you can see the Waimea Valley. When looking down from here a little off to the right and across the river you will notice a strip of farmland and the roof of a small house; this is the farm belonging to another man of Kala's generation, Carl Dusenberry Sr. Off to the left, farther up the valley, you will notice a large black pipe climbing up the ridge to a ditch above; this is part of the aqueduct that flows out of Waimea Canyon from the Camp One powerhouse. Old-time Hawaiians call this section of the aqueduct Namo´o elua (the second serpent). This area is commonly called Black Pipe by the local people. Just past Black Pipe there is a steep rocky road that leads from the river below to the ditch line above. This road and hillside are known as Keiki pueo (*keiki* means "child" and *pueo* means "owl"), an area that is a constant nesting ground for Hawaiian owls, which many Hawaiian families refer to as an ʻaumakua for foster children or to one who is lost in the mountains. The flight of an owl is said to lead to the correct path. Just past the base of this road, heading toward the canyon, the name of the valley changes from Waimea to Mahele. Mahele runs almost all the way to Camp One in the canyon, where the name of the valley changes again to Peʻe kauaʻi just before entering the canyon at Waialae.

Back toward the direction of the Dusenberry Farm, farther to the right down the valley, there is a suspension bridge crossing the river. This bridge is commonly called Obake Bridge by the local people (*obake* means "ghost" in Japanese) and the area around it is called the Obake Valley (in actuality it is the Mokihana Valley). The Hawaiian name for this place—mainly the cliff on the other side of the bridge—is Pepe kanaka, *pepe* meaning "baby" and *kanaka* meaning "man." The Japanese name harkens back to the time when there was a plantation camp here for Japanese laborers who worked the original aqueduct and the cane fields that once grew in the valley as far as Camp Four. Kala explained that the Naumu and Kua families were already living there at the time of the camps' construction, the Naumus having migrated from the valley of Koaie deep within the canyon and the Kuas from the valley that starts here at the mouth of Mokihana stream. The original aqueduct ran through Mahele alongside the river, not to the Black Pipe as it does today. Families such as the Sakais, Miyasakis, and the original Taniguchis first settled here upon their emigration from Japan up to around 1900. Just beyond Pepe kanaka, where the bank starts again on the left side of the river, there is a series of burial caves along the base of the cliff. I have seen the entrances to these caves but have never ventured inside; they give a strong feeling of the presence of something strange there. It would seem by the name the Japanese gave this place that they had many encounters with ghosts in this vicinity.

Kala told me that there once was an ancient Hawaiian village here. This village and later the Japanese camp were located at the junction of the Mokihana stream and the Waimea River where today only a lone mango tree remains. It was here, before the twentieth century, that the son of the original Taniguchi would meet and marry a Hawaiian girl named Kaliko Aukai Naumu, Kala's grandmother.

As it was for his Taniguchi and Kajiwara cousins, the valley of Koaie—

originally called Koaia`ie—was Kala's hunting ground. The *koaie* is a tree similar to the koa but smaller in size and very rare. It once grew only on the island of Kauai, in this valley, which carries its name. This is where the Naumu family dwelled in ancient times, living off the fertile land of the valley floor. Kala's grandmother told him that the people who lived in these valleys deep within the canyon would seldom venture to the sea, except, perhaps, to trade once or twice a year. In fact, there were people in Koaie who did not know what a crab was because they had never seen one. It was said that when people from Koaie and Waiahulu were introduced to the *a`ama* crab, which is a large black edible crab that lives in the rocks along the coast, they believed they were large spiders.

Kala told me what his grandmother had explained to him—that the only item these valley dwellers required from the ocean was salt. When they traveled down to Waimea for their salt they often gathered at the point known as Laau o a ka la, in front of the present-day Russian fort. Here the coastal dwellers introduced them to a variety of seafood, such as the a`ama crab, opihi, limu, and different dishes of raw and dried fish. It was said that there was once a great rock here, a flat slab like a large stone table, resting on a few smaller rocks beneath. This rock, six to eight feet in diameter, had on its surface a series of depressions resembling different-sized bowls. The largest of these was directly in the center of the slab and was filled with poi. Around this center bowl were smaller bowls filled with different types of seafood prepared for this occasion. The visiting people from Koaie sat around the slab table and ate to their hearts' content before returning to the canyon.

After telling this story, Kala went on to say that when he was a young man working in the fields near Laau o a ka la for Gay and Robinson, this rock was still in place. But later it was removed with a crane and taken to one of the Robinson family homes in Makaweli, where it now sits in the yard.

In Koaie and the valleys of Hipalau and Kawai `iki within Koaie, the hunting grounds of Kala's ancestors, there is a story known as the legend of Kumulio that was often told by members of Kala's family. Many people, when talking of Kumulio, would say that she was a sister of the fire goddess Pele in ancient times, and that she was cursed by Pele forever after having an affair with Pele's lover, Lohi ʻau. That, however, was not the Kumulio of Koae and Waiahulu within the canyon. This is Kala's story of Kumulio, though even his version is an altered form of the original.

During the days of old when many Hawaiian families dwelled in the valley of Koae, with its deep gorges and its terraces of taro patches on the valley floor, in a time not long before this valley would be deserted as a result of the coming of the white man, the girl Kumulio was born in the valley of Hipalau. Today, traveling into Koae, you will notice stone walls that span the width of the valley. These were built in the 1800s to act as large corrals for the cattle and horses that were raised in the canyon. Today, beyond the second stone wall the state maintains a campsite for hikers called the Hipalau Shelter. The valley of Hipalau is located just across the river from this shelter. Outside of the rainy season, no stream runs through it. Here Kumulio lived with her parents, not far from the river of Koae, along with a brother whose name was Ponoluʻu.

In those days the Hawaiians made it a practice to put children outside of the house at night alone, in order to stop them from crying or fussing. Such was the case with little Kumulio; at age three, when she would not stop crying, her parents left her outside in the darkness. After an hour or so it became very quiet beyond the door. Her parents went to bring Kumulio back inside, only to discover that she had disappeared. They never saw their daughter again and came to believe that she was taken by some akua or uhane (meaning here "ghost") or perhaps by some ʻaumukua. The thought never crossed their minds that little Kumulio may have wandered down to the Koae River and fallen in, vanishing beneath the surface of one of its deep dark pools.

After many years had passed a young lady began to appear at a large pool beneath a particular waterfall in Koae, not far upstream from the valley of Hipilau. She was a beautiful young lady, lying half in the water and half on the rocks below the waterfall, sunning her arms and shoulders and face. Some of the old women of Koae who had known Kumulio believed this young woman was the child now grown, so striking was the stranger's resemblance to the little girl who had disappeared. Once they called out to her, however, she vanished in the water and was never seen by them again.

As the years went by the legend of Kumulio started to grow, and the pool and waterfall would come to be known as Kumulio Falls. But now it seemed she revealed herself only to people of her choosing, and only to men, swimming and sunning her shoulders in the water on the rocks. From there she enticed them to join her for a swim. Once a man entered the water of the pool, he was never seen again. Those who looked upon her but did not answer her entreaties for company were cursed with the physical disfigurement of a crooked mouth, such as occurs when one suffers a stroke. This could be cured, but only by the strongest of kahuna, those who practiced the art of kahea (unselfish touch).

From these men who survived encounters with Kumulio it was discovered that she had become half fish—a mermaid—and this deep pool was her home. For many years thereafter the pool was avoided by the Hawaiians who hunted in the valley. Even up until Kala's day it was commonly known that this place in the valley of Koaie was not for swimming or camping—and if you were to see a beautiful woman there while passing, you were not to look at her, but should turn and leave.

Legend tells us that as Kumulio matured, she reached the point in life when her monthly periods began—and this is why the water in the Koaie River has its reddish color, which can be seen even today, especially from the pool down to the river's junction with the Waimea River. The Hawaiians who lived down the valley, close to the town of Waimea and the Menehune Ditch, noticed that the water of the Waimea River, until it joined with the Makaweli River, turned this reddish color once a month—and does so even today.

When the tunnel from Koaie to Waiahulu was dug in 1913 as part of the aqueduct Namo´o ekahi, which runs to the powerhouse at Camp One, Kumulio began to be seen in Waiahulu, swimming in the pool just outside of the tunnel entrance. During the days of my youth when I hunted in Waiahulu, the Filipino ditchman who worked in that area believed he could ward her away. He placed ti leaf, Hawaiian salt, and urine in old vases, cans, and bottles on the bank of the river outside the tunnel entrance and in the cabin. He was certain that there were now other spirits traveling with Kumulio. And yet, despite the strong convictions like those of the Filipino's that I saw and heard, I am sure that belief in the existence of Kumulio will disappear with my generation.

What made the story of Kumulio so special in the lore of Kala's family was the belief that during the 1920s a member of this family had fallen in love with the mermaid and she with him. According to the story, this affair lasted for more than ten years, ending in death and tragedy. I will not disclose the name of the family member out of respect for Kala, but will say that from the turn of the century to the early 1930s when the tragedy occurred, he was known to be the greatest mountain man of his era, possessing greater skill and knowledge of the mountains of Kauai than anyone else alive at the time.

It was said that he often disappeared into the canyon for days at a time, without anyone knowing where he had gone. At the end of the valley of Koaie, where Koaie (or Kumulio) Falls drop from the Alaka'i Swamp above, Kumulio and the mountain man would meet and carry on their affair. His wife's suspicions grew and she began to have dreams of him and Kumulio together until she came to believe in the existence of the mermaid. Thereafter she began an affair of her own. All of it came to an end in 1932, resulting in the deaths of both the mountain man and his wife. And this was where Kala's story ended.

We talked of other things besides the legend of Kumulio. Kala often mentioned a campsite in the valley of Waiahulu, close to the area known as Waiahani, that became a popular gathering place for the men of his time. Waiahani is a gorge located just past Paleapa, the cliff with the caves that can be seen from Waiahulu House and that separates Waiahulu from Koaie. Kanaka nui maintained a camp here, and it was here, during the days of his youth, that Eugene Makaaila had built a house made entirely out of leaves from the sisal plant, or malina. The sisal, which has pointed four- to six-foot rigid leaves, resembles a giant aloe plant. When picked leaves are arranged in rows, one leaf overlapping another in an alternating faceup, facedown pattern, they resemble Spanish roofing tiles and make for a very watertight roof and sturdy walls. Eugene lashed the leaves together to a frame designed as the original Hawaiian lodges were in ancient days. Here many old-timers gathered to share their drink, food, stories, and music for a weekend, and the house stood for many years.

Ka`ili (the Snatcher)

The old-timer with whom I hunted the most was Samuel Naumu, known as Ka`ili. He and his brother Nahuka, sons of Nohili, were the last two hunters in the canyon to carry the Naumu name. As I mentioned earlier in my story, these brothers were also the last of the ha builders, the last to catch the o`opu in bulk along the Waimea River during the rainy season. In 1969, because there were many more people in Hawaii, including many more who fished the waters, the Department of Land and Natural Resources began monitoring the river every year to limit catch and consumption.

Ka`ili, although born and raised in the same place and in much the same way as the other old-timers, and although descending from the same Hawaiian ancestry, did not seem quite the same as the others. This was, in part, likely due to his mother's Irish heritage. For a time it seemed Ka`ili could not decide who or what he was. Some people can adjust more easily than others to mixed ancestry, half one culture and half another, in an environment that still has strong elements of either of these cultures. In Hawaii, if a person is born half Hawaiian and half of European descent, he or she must choose to be Hawaiian or become an outcast among the Hawaiian people, including his or her own family. If this same person was born in a Caucasian environment, then he or she might take as an identity the half that is of European descent. But to go through life undecided means that one must live as two people. Nahuka Naumu seemed 100 percent Hawaiian, and there was no question that his name was Nahuka; Ka`ili, however, seemed constantly to switch from being Ka`ili, to being Samuel, to being Ka`ili again. The only time that he seemed comfortable in himself was when we hunted and spent our days in the canyon. Here he could be one with his ancestors, here he became 100 percent Naumu, and he was a much happier man.

Ka`ili once told me that he spent seven years as a dedicated Seventh-Day Adventist. During this time his family and friends referred to him as a religious fanatic. After this period, he took up the bottle, drinking for many years. Eventually he was committed to a treatment center for alcoholics in Kaneohe, on the island of Oahu. There he spent another seven years of his life overcoming alcohol abuse.

Upon returning to Kauai he also returned to the mountains and the lifestyle of his youth, and here he found happiness. He often repeated the following words to me while we traveled in the mountains of Waialae and Ka'aha.

I spent seven years in that tunnel

Looking for the light on the other end.

But I couldn't find it
So I came out the same way I went in.

And saw the same light
That I'd seen before I went in.

Everywhere people today are searching, in other people, in groups, in organizations, for the light they already possess within themselves—yet, not knowing this, they keep themselves in darkness. When we enter a dark room at night and our finger flips the switch, the room is filled with light—and whether we enter this room alone or with one hundred people, the room still fills with light. The same is true of the light within ourselves that was turned on the day we were born and does not darken until the day we die. Even when we are alone we are filled with light. Yet how many of us leave our own light and enter a tunnel seeking some light at the other end, only to find that none exists?

So many of the younger generation today are born in the center of this tunnel, not sure of the light from which they came or of the light to which they are heading. If there is no light at the other end, and you do not know the light from which you have come, then where are you to go? So many groups in our world—the social, the religious, and the political—are trying to provide direction to the young who are caught in the dark. How fortunate were our ancestors, with their belief in na 'aumakua; from our birth this light that we all should have was nurtured to shine. No one then could ever forget that from which he came, and no one would ever have to face the confusion of believing in another light that truly doesn't exist.

Whether Ka'ili's tunnel was the seven years of religion or the seven years of treatment for alcohol abuse, or perhaps both, he found his own light again when he returned to the mountains. While the other old-timers always had a piece of ancient culture or history to share, Ka'ili, although of the same generation, seldom mentioned the past, becoming instead a philosopher of day-to-day life.

I began hunting with Ka'ili in 1967, as a sophomore in high school, when he was between fifty-eight and fifty-nine years old, though still capable of walking most teenagers into the ground. We always hunted on foot, and usually traveled farther than most people hunting with horses. Because it was Ka'ili's belief that game should be caught by surprising them from above instead of from below, we always climbed the walls of the canyon to hunt them. The big old billy goats that acted as lookouts for the herd always concentrated on the river below and never noticed us descending from the top of the canyon walls. Even in hunting, Ka'ili's way was opposite the rest of his generation's.

His favorite hunting ground was the valley of Waialae, which we always approached from the top of Ka'aha, descending two thousand feet into the valley rather than entering it from within the canyon. As we headed home, though, we always traveled through the canyon and the Waimea Valley below, passing through Mahele. Altogether this made for a very long walk. On our way to hunting we entered the Mokihana Valley at Pepe kanaka, walked its entire length, and climbed onto Kapakapaia Ridge before Hihi nui Falls and to the rear of Pu'ukii Hill. Then we crossed the rolling hills and flatlands of Pu'u kii (or Pu'u tii) until we reached the top of Ka'aha Falls, from which we could look out over the Ka'aha and Waialae Valleys. Here on Kapakapaia Ridge there is a large silver oak tree just before the steep climb that leads up to Pili i kaha. Eddie Taniguchi Jr., known as Maka `po, once maintained a camp near this spot. At this point in our journey the sun usually began to disappear behind Kokee far across the canyon. We climbed down into the narrow valley above Ka'aha Falls and camped alongside the Ka'aha stream for the night, surrounded by white gingers, large lehua, and silver oak trees.

At night Ka'ili told me about camping here as a young boy, with his grandfather, Ke kanaka Aukai, and how his grandfather always slept in the exact spot that I had chosen. When we ate he told me that I leaned against the same tree that his grandfather used as a backrest after a day of work digging three-foot embankments along the steep slopes on the rim of Ka'aha and Waialae so they could ride their horses closer to the game. Today only remnants of these horse roads remain.

When Ka'ili's brother came along, we used the Kukui Trail from Kokee to shorten the walk and make it easier for Nahuka, who had a knee problem. The hunting plan remained the same, though: we would descend into Waialae from the opposite side by climbing onto Ponolu'u from the trail that leads up to it just before the junction of the Koaie and Waimea Rivers at Iao Point. We crossed the plateau of Ponolu'u beneath A'a kalepo until we overlooked the valley of Waialae from the opposite side of Ka'aha, timing it so that upon our arrival the goats would be below us moving toward the river to drink.

Whenever we reached the Waialae River, Ka'ili always headed for a special spring to fill his canteen instead of plunging into the river as we did. This spring was located just above the Ka'aha junction, on the Waialae side, about ten feet above the river, and flowed out of a little hollow in the cliff. Ka'ili always asserted this water was the fountain of youth (Waialae means "water mixed with alae") and told me to drink it directly from the earth and not the river.

When our load was too big, we had to camp in Waialae for the night. I noticed that Ka'ili could never sleep in this valley; he stayed awake into the wee hours of the morning, arguing and cursing in the dark, preaching in the dark, to whom I never knew, for I could never see anyone there. But whatever was there for Ka'ili, it would not let him sleep. Nahuka ordered me to close my eyes and not to bother his brother. Sometimes Ka'ili would cut down trees in the night, stacking them up as though preparing to build a ha. In his youth their family built ha as far as Koaie within the canyon, as well as at the Waialae junction. But as soon as daylight came, it was as if none of this had taken place, and he broke camp and headed for home as though his night's sleep had been completely restful. This same behavior also occurred when we spent the night in one of the old shacks at Camp One. Only in this place he talked to people with whom he had spent the night there before, and who had since died.

The pavement of Menehune Road in the Waimea Valley ends at the

Kapahu house. Here the road crosses the river at Waiahole and goes in the direction of Waimea Canyon. The next river crossing is known as Niuli´i, as is the surrounding area. It was here at Niuli´i that Ka´ili and Nahuka, in 1968 and 1969, would construct the last of their ha—one to the right of the river crossing, just below the sheer cliff that drops from Mokihana Ridge at the bend of the river as it turns toward the canyon, and the next just below the crossing, where the river again makes a sharp turn, this time toward Waimea.

Ka´ili was a strong and mysterious man, and of all of these old-timers I can recall, he is the most difficult to capture on the page, despite the fact that I spent over two years of my life hunting and traveling with him. After all his personal battles, he gained strength by returning to his roots, and, I believe, found happiness in the end within his `aumakua. Ka´ili's urn lies buried at the top of Ka´aha. Only one man alive knows its exact location.

The Others

There were many other men of this generation who shared with me during this time in my youth, and many who left an impression in one way or another. When I first began to frequent the upper Waimea Valley, I ventured only as far as Camp Four and Mahele, although I knew the route to Waimea Canyon from my trip with Willy Kani some years before. Here I hunted pheasant and tried to track wild pigs that passed through the area during the night and hid on the upper ridges above the valley floor during the daylight hours. It was at this time that I came to know Carl Dusenberry Sr. and his wife, whom I called Auntie Ogotto from the time I was a child. These two lived nearby and operated the Dusenberry Farm, which I have already mentioned.

Mr. Dusenberry, like George Cliff, came to Hawaii from the mainland. He was originally from Ohio, arriving here as a member of the U.S. Army during World War II. He married a Taniguchi girl—Auntie Ogotto—and settled here for the rest of his life, working for the County of Kauai for over twenty years, along with my father. While he did not have a lifelong history with the mountains, he learned a great deal from his wife's family and became quite knowledgeable over the years.

Just below Dusenberry Farm the Waimea River makes a very sharp turn. At this spot there is a small lava rock cliff, covered with sisal plants, that has a deep pool below, and it was here that I always made my camp for the night. As it grew dark, Mr. Dusenberry walked over from his farm to see whose fire it was, and often sat down to tell me about the ghosts that frequented the area, emerging from the caves of Pepe kanaka at night, and the spirits of old-time hunters that crossed over the cliff above the pond in the evening to make their way home to the Waimea Valley below. Whether or not he was trying to scare me for the night I do not know, but always before leaving my camp Mr. Dusenberry told me not to make my fire too big; doing so would attract to my camp all the lonely ghosts in the area so they could warm themselves. My last words to him were always the same: it is better that they use the fire than crawl into my blanket beside me.

Along with Mr. Dusenberry I remember Manny Noholoholo (evening star), and although I never hunted with him, I did pass him on the trail every so often. He once told me that over the years he had lost a total of four horses, all dying from exhaustion and lung collapse in trying to climb the mountain named A´a kalepo in Waimea Canyon. A´a kalepo, towering above Ponolu´u, or Red Hill, is the pyramidal mountain that can be seen directly across from Waimea Canyon lookout.

While most Hawaiians would take the trails up into the forest above Waimea Canyon on the outskirts of Alaka´i Swamp on Mokihana Ridge and then descend A´a kalepo to return home by way of the Waimea Valley, Manny would travel the route in the opposite direction, climbing A´a kalepo and returning home through Mokihana Ridge and the Makaweli Valley, his horse heavily laden with mountain meat—a much more demanding path.

When not in the mountains, Manny loved to fish in the Waimea River and catch crabs on the old Waimea pier. He was an expert at sewing nets, for both fish and crab, as was his steady drinking partner, a Hawaiian man by the name of John Keuma, a card player whose favorite game was kumau, or trumps.

Philip Fortardo, known as One Leg Philip or simply Peg Leg, was an old man of Portuguese descent and the brother-in-law of Eddie Taniguchi

Sr., who was married to Philip's sister Mary. As I mentioned earlier, Philip had lost one of his legs just below the knee in an accident while working at a stone-crushing plant in Waimea during the 1940s. With no artificial limb available to him, he used a wooden peg held on by a leather strap, much like the wooden pegs you see on sailors in old pirate movies.

This handicap did not hamper his ability to hunt, however; he knew the mountains just as well as any other man of his time and could get around on foot just as well. His favorite hunting ground in the canyon was the valley of Waialae, mainly Pue pue and Ponoluʻu. He often traveled through the valley of Mahele at night when heading into the canyon, preferring the old trail leading to Camp One over the new one that follows the aqueduct above Keiki pueo.

Once, I was hunting with two friends who would later become my steady hunting partners—my cousin Blaisedel Kaukani, whose Hawaiian name was Keo, and my childhood partner and lifelong friend from the Makaweli Valley, William Apo, whose Hawaiian name was Kaeo; along with Allen Lewis, whose Hawaiian name was Lanui, but who was called Ula, after his father (he would later be killed in Vietnam). We had a good catch of goats, three of them very large billies, and had set up camp for the night at Camp One. Philip, who was camping close by, noticed how we had dressed our game and came over to give us some advice. Because none of us owned horses, we always hunted on foot and packed our game out of the mountains ourselves. Philip told us that it was not necessary to carry the additional weight of all the bones, especially the backbones, which were the heaviest, and the leg bones, which often stuck out and poked you. He then proceeded to teach us, well into the night, how to bone these animals properly so that we might learn the skills to lighten our load.

I often ran into Philip at Camp One, where he spent the day weaving opu lio, the main belt that runs beneath a horse's stomach to secure the saddle. His brother-in-law was a ranch foreman and cowboy for Robinson, so many of these were not for him, but those that didn't go to his brother were for people who had ordered and purchased girts from him. The rope he used to weave these belts was made from the sisal plant. I sat and watched him for a while, and he told me that he would always travel into the canyon to do this work; he simply felt more comfortable here.

Kala's brothers were men I often passed on the trail. Eddie Kapahu, called Bahuk, was a very quiet man when not aggravated, and always stopped and offered to carry our packs for us on his horse. Masa Kapahu often hunted with his cousin Mitsu Kajiwara. He was known as a saddle maker, having married into the Kaohi'laulii family from Ni'ihau, who fashioned his pahu from the wood of the mango tree. He was also a cowboy and later the sheriff for the Gay and Robinson Plantation. Mitsu Kajiwara was married to a cousin of mine, the former Tootsie Blackstad, daughter of my great-uncle Alex Blackstad. Both he and his wife were known as makers of kulolo, steamed or baked taro and coconut pudding.

Masao Okamoto was a man I saw often on the Kukui Trail. Although of pure Japanese ancestry, he was born and raised in the Waimea Valley among Hawaiian families and became very attached to the canyon, where he often hunted with members of the Kapahu family. His favorite area lay between the base of the Kukui Trail and Waiahulu, which is commonly called Chinaman's Hat because its outline resembles a particular hat once worn by Chinese laborers. A tunnel running beneath this mountain, known as Tunnel Thirteen, was dug by Chinese workers and is part of the aqueduct that runs from Waiahulu to Camp One.

If you head into the canyon from the base of Kukui Trail, the first river crossing will take you to the right side of the river. On the left side is a sheer black cliff with a narrow foot trail, about twenty feet above the water. The next crossing will take you back to the left bank, where the trail continues. This is known as Keoki Crossing. Its location at the turn of the river, close to where the water sweeps against the black cliff, makes for a great deal of danger during the rainy season or any time the river floods and the waters run with force. It was here in the days of old that some men trying to return to Waimea attempted to cross during one of the many floods. A mule named Keoki, ridden by Nahuka Naumu, did not make it and was swept downriver. The crossing has borne the mule's name ever since.

From Keoki Crossing there is a good view of Chinaman's Hat. It was here that the purple haha (the purple-stemmed taro plant) once grew in abundance. As for Masao Okamoto, his ashes were scattered here, where he remains for eternity.

The Taniguchi name has appeared several times in my story up to now. Eddie Taniguchi Sr. and his brother, Sonny Hulu, were the sons of Hulu Taniguchi of the Waimea Valley, who led members of the U.S. Geological Survey in their expedition to establish the first rain gauge upon the summit of Mt. Waialeale in the early 1900s. He acted as guide for many of these scientific surveys over the years to gather information on rainfall amounts on Waialeale, the wettest spot on earth at that time.

There are a number of trails that lead to the summit of Waialeale, and while the most familiar starts above Waialae Falls, where the state today maintains a forestry cabin, there is a shorter route from above Mokihana Ridge, Naulii, and Halemanu, which, since Hulu Taniguchi's passing, has become overgrown. Much of this trail was located under two or three feet of water in Alaka'i Swamp, so that even those who often hunt there, who know of the trail's existence and have a keen sense of direction, would be easily confused. With the exception of a few members of the Makuaole family, no one today knows this trail.

The Taniguchis were very serious people when in the mountains. Passing them on the trail was like passing a war party of Comanche Indians on a raid. Each moved quickly, looking straight ahead without noticing those around him. Their horses dripped with the sweat of being pushed to the limit. Although they hunted mainly on Robinson land, the Taniguchis still visited their ancestral grounds of Koaie once or twice a year.

As a child I spent a weekend camping with a boy named Kenneth Taniguchi and his brothers Hulu and Jerry. These were the sons of Sunny Hulu. I remember sleeping in the old Taniguchi home at the end of Menehune Road, overlooking the river crossing of Waiahole. This was the same house that Kala had lived in as a child, and by this time in my youth had already seen its day. Eddie Kapahu was the last to live in it before it was finally torn down in the early 1980s. It had stood for more than ninety years, providing the comfort of her roof and floor and touching more than five generations

The rest of the men I recall were from the Makaweli Valley, which, although separated from Waimea Canyon by only Mokihana Ridge and Pu'u kii, is scenically and climatically very different from the valleys within the canyon.

Due to the fact that Mokihana Ridge on one side of the valley and Nonopahu Ridge on the other are of low elevation with no watershed or forest, the Makaweli Valley becomes quite hot and dry up to the valley of Kahana and the canyon of Olekele, at which point the ridges on either side of the valley are much higher and begin to join the forest above, making these deeper valleys a good deal cooler and greener.

Because of this hot, dry climate within the valley, the landscape in Makaweli is unique; the ancient lava flows and rock formations have not been eroded and have not been covered. Although in the canyon there is a mixture of colors—blue, purple, shades of pink and red—in Makaweli there is the darkness of black rock against a brown and yellow background of dried haole koa, pili grass, and panini, the common wild cactus, together making the landscape look like an aged and ancient world.

Whenever I hunted with Kaeo in the Makaweli Valley (he had mastered the Makaweli as I had the Waiahulu), we were often accompanied by Nani or Ernest Char, descendants of the Makuaole family. Their history in the Makaweli went as far back as that of the Naumus in Koaie, and we always hunted together in the valley of Mokuone. Both brothers hunted barefoot and Nani wore only shorts. They both seemed content to act as guides and to spot game, and would not carry any firearms.

There are many ancient stone terraces and walls in the valley of Mokuone, built with boulders so large that one wonders how they were manhandled into place so neatly. I have never seen better stonework anywhere else in Hawaii.

Mo´ole, with its stream running into Mokuone stream, is the first major valley in Mokuone. At the junction of the two streams there is a cliff that drops down from the ridge known as Waihiwa. About one hundred fifty feet above the base of this cliff and somehow fastened to it there are a number of pieces of what seem to be ohia logs, all four to five inches in diameter and six to eight feet in length. They are lashed together with rope of the type made by the ancients from bark known as kaula. Part of this log construction seems to have shifted over the years, giving it the appearance of a cross, with three or four vertical pieces still attached at the center to the pieces hanging horizontally. We often sat in the streambed and looked up at this remnant wondering who put it there on this cliff too sheer to climb. Nani and Ernest did not know and would say only that it had been there for as long as they could remember.

I later mentioned this to Pipito Makuaole, and was told it was an ancient Hawaiian scaffold once used to lower remains into burial caves located toward the top of the cliff. During one of these burials the ropes supporting the scaffold broke, and it plunged down the cliff and became caught by its lashing on some jagged rocks. The hot dry climate of Makaweli had preserved it for centuries.

Kekua (the God)

As for Albert Kekua Makuaole, known as Pipito—he is the last of the true mountain men of the entire era, and as of this writing still lives in the Makaweli Valley as its only inhabitant. He has always chosen to be separate from society, and will remain that way until the end. Pipito lives without modern conveniences; he has no need for electricity, piped water, television, or an automobile. These have no bearing on his life. He has always chosen to live outdoors, rather than in a house, and has made many campsites along both the Waimea and Makaweli Rivers. When I was a young man in high school, he dwelled about one hundred yards upriver from the swinging bridge, just below the pond known as Puna wai mano, which is where the shark man of the Makaweli Valley was believed to have lived in the days of old. Here, as today, he lived under a simple canvas roof secured to the nearby trees, surrounded by his mule, his horse, and roughly fifty hunting dogs.

Evenings with Pipito were always spent around an old picnic table made from boards taken from houses that had fallen to the ground after having been vacant for many years. His portable radio was tuned to whichever station was playing Hawaiian music at the time. He sat and drank beer and talked of his ancestors, hunting, and the days gone by. As darkness set in, his usual light came from a burning newspaper wick in a large pot of animal fat. As the night went on the radio stations left the airwaves one by one, and then he brought out his guitar and ukulele and provided his own Hawaiian music, singing songs of the Makaweli Valley that were known only to him. It was always hard to leave his camp while seeing him still sitting in his chair, full of life, and knowing that once you were gone he would be alone again in the darkness, with no one to talk and laugh with for the remainder of the night. But that was Pipito's life as he chose to live it.

From this campsite, which was washed away by a flood that occurred in 1966, he moved to the junction of the Waimea and Makaweli Rivers, and here he remained for many years, until this camp also was washed away in a flood, this time in the 1980s. The piece of land that remains at the junction, however, will always be known as Pipito's Point. From here he moved to the old A´ana estate in the Makaweli Valley, and here he remains today, still under a canvas, still sitting at an old table, still surrounded by a mule and a horse and fifty descendants of his fifty dogs.

Pipito often spoke of the days when the clans that inhabited the Makaweli Valley were always at war with the clans that inhabited the Waimea Valley. After years of fighting, it was understood that neither would trespass on the lands of the other, and the Mokihana Valley became the dividing line. His ancestors hunted only Mokihana Ridge and the forest between Naulii and back toward the Makaweli Valley, up to the summit of Mt. Waialale. Even in his day, marriage between families of the two valleys was still unacceptable. Whenever a group from the Makaweli Valley came upon Hawaiians from the Waimea Valley, a fight would still often ensue, and this continued down to his nephew Kaeo's and my generation.

Although Pipito knew Waimea Canyon just as well as anyone else, he chose to hunt strictly on his ancestral ground—the forest that surrounds Mt. Waialeale from above Mokihana Ridge to the top of the Hanapepe Valley, where all these valleys, canyons, and ridges join to form part of the summit. After the death of Eugene Makaaila, no one came close to knowing this land as he did.

He never held down a steady job, choosing instead to roam these ancestral grounds whenever he pleased, staying in the forest for as long as he wanted with a stack of Western novels, his favorite entertainment to pass the time. Pipito may well be the last true native of the entire Hawaiian Islands—except for those who dwell on Ni´ihau—who can place his family home site on his native island to a time prior to the arrival of Captain

Cook. Many Hawaiians can trace their genealogy, but very few remain on the same home site that their ancestors lived on at the time of Cook, or can even guess at the site.

Pipito, Kaeo, and I Make a Journey

A journey to the land of Pipito's ancestors begins with our climb up Kanikula to his ancestral burial site on its summit. The old cattle road leads up the mountain from the site of the old Manini house in the Makaweli Valley, as does the horse road that ascends the peak from Pu'u lima on the side of Kanikula facing the Menehune Ditch. After traveling up the cattle road to the top of Mokihana Ridge, and before walking the rolling red hills of Mokihana, we can look toward the Makaweli Valley and see the jagged rocky point known as Pe'e a mo'a and know that the old Makuaole house is directly below on the valley floor.

Pipito often repeated the story of his ancestors standing on Pe'e a mo'a, generation after generation, just prior to and after the arrival of the white man. From here they could see the lower end of the valley at the junction of the two rivers, and, looking inland, as far as Ka'aweiki Point, which separates Mokuone from Makaweli. His great-grandfather's father stood on Pe'e a mo'a and swept his hand from the direction of Mokuone across the valley, to the river junction below, and then said, "Ko'u aina keoa apauloa," meaning "This is all my land." Some time later his great-grandfather stood in this same place, but this time, rather than sweeping his hand to encompass all in front of him, he pointed from place to place in the valley below, saying as he pointed, "Ma'o mai ko'u aina"—"There is my land." Pipito's grandfather could only stand on Pe'e a mo'a and look out and ask, "A'ia ihea kana aina loa?"—"Where is all our land?"

Continuing our journey across the red soil of Mokihana Ridge, we head for the base of Naulii, following the rim of the Mokihana Valley, the ancient boundary that once marked the separation of the peoples of the Waimea and Makaweli Valleys. As the Mokihana Valley makes its turn toward Waimea Canyon, we continue straight, heading for the ridge directly in front of us—Kalua o kalani—that slopes gently enough for our horses to be able to climb into the forest above and leave Mokihana far behind. Here there is a different world of ancient swamp and forest surrounding the western summit of Mt. Waialeale.

We begin climbing to Naulii, but stop to make camp for the night when it grows too dark to enter the forest. Here at the halfway point of our climb is a place called Manini ula, just above a fence line known as the old Army fence, a remnant of the U.S. Army's presence during World War II. Early in the morning, as light first peeks into the sky, we continue climbing. When we enter the forest of Naulii we can no longer look back and see Mokihana Ridge or the ocean far below us. This forest is three thousand feet above the Makaweli Valley—and here there is a cave that was used in the 1800s as a hiding place by lepers who did not want to be sent to the leper colony of Kaluapapa on the island of Molokai.

Next we travel onto the plateau that surrounds this side of Mt. Waialeale, heading in a northeasterly direction, and enter a flat area covered with swamp grass two or three feet high and greenish yellow in color. Beneath the grass we can hear the sound of the horses' hooves as they splash in the muddy gray soil. We pick up the scent of the wild Mokihana berries and know that we are in the midst of a large Mokihana forest, which will take us an hour to navigate.

Once through the trees, we head in the direction of Kahana and begin a short descent from Hale koa Ridge into the narrow valley of Kauluwaina below, overgrown with hapu´u, or giant ferns. After climbing out of this valley, we enter onto another plateau known as Waikalipo, and here, on the rich green pangolia grass beneath the giant lehua trees, we see a wooden structure similar to an A-frame, built from lehua logs; this is Pipito's Waikalipo campsite, and we stay here for the night.

We awake the following morning to surroundings that have turned pure white with frost from the sudden drop in temperature during the early-morning hours. We once again saddle up and ride in the direction of the sun, crossing Waikalipo stream nearby and traveling onto Mo´o kahana Ridge overlooking the Kahana Valley. This valley resembles a smaller version of the Kalalau Valley from this vantage point but has no ocean at its end, only cliffs that climb up to the land of Wailenalena. Across the Kahana Valley we see Lauli´i Ridge, which separates Kahana from Olekele Canyon. Just below us is a ravine known as Hale´kauai, where there is an ancient trail that descends Moʻo kahana, allowing travel from Waikalipo into the Kahana Valley below. In the early-morning air the clouds pass beneath our horses, preventing us from seeing the ground as we proceed onto the ridge; we actually descend into some of these clouds before circling back toward Waikalipo.

From Waikalipo we follow the northeastern rim of Kauluwaina and head deeper into the forest, to a place known as Haleʻo, or Haleʻoʻu. We pass an ancient volcanic crater that has not yet been filled by swamp. This crater, almost a perfect circle about five hundred feet in diameter and one hundred feet deep with sheer black lava walls, reminds us of Waialeale's ancient pass. Living within the crater is a herd of mountain goats that has adjusted to life in the forest; each goat's hair is twice as thick and twice as long as the hair of the goats in the canyon, and the hooves of each have become very wide and flat from continuously walking in the muddy soil.

The land of Haleʻo was the workplace of the ancient bird catchers known as *kia manu* who traveled to this forest to catch the black oʻo bird from which they gathered the yellow feathers that they used in making capes and helmets. (Haleʻo means "house of the oʻo bird.") The greenish feathers of the oʻu, a similar bird, were used in making leis. Keakua, Pipito's grandfather, was believed to be the last expert in this art.

As we near the destination of our journey, we come across remnants of the old trail leading to the summit of Mt. Waialeale. We still can see places along the trail where the embankment was carved away to allow horses to pass. We are now close to Kepapaekahi, the place, in the old days, where horses were tied—those who wanted to get to the summit of Mt. Waialeale would have to walk from here.

Just beyond Kepapaekahi to the east and separated from it by a small gorge from which Wailena stream is formed is Kepapaelua. It is near here that the cave known as Keaku is located, just below the summit of Waialeale. Although once used as a sleeping cave for those who traveled to the summit in the days of old, it is also home to a tribe of white rats that dwell deep within its smallest caverns. These rats grow as large as medium-sized cats, have all the characteristics of an albino species, and are afraid of the sunlight, venturing out only during the hours of early morning or late evening.

Having reached the summit of Waialeale, our destination, we return to Waikalipo through the land known as Kaulawehi. Here a little creek forms and becomes Kaulawehi stream, flowing below the ridge and into the valley of Kaulawehi. Its name refers to a reddish ornament such as the lehua blossom.

As we descend Kaulawehi, we enter a dwarf forest of ohia lehua trees; each has grown to a height of no more than three feet, with some trees no taller than twelve inches. The formation of their branches and the texture of their bark are exactly the same as a ohia lehua tree at full maturity—only a usual ohia lehua at this stage is between twenty and fifty feet tall. This forest, first seen by Pipito over fifty years ago, has not changed at all in the interim, and it is clear that it is ancient. Whether this stunted growth is due to the climate and soil of this particular area or it is an entirely separate species of ohia lehua, only an expert on native plant life can determine. The branches of the ohia lehua were used by the kahuna lapa `au order of the priesthood, from which many of Pipito's ancestors descended, as offerings to the god Ku and the goddess Hina when medicinal herbs were gathered in the forest.

As we leave the land of Kaulawehi, we enter the land of Waikealoha at the point where Kaulawehi stream enters Waikealoha stream, which flows to the west of Wailenalena. We next approach Waikealoha Falls, which drop some two hundred feet into the valley below to join with the waters of Waikalipo. Legend has it that during the old days there was a tree that grew on a small island in the middle of the large pool just below Waikealoha Falls. This tree, it is said, imparted special magic if these directions were followed: After removing all your clothing, diving into the dark pool, and swimming out to this island, you were to pluck some leaves from this tree, dip them in the pool, and proceed to rub them all over your body—especially over the sexual parts. Upon returning home, the first person of the opposite sex whom you touched would fall madly in love with you and be passionate for life. From this magical promise comes the name Waikealoha, or "water of love."

Finally we enter the land of Waikalipo and follow the stream until we emerge once again onto Mo´o kahana to return to our campsite for the night. The next morning we take a different route home, heading back out to Moʻo kahana Ridge after crossing Waikalipo stream once again. We follow the top of this ridge, descending slowly in the direction of the ocean, but as the ridge becomes too steep, we turn back into the forest above the sloping lands of Olelua.

We now follow a trail that is barely visible, leading through a thick fern forest. This trail and the surrounding area are known as Pukipua. After working our way through the ferns, we finally emerge on the open red soil of Kalua o kalani, high above the place known as Waihiwa. Mokihana Ridge and the ocean become visible below us, and we can look down toward Mokuone and see that the streams of Kauluwaina and Waikalipo have merged into one and now plunge into the Mokuone Valley. If we were to stand in the center of Waimea Bridge and look inland toward the Makaweli Valley, we would notice the bright red soil emerging from the forest high above Mokihana; from the forest above down to the long, sloping, red soils of Waihiwa and Olelua, this is the land of Pipito's ancestors.

As we descend from Kalua o kalani and head back toward Mokihana, we pass through another small valley with a stream know as Oʻmole, which drops off into the valley of Moʻole below. From here we are once again on Mokihana Ridge, making our way back down to Kanikula, then to the Makaweli Valley and the end of our journey.

As time goes by and these place-names disappear into the past to join the people who once used them and knew their legends, we can only remind ourselves of a time when we were part of the earth and the earth was part of us. When we pass from this world, we now leave behind wills and personal wealth and property in place of love of land and family. For Pipito these last two—love of land and family—are the only wealth he has, and it is wealth that cannot be taxed or fought over or used as a means to create hate.

The men with whom I spent time as a young man left me their knowledge, their stories, and their light, but some—especially Kaʻili—knew that I would take these and make my own way. Upon my graduation from high school he told me, "Don't follow my footsteps . . . follow your own."

I asked him, "How can I follow my own footsteps? They don't stretch ahead of me. They can only be taken with me. I cannot be separated from them or they from me.

Ka'ili replied, "Just so."

So ends this chapter of my life, my time spent with the people of the 'aumakua who were our last connections to the past. During this period, Kauai began to change rapidly. Tourism replaced agriculture as our number one source of income, and this, in turn, provided the impetus for the growth of the construction industry that would become a cancer leading to the devastation of our environment and lifestyle. As is the way of human nature, most people were blind to this destruction even as our world disappeared right in front of our eyes. The one stark fact is this: When our land and culture are gone, there is no place to buy more.

After graduating from high school, while my classmates were preparing themselves for the future, I lived very much in the past. I did not realize how much Kauai had changed, and I was not prepared for it. The once peaceful and serene environment of Waimea Canyon was destroyed by the coming of the helicopter, and the placement of directional signs, and the tying of survey ribbons along our trails.

When one learns about the land by listening to a voice that has been speaking for sixty to seventy years and by looking into eyes that have seen the land for sixty to seventy years, it becomes clear that this voice and these eyes are transferring something that was inherited from another voice and another pair of eyes. It is clear that what is being bestowed is sacred to the heart of the one who is bestowing it. Thus this knowledge becomes sacred, and the land becomes sacred. However, when one learns about the land through maps and brochures, camping guides and trail signs, with no voice, no eyes, no emotions, no ancestral ties, then it simply remains roads and trails and campgrounds—just land. Hawaii's society developed without thought of the native Hawaiian and the importance to him or her of passing heritage from generation to generation. As has happened again and again to indigenous peoples in every part of the world, monetary value was placed above native rights. All too soon the years I had spent learning from these old-timers were over. One of Pipito's camps deep within the forest was spotted from the air by helicopter; later it was destroyed by forestry workers after it had been deemed an illegal structure. Ka'ili, at age sixty-one, was threatened by the new generation of game wardens; if he was caught in the mountains without proper permits, he would be arrested.

I cannot say that in my youth it would have been out of the question to react violently to the new rules and this forced, unnatural change. Today, however, it is gratifying to see the Hawaiian people rediscovering their connection to their na 'aumakua, a connection that I thought would be lost forever. Through our ancestors this light is returning. It is the way of our people to have a connection to the past—we are the people of the 'aumakua.

CHAPTER EIGHT

THE BREATH OF THE `AUMAKUA

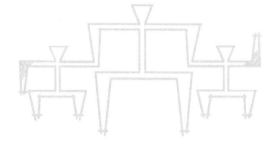

WHEN DOES A BOY BECOME A MAN? He turns, one day, inside a body that is as tall as it will be—too tall to stand in the shelter of a mother or of the elders with whom he can now see eye to eye. Inside this body is a mind that has grown tall, its height made up of dreams and wishes from the years of boyhood's fertile sleep. Whether or not they will live in the light of waking day, in a world that may be growing colder and more broken with each hour, is the struggle of manhood. If the body, the mind, and the conscience can remain working as one, the boy becomes a man. Memory—of ancestors, of his people and place of origin, and of those kahuna who have shown him the heart of both—stands close in this journey, the `aumakua that lives on his breath, whispering "I am the light that brought you life, that removes darkness from hardship and struggle; I breathe light into those who come after."

I began my journey into the world as a man, the past in which I had been living during my high school years now looking for a place in the future.

That I had no interest in what went on in the classroom during school hours and that I paid no attention while there were nothing new. From the third grade on I sat in the back row and drew pictures in my notebook of whatever came to my mind, and in this way passed the time until the end of the school day. I always picked up enough information to get by the necessary exams so that I could progress from grade to grade, but the thought of actively participating in classroom activities never occurred to me. By the time I graduated from high school, however, I had become a good artist and thus when I had to decide what I might be capable of becoming—outside of a mountain man—I chose to major in architectural drafting. I entered Kauai Community College, which was then located next to the Kauai High School campus, where the intermediate school now stands.

During the course of commuting every day from Waimea to Lihue to attend classes, I traveled through the northwestern uplands of Koloa and Omao and on through Knudsen Gap, a narrow corridor below the peak of Laau ku kahi that runs through the Ha'upu mountain range (the mountains that separate the northwestern uplands from those that lie to the east of the gap). It was a four-mile drive that served as a daily period of reflection for me. As you may recall, this is the vicinity of Kilohana Crater, and every day as I traveled to and from Lihue through this section of highway I looked toward the crater and thought of the akua that helped me that dark, lonely night many years before.

Just beyond the gap, in full view of Kilohana, gentle slopes swept down from Laau ku kahi like a lush carpet of green sugarcane to form the southwestern walls of the deep and tropical valley of Hule'ia, carved out by the waters of the Hule'ia River that pass between the gentle slopes of Kipu to the south, and the southern rim of Kilohana Crater in the distance to the north. As I entered this arcadia every morning, surrounded by the sheer walls of the Ha'upu, I had no sense of the presence of the ocean that surrounds Kauai. The walls of volcanic rock around me were covered with a variegated display of mosses and fungi; many shades of white, gray, and misty green clung to the porous lava amid the ferns, pandanus, ginger, and wild guava trees. My senses were occupied solely with this immediate beauty.

Descending Hule'ia's western slope in the midst of the encircling

Haʻupu mountains and the sheer walls of Laau ku kahi behind me was like entering an ancient Greek theater (which my ancestors would have called a *keaka*) from the very top tier of its auditorium *(puʻu noho anaina)*. In this natural theater rich green fields of sugarcane grew where seats might have been hewed from a rocky Greek hillside. What would have been the orchestra for the ancient Greeks was for me the floor of the Huleʻia Valley, which I crossed via an old wooden bridge that spanned the Huleʻia River at that time. On the other side of the bridge I ascended the eastern slope of Huleʻia. The hillside on both sides of the road was draped with ferns, and as the slope increased the ground broadened to allow shell gingers enough growing space. The southern rim of Kilohana came into full view at the start of the Kipu stretch at the top of the eastern slope of the Huleʻia Valley.

As time passed and I continued commuting and viewing the valley and its backdrop of Kilohana, the gazing place of the ancients, a chant began to evolve in my mind, and although it contained very few words or verses, it became quite natural to recite it on the way to Lihue or back to Waimea. The chant is composed of two lines—and, oddly enough, I cannot account for its words existing in my vocabulary at the time, nor could I explain its meaning. Indeed, I recited this chant for many, many years, long after leaving school, without thought of defining its meaning. It simply seemed like something natural to do to express gratitude to the ʻaumakua that once helped me many years ago, and to acknowledge its existence. Reciting the words of this chant seemed to awaken this ʻaumakua within me:

> *Kilo ha— —na ʻAuma ku—u—a*
> *ʻAumakua Mai ʻAumakua Mai*
> *Kia Pa Loa a Mai ʻAumakua Mai*
> *Hia Pa Loa a Mai ʻAumakua Mai*
> *Kilo ha— —na ʻAuma ku—u—a*

For Hawaiians *mana* simply means "power." Often today when we hear this word we think of it in the sense of supernatural, divine, miraculous, or spiritual power, perhaps because of the influence of Christianity since the arrival of the white man to our shores. In truth there are many different forms of mana, just as there are many definitions of the word *power.* The mana of our na ʻaumakua, when acknowledged and awakened, is that of our natural strength, vigor, energy, and force when they are in agreement with our natural ability to do and bear.

The mana I speak of is *mana kiaʻi,* "guardian power," inherited from our ancestors—our na ʻaumakua—who now act as guardians to our inner selves, providing the willpower, that source of power that guides us through the day and steers us toward positive results in whatever we endeavor or seek to do. It allows us to exert our natural power in the right direction, bringing together the three entities of our physical self, our mental self, and our conscience to act as one.

My chant of the ʻaumakua seemed to breathe life into the ʻaumakua within me, and as my mana increased through my acquisition of more knowledge and greater skills, so my ʻaumakua became more powerful. In recognizing my ʻaumakua I recognized that power that would keep confusion at bay and somehow preserve harmony between my thoughts and my actions.

The Chant of the ʻAumakua, the Akua's Light, and the House of the Ancients

During the course of my first school year at Kauai Community College, which would also turn out to be my last, I reverted to my original classroom habits, maintaining little interest in participating but gaining enough knowledge to carry a 3.0 grade point average in the drafting program.

One evening after staying late at school with some friends with whom I rode from Waimea, I decided that we would take a drive to Alekoko, the Menehune fishpond in Niumalu, just outside of Lihue along Hulemalu Road, around the bend from Nawiliwili Harbor. This pond, according to legend, was built by the Menehune and was once guarded by a large red eel known as Puhiʻula and a shark, the pond's namesake, known as Alekoko (*ale* meaning "to gulp or swallow" and *koko* meaning "blood"). The river adjacent to the pond is the Huleʻia River flowing from the Huleʻia Valley, bordered by Kipu and the Haʻupu mountain range on its southern rim and Kilohana crater on its northern rim. The word *huleʻia* refers to a type of porous stone that was used for polishing canoes as well as removing hair from dogs and pigs prior to cooking them.

As we parked and talked until late in the night, standing at the guardrail, I felt the desire to recite aloud the chant of the `aumakua. This time I dropped the reference to Kilohana and recited the chant directly to an `aumakua:

> `Auma ku—u—a Mai*
> *Kia Pa Loa a Mai*
> *Hia Pa Loa a Mai*
> *`Auma ku—u—a Mai*

The Ha´upu mountain range directly across the fishpond runs from Nawiliwili to Kipu and on to Knudsen Gap beyond. The first peak that can be seen directly across Nawiliwili Harbor, close to its entrance to the sea, is known as Kalanipu´u, which means "the heavenly hill," perhaps referring to a place from which heavenly bodies were viewed at night; when an *o* is added to this name—Kalani `opu´u—then it refers to a star or planet, most likely Venus. The next peak, in line with the little village of Niumalu and the fishpond, is known as Keopaweo, which means "to turn away from the light," light here referring to something like a white flash. Just past the pond is the peak known as Hoku nui, which refers to a large star or, perhaps, the moon; on the fifteenth night of the Hawaiian month called Hoku, the moon was often taken for a giant star as it rose to its fullest into the sky. From here the ridge sweeps down toward Kipu and the peak known as Ha´upu, meaning "to recall" or "to remember."

As I chanted I saw, appearing below the base of Keopaweo, a white light much like the light at Kilohana Crater many years before; it had no source but simply traveled as a beam with no beginning, as though it had just materialized out of the darkness. The face of Keopaweo became illuminated, and although the light traveled in my direction, all that was behind me remained in darkness. As I continued to chant, the light began to spread across the valley toward me.

Then, faintly at first, I heard the sound of the beating of drums, or of rocks sounding rhythmically against a hollow log. I continued to chant, and as the light grew closer, the sound of the drums grew louder until I heard with it the faint voices of people chanting, the sound of male voices that seemed to come from the rear of the beating drums. As the light approached the boundaries of the fishpond, I waited to see what would happen next; I wanted the entire phenomenon to play itself out. My two friends, however, began to panic with thoughts of one word—*ghost*—and proceeded to rush to the car, calling to me to leave with them. In the noise and confusion, my concentration was broken and I left, appeasing my friends but abandoning what I had started that night.

Experiences such as this one—like my night in the ferns on Kilohana—seem to come from a world that is beyond the `aumakua realm, a world that borders on the level of the akua, but whose opening is accessed by the `aumakua through the petitions of those who call upon it from places on this earth. There are, I firmly believe, many such places on Kauai.

Before leaving Kauai Community College at the end of the second semester, I entered a contest in the architectural drafting program only because it was a mandatory grade for the term. The contest required students to design a residence or other structure of their choice, including in their presentation detailed construction drawings and a rendering of the proposed project. The presentations would be collected at a specified time and displayed so that students could vote for the one with the most interesting design and the best architectural drawing quality.

The final display revealed "dream houses" that incorporated the latest architectural features and materials, reflecting a standard of what an upper-class residence should look like and revealing the types of houses students seemed to admire or hoped to live in some day.

I chose to create something different. My project, in contrast to the predominantly residential creations of other students, was entitled "Ancient Hawaiian Architecture." I designed a house of worship called Hale Heiau, because it was built within the walls of an ancient heiau. While other students worked under the supervision of our instructor and used the resource materials available in the classroom, I turned to David Malo's book, *Hawaiian Antiquities*, and followed his descriptions of the construction of the Hawaiian house in ancient times. While other students sited their projects in the prime subdivisions on Kauai, mine was located in Waialua, at the site of Poli'ahu, a heiau situated above the Waialua River and dedicated to the god Lono.

Their sites were enclosed with redwood or concrete block fences, but mine was enclosed with walls of waterworn stone, built in the ancient way, from stones that were still in their natural state—a fence that also acted as the sacred walls of the structure within. I layered the ground around my structure with pebbles and flat rocks, allowing the sacred land beneath to show through instead of incorporating the landscaped shrubs, miniature trees, and manicured grass of the other projects.

While other students used concrete foundations and floors of wood or concrete, my foundation was embedded directly into the earth and the floor was earth itself. My walls, blessed instead of finished, were made from the wood of the ohia tree and pili grass rather than timber and manufactured panels. My roof was of simple pili grass, cured in kukui nut oil, rather than expensive shingles or shakes. In place of nails and metal fasteners, my plan called for fasteners of simple cord made from the bark of the olona plant; in place of columns, studs, and headers I used posts known as *pou*, *pou hana* (posts at the ends of a structure that support the ridgepole), *pou kihi* (corner posts), and *pou kukana* (intermediate posts); and for rafters, beams, and girders my plan incorporated *oa* (rafters) and *kauhulu* or *kaupaku* (ridgepoles). Whereas their plans called for purlins and sheathing, I used *aho* and *pa* of many types, and for seat and angle cuts I used notching known as *kole* and *ule*.

Only the entrance to Hale Heiau, which was located in the center of the wall of stones enclosing the courtyard and surrounding the structure, was a bit more contemporary, an entryway of the 1800s built in the form of an arch made of the same type of stone slabs that were used in the Kawaiahao Church on Oahu. With regard to this entryway, my rendering could be understood from a perspective in the present, but investigating it more fully required entering the past. I chose to bring back to life graphically and artistically what was written by David Malo some one hundred twenty years ago to illustrate the fact that Hawaiians did have a form of architecture, and when presented in the form of my project, it was clear that there was much more to it than little grass huts.

In the process of trying to communicate this, I won the competition.

The Three Entities: the Physical Self, the Mental Self, and the Conscience

The person in ancient Hawaiian society who was closest to what could be termed an architect was the *kahuna kuhikuhi pu'uone.* This kahuna was actually both a priest and an architect combined into one; in selecting sites for his projects, mainly heiau, he was required to feel the presence of openings and leaping points between the worlds of the 'aumakua and the akua and between the ao and the po, as well as to recognize that the akua that comes forth from this opening and the akua to which a heiau is being built are one and the same so that the heiau can attain its *aha* (connection to the gods). One should not worship Ku at the house of Lono unless both dwell in the same house. This, then, is the reason that heiau were reconstructed on the same sites again and again—such sites were few in number and the priestly powers to recognize them did not exist in every generation.

The very title of kahuna kuhikuhi pu'uone embodies the dual nature of this position: *kahuna* in this context, in addition to referring to a priest, refers to an expert in any profession. *Kuhikuhi* refers to showing, pointing out, or illustrating the desires of others or oneself, to make these desires materialize in physical form from intangible ideas, as is accomplished with a blueprint. *Pu'uone* means "to mold in sand"—because Hawaiians had no written language, ideas were molded in sand much as a sand castle is built at the beach.

The kahuna kuhikuhi pu'uone was a kahuna by virtue of the existence of the 'aumakua within him at birth, the development of which could not be taught but only nurtured by elder kahuna or kupuna. The other aspects of his position could be learned as one would learn any other trade. In ancient Hawaiian society this was accomplished through apprenticeship because there was no form of institutionalized education. In many cases the ohana—family or extended family—and connection to ancestors through the 'aumakua belief played the role that institutionalized education plays today. Values and knowledge of trades were passed on, from breath to breath, generation to generation, much like a family heirloom.

When this system is replaced with institutionalized education, the main intent of which can be to prepare students for employment and a higher standard of living rather than to pass on knowledge, the informed mind of each student is made finite, coming to an end when the student's life ends, rather than living on in the knowledge of the ensuing generation.

I left Kauai Community College after a year with my three entities—my physical self, my mental self, and my conscience—working as one. I was ready to enter society and follow my destiny in the only way I knew how: by learning from each individual experience and in the process fortifying my personal knowledge in my own way; by going farther in the direction of my choosing, yet taking care to stay within the capabilities of my body, mind, and conscience; by patiently letting these capabilities expand over time as I collected knowledge of our world, taking care never to allow one to leap in front of the others.

Over the course of time I met three people who helped me develop my drafting skills to such a level that many people in the community of Kauai in the 1970s believed me to be an architect, although I never made this claim. These three people, through their existing knowledge in their individual trades, which, when combined, totaled more than one hundred years of experience, provided for me the building blocks that in ancient times allowed the kahuna kuhikuhi pu´uone to practice his profession.

Hanis Therkelsen's Gifts

The first of these three individuals was Hanis Therkelsen, a man of Norwegian ancestry in his late fifties who was a registered professional architect and a member of the American Institute of Architects. At the time I met him he had just recently arrived from California and had moved to Hanalei, Kauai, after a battle with alcohol, which had toppled him from his standing as one of the more notable architects in California to his place now as a man who was using his knowledge for simple room and board and the advancement of others who possessed no skill at his trade. In this work he seemed to find peace of mind and freedom from the pressures of dealing with the business side of architecture. Others dealt with the business end and I was hired to be the hands that created the renderings of its product. His role was to be the instrument for those who desired the fortune of his profession, but who had no interest in its art or in the responsibility of transforming the ideas of others into the physical.

The year was 1972 and the company was Hanalei Homes, Inc., owned and operated by Richard Johnson, known as Red Johnson, who was a trained helicopter pilot (and who would later start a company called Papillon Helicopters). During my short tenure at Hanalei Homes, I met Hanis Therkelsen on only a few occasions to discuss some of his sketches that required scaling and detailing; within a few months of my arrival he was again incapacitated by alcohol and the company seemed on the verge of dissolving. Even so, his work had a direct impact on the development of my skills and furthered my understanding of architecture as an art form—the art form that we come into contact with daily, that shelters us from the elements, provides us with homes, and enshrines the sacred symbols of all religions.

The last time I saw Hanis Therkelsen was shortly before he moved back to California, when he dropped by the office to pick up the few items he had on his desk. As he sat in his chair and proceeded to place these items in a brown paper bag, I began to chat with him about how I admired him, a man who had mastered the art of architecture. The thought of the alcohol that possessed him did not cross my mind. I knew that he would always keep the knowledge that he held, even if he did not value it himself. Our world is strange; so many people place a market value on knowledge, and when it no longer becomes feasible to gain a market return on it, it is thought of as useless. If the bulk of one's knowledge has no real market value, it becomes easy to imagine oneself as useless. It is rare to find any who value and appreciate knowledge for its own sake rather than for any financial gain it may promise.

Before leaving he handed me a book to keep, one that he had carried with him since his collegiate days, and told me that it had always reminded him of the true nature of architecture, and there was nothing more I truly needed to understand about the art outside of what was in this book, other than the importance of natural creativity. The book, *A History of Architecture: On the Comparative Method,* by Sir Banister Fletcher, an Englishman, was first printed in 1896 in Great Britain and traced the history of architecture in the form of a genealogy, a "family tree" of architecture with the Egyptians, Assyrians, Peruvians, Chinese, and Japanese on its lowest branches and the United States at its very top. Downward from the base of its trunk there extended six major "roots" or factors that influenced the growth of the tree as a whole as well as each individual branch: geographical, geological, climatic, religious, social, and historical.

This book gave me such a strong understanding of the creation of architecture and its practice as it has been influenced by place of origin and people of origin around the world that if Sir Banister were still alive I believe I could argue the subject with him at a learned level. In addition, while reading this book it seemed as though the ʻaumakua within me experienced its first encounter with other civilizations of the world and, beyond their differences in architectural character, gleaned the fascinating differences in their religious beliefs.

This book helped me to realize that architecture can preserve the historical, social, and religious beliefs of civilizations, and by destroying it, we destroy the roots of our own civilization. This destruction can occur, as it did in Hawaii with the arrival and overwhelming influence of Western culture, when one civilization grafts its branch onto the existing branch of another, in effect cutting short the life of the latter and its opportunity to grow and flower.

The other items that Hanis Therkelsen left in my care were the files for three custom homes that he had designed in the Hanalei area, along with the original tracings that were drawn by him to provide its blueprints. While the book he gave me equipped me with the historical and cultural background of architecture, these tracings taught me a lesson about developing drawing or illustrating skills better to translate ideas to physical form so that others can make them a reality.

It is a powerful thing to look beyond the *purpose* of a physical creation to see the *substance* that brings this creation to life, and in the process feel the artistic sensibility of its creator. Such was the perception of the kahuna kuhikuhi puʻuone as locator of sacred sites, and of his close cousins within the priesthood, the *kahuna papa hulihonua*, who knew the configurations of the earth; the *kahuna papa kilokilo lani*, who could read the signs in the sky; the *kahuna papa kilo ʻopua*, who read the clouds; the *kahuna papa kilo hoku*, who read the stars; and finally the *kahuna papa kilo honua*, who read signs within the earth.

In reviewing Hanis's plans, I sought not to gain technical knowledge or to appreciate the aesthetic value of the design they presented, but to study his drawing style, which was the substance that made up these drawings, the markings of graphite that flowed from his hand in coordination with his mind so that all could see what was to be built and understand technically how to create it. Hanis Therkelsen was an architect of the old school in the days when, rather than science creating art, art created science.

From his inspiration I went on to develop my own style of architectural rendering, a style that expressed science through art. I aimed for a style that used line—fine, medium, or heavy—shade, and shadow to convey the same information that technical rendering did, but in a way that deferred more to art. I came to establish my own style of handwriting and pictorial representation as a result of spending thirty minutes with Hanis himself and many hours with the book and drawings he left behind.

Gallo's Gifts

Russell P. Gallo, a general contractor who was the second person to influence me strongly in my early professional years, was born on January 29, 1917, in the small town of Walla Walla, Washington, the son of a shoemaker who emigrated with his wife from the southern part of Italy just seven years prior, in 1910. Gallo was a first-generation American whose values were established by people who still practiced the traditions of the Old Country, which had yet to be dissolved in the American way of life.

He first arrived in Hawaii in 1959, coming directly to the island of Kauai to build the Prince Kuhio Apartments, which were constructed on the old Waialeale estate next to Prince Kuhio Park in Koloa, on the way to Spouting Horn. After its completion he left Hawaii for Alaska, where he built the Arctic Bowl, an office complex and bowling alley in Fairbanks. After this he returned to Kauai in the early 1960s to settle permanently. I first met him in 1973 while working as a planning consultant for A & B Commercial, a materials house that was located at Port Allen in Eleele, Kauai. Gallo was impressed by the artistic quality of my drawings, and though I still did not possess the practical knowledge necessary to structurally produce my work, I shortly thereafter became closely associated with him.

After spending time with him, I could see that the Italian family, with its close relationships, was quite similar to the Hawaiian concept of ohana, and that once taken into the confidence of its members one was accepted in much the same way as we accept extended ohana, which is to say that one would be treated as a blood relation. In addition, Gallo's willingness to share his knowledge of his trade was much like we share our mana'o.

His Italian heritage seemed to give Gallo a great appreciation for art, which was reflected in the quality of his work. His old-church Catholicism gave him a sense of spirituality that was powerful but subdued, rather than overbearing. And finally, because he was merely one generation removed from them, his relationships to his people and place of origin were still close to his heart and mind. I related strongly to him and viewed him, a descendant from the Old World, much as I viewed the elder Hawaiians among whom I had been raised; I saw him as a kupuna, based on his age and wisdom rather than on his social status or wealth. From my kupuna Gallo I learned the practical application of my trade, which gave me the power to make any architectural creation real.

Clarence's Gifts

The third person from whom I learned was Clarence S. Koike, who was born on May 18, 1906, in the village of Holualoa on the island of Hawaii. Clarence was also a first-generation American, his parents having emigrated from Japan in the late 1890s to Holualoa, where his father worked as a carpenter. Clarence attended Mid-Pacific Institute, a private high school on the island of Oahu, and graduated in 1925 as a member of the school's second graduating class. From high school he went on to the University of Hawaii, where he majored in civil and structural engineering, after which he moved to the island of Kauai to work, for the next fifty years, for the Kekaha Sugar Plantation.

His first job assignment at Kekaha was to act as a navigator in tunnel construction in the Kokee area, where many aqueducts or ditches were under construction to bring water to the cane fields on the lower ridges above Mana, Kekaha, and Waimea. A number of these tunnels were dug simultaneously from both ends to meet hundreds of feet underground. It was Clarence's job to enter the tunnels and take compass readings to ensure that both ends were heading in the proper direction for joining. He found it humorous that his Caucasian supervisors would never enter the tunnels, and he explained that the laborers—who were largely Japanese, Chinese, and Korean—would joke with him underground about being an expendable Japanese engineer. When talking about this phase of his life, Clarence always mentioned that the Caucasians who ran the plantations would never allow a non-Caucasian to attain the title of supervisor or engineer, which, in his case, was quite ironic because he was the only one there at the time who actually held an engineering degree. For many years he was the only structural engineer on the entire island, though he possessed no official title on the plantation that would indicate this status.

Through the years Clarence provided all the structural steel designs and improvements both to the Kekaha Mill, which was originally built in 1898, and to the Lihue Mill, built in 1934, as well as to the old Waimea Mill, which was closed in 1946. He was instrumental in providing the structural design for the new Main Office of the Kekaha Plantation, a building that was constructed in 1939 and is still in use today. A little building that he took great pride in was the old Kekaha post office, located just past the Kekaha Main Office, which at present is used as a hardwood shop; this was his first solo design project.

I first met Clarence around the same time I met Gallo, in 1973 while working for A & B Commercial. He often dropped by to pick up plans that required his structural certification in order to be approved by the County of Kauai. At that time he was already sixty-seven years old and semiretired, but he still worked for Kekaha Plantation and was one of only two structural engineers on the island. Clarence, like Gallo, was impressed by the artistic quality of my drawings, but noted my weakness in engineering skills. Besides making general corrections and notations on my work, he often invited me to his house to explain these corrections, and thus began a relationship that lasted for seventeen years.

Through Clarence I learned the science behind the art of architecture. As an engineer he looked at architecture from the standpoint of one who must select and arrange materials to create the proposed form in a manner that meets safety requirements, yet does not interfere with the beauty or utility of the form.

As time went by, in the 1970s Gallo, Clarence, and I worked together to create and construct many projects on the island of Kauai, from customs houses and condominiums to restaurants and churches. I provided the architectural form and arrangement, Clarence the proportioning of the elements that gave structure to this architectural form and met all institutional codes, and Gallo the physical arm to construct it. Together we created the Beach House Restaurant; the Lawai Beach Resort Phases 1 and 2 in Koloa, Kauai, on the way to Spouting Horn; a multipurpose building for St. Raphael's Catholic Church in Koloa; Village Manor, a twenty-four-unit condominium complex in Kapaa; Waimea-by-the-Sea, a ten-unit condominium complex in Waimea; and St. Theresa's Catholic Church in Kekaha, which later became a "Prodigy of the `Aumakua."

The Institution or Apprenticeship?

These years formed my apprenticeship, the time in which I learned my profession away from formal institutionalized training and education. For me these years of learning were valuable in ways that formalized education could not be. While my intent is not to condemn institutionalized education in favor of an apprenticeship model, the former does draw us away from our origins, and when we return, many of us can no longer relate to our people or place. In essence, the institution separates us from our na `aumakua within.

Often formalized education eliminates the true sharing of mana´o, which is the sharing of one's expertise and one's personal belief. For most Americans the institution is fully acceptable; most have been removed from their original places and people for many years. But for native peoples of the world, the concept of the `aumakua still plays an important role and still has influence in their daily lives. In addition, it is our heritage to transfer knowledge and to attain knowledge through apprenticeship. All through our growing years we are introduced to knowledge through this method, as the story of my childhood and youth has shown. If you were from a musical family, you would surely become a good and well-versed musician, not necessarily from being trained in the art, but by listening to, seeing, and communicating about music with your kupuna and kahuna as you grew. To learn is a natural instinct, and to remember the source of what is learned is also a natural instinct—this is true for our families that mastered the hula, or grew taro, or excelled at many other arts and skills of our culture. It is through this strength from our na ʻaumakua within us that we have managed to save the portion of our culture that remains alive today for those who are beginning to return.

It is true that the state or a government requires that education be documented, accredited, and recognized by an institution's ruling bodies to confer professional status. But even this can be overcome without losing one's physical self, one's expertise, or one's personal belief (one's body, mind, or conscience) to the homogenizing tendency of the institution. We can seek out knowledge selectively from the required sources, and then use this knowledge to participate in society much as a spear was used for fishing in the days of old: when our forebears were through with fishing and the dinner was on the table, the spear was left outside until they needed to go fishing again.

Ultimately, if an individual's or a people's conscience is lost through the impact of a government or an institutionalized education, however good or bad its intentions, the ramifications for the individual's or people's past, present, and future can be devastating. Such was the case for the Hawaiian people when, in 1819, the kapu system was abolished by Liholiho and Kaahumanu, in collaboration with other chiefs and chieftesses, to establish the monarchal institution of the Kingdom of Hawaii. The only obstacle that stood in the way of this change was the priesthood, in many ways the repository of the arts and sciences in Hawaiian culture and upon which the kapu system was established. It is understood that Liholiho was under the constant influence of foreign visitors to our shores—those whose countries had already undergone the change of separation of church and state, those who could see the tight grip that the kapu system held not only on the people, but on the chiefs as well, which prevented these chiefs from accommodating many of their wishes. Thus the priesthood was disempowered. If we look at the whole of Hawaiian society prior to the shift to monarchy as we would look at an individual, we might define the makaʻainana, the commoners, as the body; the ali´i, the leaders, as the mind; and the priest-hood, the repository of art, science, and knowledge, as the conscience. When the priesthood was disempowered, the "individual" of Hawaiian culture and society was no longer whole. Its conscience was no longer alive.

Even so, the light of the `aumakua did not burn out. Men like David Malo recorded what they could for future generations—and parents like my mother and men like Willy Kani and Eugene and Ka´ili and Pipito breathed the life of the `aumakua, and thus the life of the past, into the young like me who waited to inhale it. The `aumakua has become our conscience.

Preserving the `Aumakua

The survival of the `aumakua, however, depends upon several things. First, it depends upon learning—not the sort to be had in schools or formal institutions, but the learning received through apprenticeship and through the kahuna and kupuna such as those who shared with me during my growing up, the learning I, in turn, share with those who are young. When we look at our kupuna in their old age, we can see that though they may not have lived lives of riches, they have lived rich lives—and the knowl-edge they pass on to us becomes our responsibility to pass on to the next generation, and theirs to the next, and so on.

Yet another thing necessary to preserve the `aumakua may be best illus-trated with a story. One day not long ago, during the early stages of writ-ing this book, I traveled to the Makaweli Valley—Pipito still lives there and I still visit him as I did in the days of my youth. Often on this journey I stop near the old Kualu house, which no longer stands, to lie on the bank of the Makaweli River under the shade of the large Java plum trees, where I can dream of the old days and the kupuna and kahuna I knew while growing up.

One day as I lay there half asleep, in the state that the Hawaiians refer to as *hihi´o*, the moment of falling asleep, I could hear a voice speaking to me in Hawaiian. At first it said only, "Listen to the river." So I began to listen to the water flowing and the faint knocking sound of the stones in the river as they rolled and shifted against each other from the force of the water through the riverbed. After a while I could hear separately the sound of the water flowing, and then the sound of the stones knocking against each other, and then the force of the water.

Once again the voice spoke in Hawaiian, repeating itself several times, saying, "Follow the sound of the water back to its source, not to its ending, for there is no sound of the water flowing thereafter." Then I listened and separated all the sounds of the water, first the loud, then the faint, then just the pure sound of water in its flowing movement. Once again the voice spoke, saying that the source of the past lies in the opposite direction of the flow, and one must remove the sounds of the present to hear the sounds of the past.

Those of us who have children can watch them spend time with their kupuna, our parents and other elders within our family, and with the kahuna who associate with our family. As we watch and listen to these elders share their mana´o with our children, we think of our own experiences with our kupuna and kahuna during our own childhood. The way our parents and other elders now relate to our children refreshes our own memories of these experiences, reminding us of what we may have forgotten, overlooked, or were too young to understand. With our children around us we are now in a kupuna apprenticeship; time is the flowing water, and in hearing first the present sounds of our children and their kupuna, we can hear the sounds of our past and learn from them again.

Marriage, too, is something upon which the ´aumakua depends for survival. For the preservation of the ´aumakua among Hawaiians—indeed, for the preservation of Hawaiians themselves—the most obvious path is for native Hawaiians to marry other native Hawaiians. But as men like Russell Gallo and Carl Dusenberry and George Cliff have shown, the ´aumakua can be alive in anyone of any race or origin. It is most important that neither partner compromise on exercising and sharing cultural beliefs and the ways of family origin—especially since marriage so often flows directly into the rearing of children. In addition, for Hawaiians, or for anyone, in marriage it is important to seek out elder family members, to cherish them and accept and acknowledge them as ohana. Listen when these kupuna speak; they still share mana´o in the old tradition. And when you absorb their mana´o and closeness to past family, your ´aumakua will live within you.

Lihue

One final factor upon which the `aumakua depends for survival is the environment in which we live. In 1972, due to the circumstances of marriage and ambition, I moved from the country town of Waimea to the more urban environment of Lihue. I knew no world other than the little town of Waimea, aside from my short stay in Anahola many years before. My eleven years in Lihue, where I lived near Kelena Street, marked a number of firsts—for instance, it was the first time in my life that I lived in a house that was not more than one hundred years old, and it was the first time I lived in a place without knowing its history firsthand or its people and their origins. It is remarkable that I was feeling all of this merely twenty-six miles from home, on the same island.

During my time in Lihue I became close friends with two natives of the area, Ronald Kelii Kealoha—who was called Squeaky—from Pua loke, and Leopold (or Butch) Durant, who descended from the Kaliloa family from the Kapaia Valley between Lihue and Hanamaulu. I understood that these two related to Lihue, Nawiliwili, and Hanamaulu, along with the beaches and ocean, the valleys, and mountains that surrounded Lihue, in the same way that I related to Waimea and the Makaweli Valley.

In the time I spent in this city I often thought about those who had moved to Oahu or to the mainland United States and the adjustments they would have to make to adapt to a new environment without losing their connection to their place and people of origin. They would have to maintain this connection without daily contact and interaction with their people and those surroundings that gave them their first perception of what it means to be Hawaiian. This first perception, however, developed in the course of the growing years, can often determine how we perceive being Hawaiian in relationship to our environment for the rest of our lives.

The Three Perspectives of the Hawaiian People

There are three possible perspectives that Hawaiians may have depending upon the environment in which they were raised. The ancient perspective, which I term *i kahiko ka ike* (*kahiko* means "old"), is that which one has if raised on konohiki or kuleana land—land that was originally ruled by the family or that came into the family before or during the period of the Great Mahele in 1848 and still continues to be used as it was originally intended at the time of its awarding, mainly for the growing of taro. Kuleana lands are those still surrounded by their ancient environment to a large degree, such as Makaweli and portions of the Waimea Valley. The people who have this perspective are those who have never moved from their place of origin, such as the majority of the mountain men with whom I spent time in my youth. The heart of the Hawaiian with this perspective aches every time he has to bear witness to another piece of land being changed from its natural state; he knows that soon ancient land will be urban land.

The traditional perspective, which I term *i ku´una ka ike* (*ku´una* means "traditional"), is the perspective one has when raised away from one's family's place of origin at the time of the Great Mahele due to the loss of one's original kuleana either by sale, deception, failure to apply and thus becoming absorbed by the plantation system, or relocation to Oahu or some other more urban location. For those with this perspective, home and work become two different entities; in one place culture can be expressed, in the other it cannot. Many of our surviving kupuna today have a combined perception of i kahiko ka ike and i ku´una ka ike, and feel strongly that our lands were stolen.

The modern perspective, which I term *ka nupaikini ike* (*nupaikini* means "modern"), results when one has been raised in an urban environment and relates to the traditional and ancient perspectives only in an institutionalized sense. One who has this perspective has had to learn culture from an institution because either there are no more practicing kupuna within the family or, because of location, there is no longer an association with these kupuna. Those with ka nupaikini ike may see their culture only through the lens of what has been created by the tourist industry, and may attend a luau but have never participated in its preparation or gathering of food. These are the Hawaiians who think our present system is within our best interest and that our culture is merely our history.

There are no guarantees that one will maintain the same perspective throughout life. Circumstances such as relocating may, over the years, alter the way one views our culture. Maintaining one's original perspective requires choice and conscious effort. In Waimea, for instance, my perspective was very much kahiko or ku´una. In Lihue I knew I had to make the conscious effort to keep my ancient perspective from being altered so that I might keep my `aumakua alive. In addition, I had two sons while living there—one I named Keola after my great-uncle Charles K. Johnson and my younger brother, and the other I named Kimo after my boyhood friend Hiriam Ka´ili—and I was responsible for instilling in them a belief in the `aumakua. Before each reached the age of five years I journeyed with them to Waiahulu, Koaie, and Waialae to accomplish this and to help their perspectives to be as close to kahiko and ku´una as possible. I also frequented such areas near Lihue as Niumalu, Alekoko, Halehaka, and the Hule´ia Valley, areas that still resonated with the `aumakua, that were still in their natural state, and where one felt the presence of the ancient. My time with Ronald Kealoha and Butch Durant, who still dwelled on kuleana land and continued to raise taro, also served to support me in my original views. But what of those who have no traditional environment to frequent or people like Ronald or Butch to communicate with?

A Kuahu within My House

To preserve the ancient or traditional perspective, one can look for support in the environment created within one's own house. This is as true for those of other cultures as it is for Hawaiians. In the days of the ancients under the kapu system, when eating quarters were separated according to gender into hale´aina (the women's eating house) and hale mua (the men's eating house), a small altar was constructed in one of the corners or on an end wall of the hale mua. This altar, called a kua´aha or more commonly a kuahu, is where the men of the family worshiped their personal god or ancestral gods. It was here that they also consecrated their sons to their religious beliefs as well as to the tabus of the kapu system. Here, daily and during special ceremonies, offerings were made to family deities. This is a tradition that is thought of as being nonexistent today, but it has never really perished—it has simply taken a different form.

If a Hawaiian goes back in his memory to his tutu's house—his grandmother's house—or, if he is older, to his parents' or an elder's house, an old table can be recalled in a corner of the parlor or along one of the walls, in view of the dining room, and it was covered with family heirlooms, from poi and salt pounders to old pictures, seashells, leis, calabashes, musical instruments, kapa cloth and lau'hala mats, and hats—on display for everyone to see.

Tutu carefully cleaned and dusted these items once a week, holding each in her hands, mumbling to herself, and then returning them carefully to the same position. Whenever Tutu came home from an event at which she received a lei, she placed it on one of these items, or on her favorite kupuna's picture. She also placed a decoration of ti leaves or gingers in a large vase on this table of family heirlooms. If a party took place in the house, a pu'olo or ho'okupu (a bundle) made from ti leaves containing a portion of the type of food prepared was placed upon this table. In fact, this was not a display for Tutu but, rather, was her version of a kuahu. These heirlooms were icons of a sort. They were possessions of our ancestors that enabled us to feel the presence of their na 'aumakua within us.

These kuahu become especially important when one is away from one's place of origin. Building a display of family heritage and keeping this kuahu in mind will help preserve a connection to original culture, and will help children particularly to establish a connection to their people and place of origin.

During my stay in Lihue I created my own kuahu in my house. For many at my age it would be almost impossible—kupuna will not usually part with their possessions until they are close to the end of their lives; thus, most are quite a bit older than I was when they begin to collect items for a kuahu. But because most of the kupuna and kahuna of my youth were quite elderly, especially Willy Kani, Roland Gay, and Eugene Makaaila, they had given me valued possessions when I was very young. In addition to these items, I placed at my kuahu my book by David Malo, which was my most prized possession. Stones from one's place of origin may also be used. These should be of the porous "female" type and should have a natural shape similar to that of a bell. If they are small, such as those that might fit in a large jar, then they should be kept immersed in water; if they are larger, then they should be watered often under a tap for a few minutes. If at first the stones are watered once every ten days, then this is the routine that must be continued. If one wants to keep a male stone from a birthing stone, such as those that came from the stone my mother watered in my childhood, it should be kept in a bottle of Hawaiian salt.

Whatever the objects at your kuahu, they are reminders of who you are and what you have come from. Your kupuna who see them will treat them with reverence. Even those beyond your family will be moved as these objects remind them of treasured possessions in their own families that may have been forgotten until they saw yours. In these ways it is clear that these objects are sacred and alive, and that they speak.

Hule´ia Calls

During my stay in Lihue I often had a recurring dream that I could attribute only to the memorabilia at my kuahu, but in time I discovered an entirely different connection. The dream was always the same. I saw myself wandering around in a massive cavern, the ceiling of which was ten feet above me in some areas while in others I was forced to bend my head as I stood. The cave was dimly lit with the yellow light that comes from the flame of a candle or an oil lamp, though I could not see its actual source. The rooms and areas that branched out from the main cavern resembled a series of catacombs and terraces. All along the walls there were rock ledges, like shelves, upon which individual bodies were laid. In the main room, however, where I found myself at first, some of the rock platforms were covered with numerous bodies that had been placed there together. All of these remains were wrapped completely, some in kapa cloth, some in finely woven lau´hala mats, preventing me from seeing the bodies themselves.

As I made my way through the main cave, passing burial after burial, I began to sense that it was not possible to find my way out of this subterranean space through the opening I had used to enter it—I could sense that it was sealed, and any thought of the entrance left me with a feeling of darkness. Soon, however, I became aware that there was another entrance to this cave, one that, though much smaller, was much closer to the surface of the earth than the one I'd used to access the cavern. This instinctive knowledge spurred me on, and I began climbing onto some of the terraces that led farther into the catacombs, knowing that in one of them there would be a way out.

Every time the dream occurred it was at this point that I sensed the closeness of something that seemed alive, yet exuded an aura of death. I turned to look back toward the lower main cavern from which I had just climbed and could see that most of the bodies I had passed no longer wore their wrappings, and although some were still lying down, others were sitting up, held in position by wooden braces.

These were different burials from those that I had seen in my youth; these were not merely skeletal remains, but bodies that still had skin on their bones. It was as though an attempt had been made to preserve them, and in this processs the flesh had lost all moisture, leaving dry, leathery skin, like hide, clinging to the skeletons beneath.

Although these bodies were clearly emerging from their wrappings, whenever I looked I could see no sign of motion; I could only sense that things around me were moving. Just the same, I continued walking the dim catacombs in an attempt to find a way out, and whenever I seemed to near the other entrance, I would be distracted by the sense of a moving presence in the cave, of death moving and surrounding me.

And then I would wake and wonder what might bring out such a dream—and what it might mean.

Niumalu, the Sacred Palm

After my eleven years in the urban environment of Lihue, I lived for the next six in Niumalu, where, though still removed from my place of origin, I found an environment suited to my perception of being Hawaiian and my increasing awareness of the ʻaumakua within me.

Niumalu, which refers to a sacred palm tree, is located just below Lihue and around the bend from Nawiliwili Harbor. When one approaches Kauai by air from the southeast, the first mountain range that can be seen rising from the ocean is the Haʻupu range, with its peaks Kalanipuʻu and Keopaweo. As the plane passes over these peaks, toward the west the river called Huleʻia can be seen entering Nawiliwili Harbor, just inland from the small boat harbor. The little village that can be seen there is Niumalu, located between the mouth of the Hule'ia River and the Alekoko (or Menehune) fishpond to the west.

Lihue was merely a barren plain before the arrival of the white man and was not inhabited until the 1830s. It was then that Kauai's first governor, a high chief named Kaikioewa, from Maui—who was sent to Kauai in 1824 by the kuhina nui Kaahumanu to be its administrator under the new Kingdom of Hawaii—chose this area for his residence, probably to separate himself from the ancient villages where people still detested the fact that their lands were taken from them to be given as gifts to high chiefs from Kamehameha's regime. In any event it seems that Kaikioewa named Lihue. Niumalu, on the other hand, like Waimea, was inhabited in ancient times, as were all of the rich valley lands, such as Waialua, Hanalei, and Wainiha, that ran adjacent to the great rivers of Kauai.

Niumalu had a sense of the ancient—altogether missing in Lihue—that made me feel more at home. It was an environment that at the time was still largely untouched by the often destructive hand of modern development. Niumalu's more recent history was similar to that of the other small valley villages, such as Hule'ia, Kipu, Nawiliwili, Kapaia, and Hanamaulu, that surrounded the plain of Lihue. Each experienced the cycle of moving from ancient village, to small town, to rural community when Lihue, in the 1930s, began to be the dominating commercial center that it is today. In each, many of the old general stores—the mom-and-pop operations—closed or steadily declined and the youth of each abandoned the old lifestyle in search of a more urban way of life.

I moved to Niumalu in the summer of 1982—which is not long ago as compared to the times we have previously passed through in my story—however, in the years up to today the area has changed enormously, with the development of the Kukui Grove Shopping Center, the Ulu ko subdivision, the Westin Kauai Hotel, the Lihue Airport and the urban sprawl in Puhi, and the improvements to Nawiliwili Harbor. This development, which occurred in the late 1980s, changed forever the once serene environment of the town. When I moved to Niumalu, there were only eight families living there: the Chows, the Pias, the Achis, the Ana'kaleas, the Mizutanis, the Ellises, the Valejoses, and the Olivases.

In 1982 Niumalu could be reached by approaching it from Nawiliwili

Harbor, along Wa'apa Road, or from the top of Nawiliwili Road, which connects with the Wa'apa Road on the valley floor. Here at this intersection were the homes of Hiram Pia, his brother, Arthur, and their families, the last holdouts of a mass eviction that was carried out by the Trust Company that managed the estate of the late governor, Paul Kanoa, appointed by the Kamehamehas to rule and caretake Kauai from 1846 to 1877. Kanoa, in return for his duty, came to own the majority of the lands that were known as Niumalu.

Continuing into Niumalu the road crossed a small concrete bridge that spanned Pu'ali stream, which flows from within the Niumalu Valley where, as in the Makaweli and Waimea Valleys, there are still remnants of what were once taro and rice fields. Just before this bridge was the Motel Frances, owned and operated by Frances Mizutani, the former Frances Walker, whose Hawaiian lineage was of the Konoho family. During the old days the original Motel Frances served as a rooming house for sailors whose ships had docked in Kalapaki Bay and Nawiliwili. Just past the bridge and before the Hulemalu junction were the remnants of the old Tsuchiyama General Store, which once served Niumalu when it was still a little town. Past the Hulemalu junction and Niumalu Beach Park to the end of the pavement of Niumalu Road were the remains of the old Lovel's Tavern, which was a popular bar in Niumalu's heyday. Back at the junction, Hulemalu Road leads past the old Kauai Inn, which was operated as a motel in 1982. These buildings were once part of the original Kauai Inn in Lihue, at the present-day site of Kalapaki Villas, just across from Pay & Save, and were moved to Niumalu in 1962, when the Kauai Inn there became the Kauai Surf Hotel on Kalapaki Bay, which later still became the Westin Kauai. On the right of Hulemalu Road, in the rear of the old Tsuchiyama store, lived the Ah Hing Chow family, and also on the right was the Kaiwi estate, which bordered the road from the intersection to the base of the hill that Hulemalu Road climbed as it continued on to Hule'ia. I lived here on this estate in a house that was estimated to be one hundred thirty-six years old.

My landlord was Mercedes Leinaala Kaiwi Olivas, a beautiful Hawaiian woman married to the son of a Filipino immigrant named Emilio, or Spud, Olivas, who was originally from the Waimea Sugar Mill's old mill camp in

Waimea, which is currently known as Waimea Plantation Cottages. Mrs. Olivas was a retired schoolteacher who had taught the third grade at Wilcox School for more than thirty years. It was she who, in sharing her mana´o, told me the following history of the house where I lived.

During the time that Governor Paul Kanoa held his position, he proceeded to build a beach house to serve as his residence at Nawiliwili. At this time there were no manmade obstacles to separate Kalapaki, Nawiliwili, and Niumalu from being one continuous white-sand beach, and while the location of the governor's house was recorded in history as being at Nawiliwili Beach, in actuality it was built along the beach within Niumalu. The house that I lived in was not the main house that he built, which was located farther in at the current site of the Stanford Achi residence close to the Alekoko fishpond, but was built to be used as a recreational house, being closer to the beach, and as an entertainment center for visiting guests and dignitaries from off island. It was probably built in 1846 or 1847, before his residence, and was used temporarily as his living quarters until the main house was completed.

Governor Kanoa left Kauai in 1877, and was appointed minister of finance by King David Kalakaua in 1882. Over the course of time he gave a portion of his lands on Kauai to his sister, whose name was Beatrice Kanoa. These lands consisted of large tracts in Nawiliwili and Lawaikai and a smaller tract in Nuimalu with his beach house and its surrounding grounds. Beatrice Kanoa had a son whose name was Kanihewa Kanoa, and over the years she passed the titles to these lands to him. Kanihewa went on to marry a woman named Kukiaka Kalili, who already had children, including a son born in 1904 whose name was Edward Kalili Kaiwi. Before his death, Kanihewa passed the titles of his remaining lands to Kukiaka, among which was the Niumalu property with its beach house.

When Edward Kalili Kaiwi grew up he married Malu Kauai Ho´ona, known as Fanny, who was the half sister of Pi´ilani, the wife of Koolau the Leper. During the course of their marriage Edward and Malu Kauai had a daughter whom they named Mercedes Leinaala Kaiwi, my landlord, and she inherited the same beach house that her grandmother Kukiaka gave to her father, Edward, the same house that had been built in 1846 or 1847 by Governor Paul Kanoa. Thus is the genealogy of my home in Niumalu.

Also living on the estate at the time was a family named Chow. Their house, which was also very old, was just inland of the house I lived in, and farther inland, at the end of the estate, was my landlord's house, which was built in the 1950s. In front of me, or at the *makai* end of the estate (the end closer to the ocean), lived a nephew of my landlord, Edward Kaiwi Valejos, who was the son of my landlord's sister, Kamaile. Just across the street and inland of the old Kauai Inn was another old house with a beautiful old-style Hawaiian yard; this was the home of the old lady Ellen Ana´kalea, the widow of Ili Waialani Ana´kalea, who was originally from the Waimea Valley and a cousin of Maraea Kaialau Cox, my auntie Maraea. From her house to the dirt lane that leads to the Alekoko fishpond, at the point where Hulemalu Road starts to climb up to the lookout above, there was a swamp and a freshwater spring. Toward the end of this swamp and close to the dirt lane there was another old house where a Hawaiian man named Henry Pia lived, who was the uncle of Hiram and Arthur. Farther up the dirt lane were the remnants of Governor Kanao's main house, which was once restored by a man named Stanford Achi, who made it his residence. Mr. Achi descended from the Ala´pai family from the island of Hawaii, and claimed his lineage from the High Chief Ala´pai nui, who became king of the island of Hawaii prior to Kamehameha the Great.

Here, close to the Achi house, on the hillside facing it, are two very large boulders, each sixteen feet high, black in color, and tapered to a rounded point toward the top. Once while visiting this area with Kala—my kapuna from Waimea—he told me that during the days of his youth his kupuna said these were akua stones, but whether they were stones of the gods themselves or of na ´aumakua he could not recall. He also mentioned that a heiau of the type used by fishermen, known as a ko´a, which was really more of a shrine, was known to be located close to these two boulders, and was used in association with the fishpond nearby.

As the dirt lane approached the Hule´ia River, it passed the site of the old Kauai Canoe Club, which was built on a little islandlike delta. Mr. Achi managed this club for many years, until its destruction by Hurricane Iwa in 1982.

The Kaiwi House

I was at home in the old Kaiwi house. I came to feel that the time I spent away from it during the day when I conducted my business was just a necessary participation in the present, and once back in the house I would again be in a time to which I was more closely connected.

The roof design consisted of a double pitch, with a very steep pitch over the main hall and a lesser pitch over the lanai. The intent was for rainwater to flow faster from the steep pitch and be thrown farther from the house by the lesser pitch below. The footings were likewise practical, consisting of flat river stones, just as at my mother's and grandmother's houses in Waimea and at many of the older houses that had survived into my time.

Its interior also resembled the majority of the old houses that I was raised in and visited during the days of my youth. The *pala* (parlor) was actually the original hall and had four doors, each located in the same spot as those of my grandmother's and mother's houses. The doors were all centered in their walls, giving access to the lanai that originally surrounded the hall. The windows were the same double-hung windows of my grandmother's house, and the main entry—a French door—was located between two of these. The doors from this parlor to the bedrooms were also the same as those in my grandmother's house—screened at the top half and dressed with curtains. The ceiling, which was over nine feet high, was solid Douglas fir planking, as were the walls, with moldings I had seen in my youth.

The parlor was white with red trim, and along with the woven lau'hala mats that covered the floor and the koa furniture (made from koa wood), it had the appearance of Hawaiian antiquity. In this room I created my kuahu.

Many years before, in 1891, when it was still used as a recreation hall, the house experienced its most memorable moment. In that year a banquet was held in the hall for Liliuokalani, the last queen of the Kingdom of Hawaii.

Leinaala

In the first few years that I spent here I often talked with Leinaala, whom I looked upon as a kupuna, and she would always share with me some of the history that surrounded this house. In the days of old when it was still being used as a recreational house, there were no bath facilities available for its guests and the Hawaiian women would have to walk along Pu'ali stream, which ran on the Lihue side of the house back then, to a waterfall that is located at the end of the Niumalu Valley, where the stream drops down from Halehaka above. Here they would gather and bathe and came to give the waterfall a *kolohe* (naughty) name: Waikohe nui, which I shall not define but leave to the reader to look up for himself.

In ancient days there existed a Hawaiian school for children toward the end of the Niumalu Valley at the base of the hills that climb up to Halehaka above. Here there existed a series of petroglyphs, all carved into individual rocks that were no larger than the average-size suitcase. The rocks were illustrated with the likenesses of humans and animals, and with representations of events of the past. Once lining the bank of Pu'ali stream, these stones were perhaps used in teaching. As time progressed to the modern era, the ancient school was forgotten and the rocks, over the years, were eventually swept down Pu'ali stream and became buried in the mud of the streambed.

Once while cleaning the tall grass from the stream so that it would not back up and overflow onto her property, Leinaala uncovered a few of these rocks. She continued cleaning the stream the whole day and decided to return the following day to study the petroglyphs more closely. Upon her return, however, she could no longer find them. She then repeated the same words to me that Roland Gay said to me many years before up in Paliuli: Sometimes the na 'aumakua show you something only once. I have often wondered how many of these rocks are buried in the earth of this area, which has since become housing lots.

One day Leinaala told me a story of the Dry Cave at Haena as told to her by her grandmother Kukiaka. As a child Kukiaka often accompanied her grandmother and other kupuna in their annual visit to the Dry Cave to treat the bodies of their ancestors. During this time the cave, with its many smaller caverns leading off from the main cavern, served as one massive burial chamber for many Hawaiian families. Within the smaller caverns there were ledges and terraces that were layered with mats holding the remains of ancestors in a semi-preserved state, their skin resembling dry hide or leather. During annual visits from descendants these bodies would be removed from their wrappings and rubbed with a solution that was made from the *uha'loa* plant, after which they would be wrapped again with fresh cloth and returned to their original places of burial. This tradition eventually came to an end due to the influence of the missionaries and the curiosity of white men, which resulted in the relocation of most of these remains. In 1946, during a tidal wave, the Dry Cave was filled with sand and it remains so today. In this telling Leinaala had described to me the recurring dream that had haunted me in Lihue but had ceased once I moved to Niumalu

Often while Leinaala worked in the yard in and around this old house, she shared with me what she knew of the plants she raised, mainly the *olena* ginger. This plant—most recognizable by its roots, which are orange in color when broken open—was commonly used medicinally in the days of old, often for the cleansing of the bloodstream. Leinaala raised the olena for her husband, who had a bad case of stomach ulcers. She often harvested its roots and removed their liquid by wrapping them in cloth and pounding them, after which she gave the juice to her husband to drink. This differed, however, from my mother's practice; she used aloe instead of olena for this condition. The olena was also an excellent cure for what is often called swimmer's ear. The liquid removed from the roots is warmed in a spoon held over a flame, then is poured into the ear canal.

Because she was a heavy smoker, Leinaala grabbed and ate a handful of the weed *wawae'e* from time to time. It grew in the lawn and resembled clover with thicker stems, and grew to no more than two inches in height. It was believed that wawae'e healed the lining of the lungs.

Once I walked with her to check on a few *noni* trees that grew in the brush close by. Although it is common practice today to use the noni fruit for medicinal purposes, she told me that her grandmother Kukiaka could remember the kupuna of her day avoiding the fruit and using only the leaves and flowers of this plant, from which they made a tea, and this was the practice she followed.

Sometimes as we stood in the yard Leinaala looked at the house and reminisced about her father enclosing the original lanai when she was a child living in the Nawiliwili Valley. She went on to explain that the walls of the original hall had a double layer of boards, similar to double-wall construction, but of post and beam rather than studs. The inside layer of these walls was removed and the boards were used to enclose the lanai. The double-hung bedroom windows that were originally removed to give the bedrooms privacy were then reinstalled horizontally as sliders. Such were the modifications made to many old halls that were converted to houses, thereby extending their usefulness and purpose—and lives—as a people's architecture.

The Old Ways—and Change

In Niumalu I often took walks, either in the early morning or late evening, up along Hulemalu Road where I could look our over Alekoko fishpond. My mother once told me that the Ha'upu range and the Hule'ia Valley were, at one time, the home of the Mo'o, a tribe of beings who were rumored to be half lizard and half human and supposedly still exist today, hidden within these mountains, venturing out only at night when there is no moon. During these walks I often traveled as far as Hule'ia and Kipu, where I could get a good view of Kilohana Crater toward the north, and sense even more the presence of my `aumakua.

At the house I constructed an imu to kalua turkeys at Thanksgiving and to cook other foods such as taro, yams, and sweet potatoes. I learned the art of imu construction and cooking from Harry Kane'akua Sr., who was originally from Kapaa and was married to the former Helen Naumu of the Hanapepe Valley. The burlap bags I used to cover the imu to hold in the steam and keep out the dirt came from the mountain man William Kanaka nui Kualu. Leinaala, especially, seemed to enjoy my efforts; it was the first imu to be maintained on her property since the death of her father.

With friendships and attention to tradition, life in Niumalu was enjoyable and good. During this time we added a daughter to our family, whom I named Kathleen Mahina O´hoku malamalama, after my grandmother. Within four years, however, major development began to encroach upon Niumalu as it had around Lihue, in my eyes changing the town forever. At the inland end of the estate a ridge begins to rise up to the plateau of Puhi, which forms the northern rim of the Hule´ia Valley and the western rim of Niumalu and Halehaka. At the top of this ridge that forms the junction of the Hule´ia and the Niumalu Valleys there was a hill very similar in nature to Kanikula. Like Kanikula it jutted above the intersection of the two valleys and overlooked two streams as they met. It resembled an ancient volcanic cone connected to the ridge at its rear by a spine, as Kanikula was connected to Mokihana. Its lonely peak stood at least one hundred fifty feet above the valley floor and Pu´ali stream as it flowed to the northeast heading for the bay. It was a beautiful hill of solid black lava rock with large sisal plants scattered here and there on its red-earth ledges and peak. Its base was surrounded by the large Java plum trees that are common along most riverbanks on Kauai. I viewed this hill every morning through my kitchen window, and it always gave me a strong feeling of the presence of the `aumakua within me.

To gain an idea of exactly what this hill looked like, you would have to journey to the Waimea Valley and gaze at Kanikula and imagine a peak with more green. It must be imagined—this hill no longer exists. Though no one knew its name, if it had a Hawaiian place-name it would surely include the word pu´u (in this use, "hill" or "peak"). In this story I will give it a name that you will remember when visiting Kauai. When you land at the Lihue Airport, remember the hill called I lalo pu´u ka mokulele, which means "the hill beneath the airport." When the decision was made in 1984 to extend the runways at the new Lihue Airport, Rego Trucking won the contract to supply base course and gravel to be used for these improvements and somehow the company acquired permission from the Kanoa estate, the County of Kauai, and the state Department of Land and Natural Resources, with no prior plan or study of impact or archaeological review, to construct a temporary rock quarry, its material being supplied by this hill. Within one year the entire hill had been consumed by machinery, and it now lies beneath the pavement and asphalt of the Lihue Airport. Today it is as though this hill had never existed in Niumalu.

I awoke every morning to look through my kitchen window and view the destruction of I lalo pu´u ka mokulele, the hill that was a source of life of a kind. To the contractor this was excavation and demolition as allowed by law—such are the thoughts of those seeking profit. When the hill was reduced to about a third of its original height, I saw one morning a fog-like cloud that seemed to come from within its shattered rock, and as this cloud disappeared into the air of the outside world I knew that this was the death of whatever dwelled there. It is thus that I remember I lalo pu´u ka mokulele.

By 1987 the conversion of the Kauai Surf Hotel into the new Westin Kauai Resort was in full swing. The need for full-grown coconut trees was great and the project's landscape contractor hired a county councilman named Jesse Fukushima to go out into the communities of Kauai and purchase these trees, with license to offer anywhere from three hundred to one thousand dollars per tree. The coconut trees that once lined Hulemalu Road at the front of the estate all disappeared to become part of the Westin landscape design. Niumalu, which means "sacred palm," was not sacred at all to the mighty dollar.

The Ana´kalea and Pia houses were soon destroyed by the Kanoa estate to make way for a new subdivision. The cane fields that I passed on my long walks along Hulemalu Road were abandoned to accommodate the urban expansion of Lihue and Puhi. Eventually the Alekoko area and Keopaweo became dormant, and today Niumalu survives solely within the confines of an old house that has stood through time and two major hurricanes to remain a symbol of the town's entry into a world of traditional Hawaii.

Return to Waimea

I decided to move back to Waimea seventeen years after I'd first left. I returned to my place of origin, to the place where our family has dwelled since 1901, to the lands of Namahana and Papalekoa, and here I remain today. I have journeyed outside of my home and have faced the influence that can shake, or stun into dormancy, one's belief in the ʻaumakua—and have survived with a belief that is even more powerful. I have shared my story to help ensure the survival of our people in relationship to their place of origin, and to help any who seek to maintain such a connection. Belief in a genealogical tie to one's ʻaumakua and a place of origin is the first step toward this survival.

To Hawaiians I say, seek out your origin if it has not already been instilled in you; there will always exist kupuna and kahuna outside of the institution who will share with you the ancient or traditional perceptions of Hawaii nei. To all those who wish to know a living past—feeling alive within you the light of your ancestors and the place from which they've come—seek out the kahuna and kupuna who will teach you what you must learn about who and what you are. Even in the face of change, my original place and your original place still live upon the breath of those who choose to keep them alive.

I leave to you the prayer to your ʻaumakua:

> ʻAuma—ku—u—a Mai
> *Oh ancestors of the past, come to thy breath.*
>
> Kia pa loaʻa Mai
> *Bestow thy blessings onto thee.*
>
> Hia pa loaʻa Mai
> *Thy desires, thy blessings of birth.*
>
> ʻAuma—ku—u—a Mai
> *Oh ancestors of the past, come to thy breath.*
>
> ʻAuma—ku—u—a Mai.

GLOSSARY

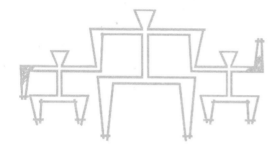

WHILE THE FOLLOWING LIST IS BY NO MEANS a complete glossary of every Hawaiian person, place, or significant term mentioned in the preceding text, included are those terms and names used most often or those that readers might find most helpful to their understanding of the author's world and culture. Please note that people are listed according to their first names.

`ai kapu Religious law of pre-monarchal Hawaii forbidding men and women to eat together.

ao Light; the earth, the living world.

ao ho`i`ho` Return to light.

ao kahea Call to light.

ao o ka ho`omana Light of religion.

ao panina Closing light.

ao uhane Light of the soul.

ao `aumakua The light of our ancestral spirits.

`aumakua  Ancestral spirit. Plural form is *na `aumakua*.

a`ama crab Large black edible crab.

A`ia ihea kana aina loa? Where is all our land?

aa A kind of rough lava rock.

aha Connection to the gods; ceremony to verify a god's recognition of a temple.

aha cord Umbilical cord (*aha* here means "meeting or gathering point").

aha moku puni An island conference.

aho Purlin.

ahu A heap (here, an *aha* of stone used to mark the boundary of an *ahupuaʻa*).

ahupuaʻa A land division usually extending from the uplands to the sea.

aina Land.

akala tree Hawaiian raspberry.

akua A creator-type god.

akua mana mana The right hand.

akua ʻaumakua Earthly incarnation of a god and the progenitor of a line of descendants.

akuaʻlele Fireballs noticed at leaping points such as the area around Kilohana Crater, indicative of connection to divine power.

akule A variety of fish.

alae (or **alaea**) A mineral containing hematite, used in the making of Hawaiian salt.

Alakaʻi Swamp Area on Mokihana Ridge above Waimea Canyon.

ale To gulp or swallow.

Alekoko fishpond Pond in Niumalu where the author recites his chant to the ʻaumakua and sees a powerful light like the one he had seen in Kilohana Crater as a boy (see chapter 8).

aliʻi Ruling class; chief or monarch, ruler; officer.

aliʻi ai moku High chief or king of the island.

aliʻi kuʻi Power behind the throne, held by the priesthood.

aliʻi nui High chief of a district.

ama The float or outrigger on a canoe that aids in balancing and stabilizing the craft.

ana ʻana ʻaihue A type of *kahuna* who attained another's property through the use of sorcery.

anae Mallet fish.

Anahola, Kauai Town to which the author is sent to live with the Lemm family as a twelve-year-old for "reform" after his gun prank in Waimea (see chapter 6).

Annexation Club A foreign conspiracy that secretly plotted the overthrow of Queen Liliuokalani with the hope of Hawaiian annexation by the United States.

anuʻu The oracle tower of a *heiau* (temple).

Ao Earth.

ao ʻauwana A place of wandering spirits; a place to which those souls not claimed by a family ʻaumakua after death can go in order to move on to the *ao kuewa*.

ao kuewa Realm of homeless souls.

Apo family Sam and his wife, Ka´luna. As a boy, the author attended many luaus at the Apo house in the Makaweli Valley.

au Endless chain of time.

au wai Irrigation ditch.

auku´u Black-crowned night heron.

awa `puhi White or yellow ginger.

Blackstad family The Norwegian family from which the author has descended on his father's side. Lena Katherine becomes Lena K. B. Wilson, the author's grandmother.

Camp One Site of a hydroelectric plant maintained by the Kekaha Sugar Plantation, located at the base of Waimea Canyon; a stopping point for many of the author's hunting trips and hikes as a youth and young man.

Carl Dusenberry Sr. An old-timer and mountain man of the Waimea Canyon, who, as a young man, moved to Kauai from the mainland. In his youth the author spends time learning from him (see chapter 7).

Catherine Mahina O´hoku Malamalama (or **Catherine Mahina Wilson**) The author's mother.

Char family Old Lady Char and sons Barney, Ernest, and Nani. Friends visited by the author and his mother on trips through the Makaweli Valley during his youth.

Clarence S. Koike A structural engineer who is one of the author's three mentors during his time in Lihue (see chapter 8).

David Malo Author of *Mo´olelo Hawaii (Hawaiian Antiquities)* and ancestor of the author.

David Malo Kupihea (or **David malo Lono hauoli mai kini nui a i mamao**) The author's great-uncle.

ditchman Person assigned to maintain the irrigation ditches and watering on plantations.

Dry Cave at Haena Burial place for many mummified Hawaiians and the subject of the author's recurrent dream while in Lihue (see chapter 8).

Eugene "Capri" Makaaila (or **Makaila**) A mountain man of the Waimea Canyon with whom the author spends his teenage years. He gives the author his backpack and a jar of Hawaiian salt, which later become objects placed at the author's *kuahu* in his home in Lihue (see chapters 7 and 8).

Gay and Robinson Plantation A large ranch and plantation begun in 1865 on Kauai. The plantation is still in existence today.

George Cliff A friend of the author's family who often visited their home during the author's boyhood. He moved to Kauai from the mainland and became an expert in the geography, geology, and natural history of the Kokee area of the island (see chapter 5).

ha A kind of sluice and trap made of trees and branches and used in catching black goby on the flooding rivers fed from the gorges of the Waimea and

Olekele Canyons during the rainy season; the Naumu brothers were experts in ha constuction.

ha'ha To inhale; to exhale.

haha Purple-stemmed dry land taro.

halalu A variety of fish.

hale mua Men's eating house under the *kapu* system.

hale'aina Women's eating house under the *kapu* system.

Haleole A noted Hawaiian scholar.

Hanau ka po i ka po, po, no Things born in the night are of the dark.

Hanau mai a puka i keao, malamalama Things born from and sprung up in the day are of the light.

Hanis Therkelsen An architect who worked with the author in Hanalei and who became his first mentor, giving the author the book that influenced his entire understanding of architecture, *A History of Architecture: On the Comparative Method* (see chapter 8).

haole Foreigner.

haole camps Housing for supervisors on a plantation.

haole koa A variety of tree, the wood of which is used in building a *ha*.

hapai To carry.

hapu'u Tree ferns, giant ferns that grow to the height and width of trees. The author encounters these the night he is lost in Kilohana Crater (see chapter 6).

Harry Kane'akua Sr. The Hawaiian who taught the author the art of *imu* construction and cooking.

hau tree The wood of this tree is used for building *iako*, the outrigger on a canoe.

Hawaii nei All of Hawaii; Hawaii as a whole.

he'e Squid.

heiau Temple.

hema mana mana The left hand.

hihi'o To dream while dozing; the dreamy moment of falling asleep.

Hiki au, e ola I have come; live.

hikimoe akua Northwest.

Hikina akala A platform *heiau* that was used as a place of refuge for travelers.

hikina hema Southeast.

Hili o holo January; or to appear and disappear, like fog.

hinana Young *o'opu*, or black goby fish.

Hiriam Kimo Ka'ili (or **Kimo**) The author's boyhood friend, nephew of Kanaka nui.

History of Architecture: On the Comparative Method A book by Sir Banister Fletcher given to the author by his mentor Hanis Therkelsen that influenced the author's understanding of and perspective on architecture.

hoʻi hoʻi To return, to come.

hoʻokupu A bundle.

hoʻopai Literally, "sharp ridges"; a particular design of *iʻekuku* used to make *kapa* cloth.

ho ʻuhane o ke ao Deified spirit of light.

hoe Oar.

hohoa Round beaters used in making *kapa* cloth.

honohono grass Used in cooking in the same way that watercress is used; introduced to the author by his *kupuna* Kanaka nui.

hooma hanahana Period of refreshment celebrated in ancient Hawaiian culture.

hua tree The bark of this tree is used to make fishing line and cord.

hui Business partnership.

huki lau Fish-harvesting ritual and celebration; literally, "to pull ropes" (see chapter 3).

huleʻia A kind of soft pumice stone.

huli Taro tops, planted in prepared ground to produce taro.

hulu Type of fishhook with one outward barb at the end.

hulu lio Horse blanket.

i kahiko ka ike The author's term for the Hawaiian ancient perspective (*kahiko* means "old"), exemplified by those who preserve the old ways, who live on the lands of their ancient ancestors, and who are most heartbroken by tourist development and the rising influence of the modern perspective on the islands. All of the Hawaiian men the author hunts with and learns from in chapter 7 have this perspective, as do men like Willy Kani (see chapter 4).

i kuʻuna ka ike The author's term for the Hawaiian traditional perspective (*kuʻuna* means "traditional"), exemplified by those who were raised away from their family's place of origin at the time of the Great Mahele, becoming either absorbed by the plantation system or relocated to a more urban environment. For these Hawaiians, life is divided; culture can be expressed at home but not at work. This is the perspective of many *kupuna* living today.

iʻekuku Beaters used in making *kapa* cloth.

I lalo puʻu ka mokulele Literally, "the hill beneath the airport"; a hill in Niumalu originally visible from the author's kitchen until it was destroyed in the process of expanding the Lihue Airport.

iako The outrigger on a canoe.

imu An underground oven.

inia tree The tree providing wood for the frame of a saddle.

ipu hoolele waa The gourds of stars, which are the gourds traditionally used as navigational instruments on canoes.

`ko`ko`lau A kind of tea commonly drunk on the island of Kauai.

Ka Mahele, the Great Mahele The great land division of 1848 instituted to give landownership to the *konohiki* under the kings who claimed specific lands, and to allow foreigners their claims to lands.

ka nupaikini ike The author's term for the Hawaiian modern perspective (*nupaikini* means "modern"), exemplified by Hawaiians who are completely disconnected from their ancestral ways and culture.

ka papa o laka Place of sacred births.

ka´aha stick A wand held by ancient Hawaiian priests during sacrifices in the temple.

Ka´ili (or **Samuel Naumu**) A mountain man of the old ways with whom Moke spends time hunting and traveling in the Waimea Canyon during his high school years. He is something of a philosopher who survived personal difficulty, and his effect on the author is profound (see chapter 7).

kahea Literally, "to call," these are the healing prayers used by Cecilia Kamai to help those who are ill.

kahili A large feathered standard for royalty, often waved like a fan.

kahu A spirit's keeper; a guardian.

kahu malama Duties of a caretaker.

kahuna Priest who was the repository of science, art, and knowledge in ancient Hawaiian culture; teacher.

kahuna ana ana aihue Sorcery used to steal another person's life, property, or kingdom.

kahuna ana ana Literally, "praying to death," this is the art used to determine which of a group of *kahuna* was most powerful; it involved a group of kahuna taking turns to try to will a *moa*—chief—to death.

kahuna kuhikuhi pu´uone The *kahuna* who most approximated an architect in ancient Hawaiian culture.

kahuna lapa `au An order of the priesthood.

kahuna papa hulihonua Land experts in ancient Hawaii who could read the configurations of the earth.

kahuna papa kilokilo lani *Kahuna* who could read signs or omens in the sky.

kahuna papa kilo `opua *Kahuna* who could read signs in the clouds.

kahuna papa kilo hoku *Kahuna* who could read the stars.

kahuna papa kilo honua *Kahuna* who could read the omens within the earth.

kahuna po´o ko´i Called "adze heads," those *kahuna* who practiced the darker arts.

Kala Kapahu One of the old-timers with whom the author spends time as a youth traveling in the Waimea Canyon (see chapter 7).

kalo Another name for taro.

kalua To bake.

kamaaina A native; one born in Hawaii.

kanaka Man.

Kanaka nui (or **William Kualu**) An old-time mountain man with whom the author travels as a teenager. He knows a great deal about the land in the Waimea Canyon and reading its signs and is very familiar with its plants and herbs and their many uses (see chapter 7).

Kane nui akea Kane of the great expanse, the god Kane, creator of Heaven, Earth, and all on the earth; one of the four primary gods of the ancient Hawaiians, along with Ku, Lono, and Kanaloa.

Kanikula High hill near the Makaweli River in the Makaweli Valley.

kao, kunana Goat.

kapa Kind of cloth made by ancient Hawaiians.

kapa lau Ritual preparation of the remains of the dead.

Kapalawai A village east of Waimea, site of ancient priestly fishponds.

kapu Religious laws; a ban; off-limits.

Katie Kamai Koani An older Hawaiian woman who spends time at the author's home during his childhood and shares her stories with him (see chapter 5).

Kauai The name of the author's island, located at the end of the Hawaiian Islands that is farthest from the mainland, United States.

kauhulu Ridgepole.

kaula Bark used to make rope; seer or oracle.

kaula waha Bridle.

kaupoku Ridgepole.

kauwa In ancient times, the lowest caste; outcasts.

kauwa `ainoa Free-eating, godless outcasts.

kauwa ha´alele loa Despised things.

kauwa kuapa´a Load-carrying outcasts.

kauwa laepuni Outcasts with a tattooed forehead.

kauwa lepo Base-born slaves.

kauwa makawela Red-eyed outcasts.

Ke na wa The Wa, one of the three original peoples of Hawaii nei.

Ke na mu The Mu, one of the three original peoples of Hawaii nei (the Menehune are the third).

ke unihi pili o po`ele`ele Deified spirit of darkness.

keaka Open presentation space, like a theater.

kia manu Ancient bird catchers who hunted the o`o bird.

kilo Observer; man in the bow of a canoe who used the gourd of Lono to navigate.

kilo hoku Stargazer, or astronomer of sorts.

Kilohana Crater Crater in which the author was lost in his youth while on his way home to Waimea from his exile in Anohola.

King Ola Ancient king who struck a deal with the Menehune to build an aqueduct that would deliver water to the village of Pe´e kaua´i.

kino lau Earthly bodies of the god Lono; the ancients believed the giant ferns *(hapu´u)* to be such bodies.

ko ono White crabs.

ko´a Shrine.

koa tree The wood of this tree is reddish in color. The hardwood is used in building furniture.

Ko`u aina keoa apauloa This is all my land.

kohe Type of fishhook with one inward barb.

koko Blood.

kole Type of notched joint used in building.

kolohe Naughty.

komohana hema Southwestern.

konohiki Lord over a land district or fisheries.

konohiki nui o kiholo Principal lord over the *ahupua´a* of Kiholo, Kono, Hawaii.

Koolau the Leper A man ordered to go to the leper colony on Molokai in the 1890s who fled instead with his wife and family and hid in the remote valley of Kalalau.

Ku nui akea One of the four primary gods of the ancients. The others are Kane, Lono, and Kanaloa.

kua kuku, kua la au Wooden anvils used to make *kapa.*

kuahu Altar; refers expecially to altars placed in the home.

kuali´i A specific priesthood order.

kuapo´i Covering piece over the bow of a single-hull canoe.

kuauhau The genealogist of court.

kuhikuhi Showing, pointing out, illustrating; giving to the intangible a physical form.

kuhina nui queen regent, vice king.

kukui Candlenut tree.

kuleana Family lands handed down from Great Mahele.

kuli kuli Be quiet.

kulolo Steamed or baked pudding made from taro and coconut.

kumau A Hawaiian card game similar to trumps.

kumu ao Out of light.

Kumulio The main character in a legend told by Kala Kapahu, about a girl who becomes a mermaid.

kumulipo Out of darkness.

kumupa'a A fixed origin; immortal light of the *akua*.

kumupa'a o ke ao Light of origin.

kupuna Elders.

laa Life.

laau palau Club.

lapu Ghost of one's own creation.

lau lau A dish usually containing pork and steamed with young taro leaves.

lau ma'u Fern leaf; a particular design of *i'ekuku* used to make *kapa* cloth.

lau'hala mats Mats woven from the leaf of the pandanus tree.

lau'ulu Leaves of the *ulu*, or breadfruit, tree.

leho Cowrie shell.

Lehua Island off the southwestern shore of Waimea town.

lehua trees These trees once existed on the slopes of Kilohana, but according to legend were used by the high chiefs of Kauai in the trickery employed to ward off the invading Kamehameha.

lei haka Pandanus leaf; a particular design of *i'ekuku* used to make *kapa*.

lei niho palaoa Necklace worn by a high chief.

leina a ka'uhane Leaping points or spirit openings from which spirits leaped into their world after death.

Leinaala The author's landlord in Niumalu who acted as a *kupuna* to him.

Lihue, Kauai Town where the author lived directly after moving from Waimea as a young man.

lima mana mana Hand of man.

limu Seaweed.

lio Horse.

lo'i Terrace.

lokahi Unity.

loko i'a kalo Method of raising fish in ponds surrounded by taro fields, usually at the mouths of rivers and streams. *Loko* means "inside"; *i'a* refers to fish when eaten; *kalo* is the Hawaiian word for taro.

lomi To massage with the hand, as is done to the salt in the making of Hawaiian salt.

Lono nui akea One of the four primary gods of the ancient Hawaiians. The others are Kane, Ku, and Kanaloa.

lu`u To plunge.

luna Heights.

Ma`o mai ko`u aina There is my land.

Maha Leoiki *Maha* means temple (side of the head); the man who conducted the *huki lau* that the author participated in with his mother when he was a boy.

mahele ana Apportioned in time.

Maile Naumu (or **Auntie Maile**) Maile Kupau, or Lydia Aha o mokupuni Kupau, wife of Nahuka and sister-in-law of Ka`ili. She was one of the author's mother's best friends, and often traveled with the author on trips to the Makaweli Valley when he was a child.

maka upena Literally, "net mesh"; a particular design of *i`ekuku* used to make *kapa.*

maka`ainana The commoners in ancient Hawaii.

makahiki The ancient time of sports, games, and tax collecting.

makai Toward the ocean.

Makaweli Valley Valley on Kauai adjacent to the Waimea Valley. The author often traveled there as a boy and young man.

maku`u Pommel.

makua Parents.

makua ea Turtle shell.

makua iwi ilio Dog bone.

makua iwi kanaka Human bone.

makua iwi kohala Whalebone.

makua kolea Foster father.

Makuaole family Family that has lived in the Makaweli Valley since ancient times. Albert Kekua Makuaole (Pipito) is the last mountain man surviving today, and the last to live on his traditional ancestral lands.

malina Sisal.

malo Loincloth.

mamake A member of the nettle family.

mana Power.

mana kia`i Guardian power.

mana mana To impart *mana* to objects.

mana mana iki The little finger. As used by George Cliff, the lesser spirit of nature in man (see chapter 5).

mana mana lima nui The thumb. As used by George Cliff, the aggressive spirit of nature in man (see chapter 5).

mana mana loa The middle finger. As used by George Cliff, the distant spirit of nature in man (see chapter 5).

mana mana miki The index finger. As used by George Cliff, the active spirit of nature in man (see chapter 5).

mana mana pili The ring finger. As used by George Cliff, the clinging spirit of nature in man (see chapter 5).

mana'o Thoughts, ideas, experience.

Manny Naholoholo A mountain man and old-timer in the Waimea Valley (see chapter 7).

mano A wall made of stone positioned so that water in a river is diverted; a shark.

mano wai Water intake.

Mano'eha The legendary "shark man of Pili."

Maraea Kaialau Cox (or **Auntie Maraea**) One of the author's mother's best friends, who travels with the author and his mother in the Makaweli Valley during the author's boyhood. She treated the author's mother after her stroke.

mele Songs.

Menehune Ditch A ditch that runs in the Waimea Valley, supposedly built by the Menehune, a small tribe in ancient times who were one of the three original groups of people of Hawaii nei.

mo'o Serpent or lizard; also refers to genealogy.

Mo'o tribe A tribe of beings rumored to be half lizard and half human.

mo'o kahuna A line of hereditary priests.

Mo'olelo Hawaii (Hawaiian Antiquities) The book, by David Malo, about the practices and way of life of the ancient Hawaiian peoples.

moa A red jungle chicken or rooster; refers to a chief.

moi A variety of fish.

moki Literally, "to shoot forth."

na ao ka po'e Light of the people.

Na mahoe hope Castor.

Na mahoe mua Pollux.

Na Pali coast Northern coastline of Kauai.

na'au The gut; intestines.

na 'aumakua o ka po Ancestral spirits of the distant past.

na 'aumakua o ke ao Ancestral spirits of the immediate past.

naiupi'o class Children of the mating of a brother and sister in ancient Hawaii.

Namahana The name of one parcel of land on the Blackstad homestead in Waimea.

Naulii The ancient high chief of those in the Makaweli Valley; also the name of a red dirt hill on the rim of Kaluaokalani.

Naumu brothers Nahuka and Ka'ili, *ha* builders and two of the last mountain men in the Waimea Valley.

Ni'ihau An island near Kauai, home to many expert Hawaiian saddle makers.

niho mano A shark tooth.

niho palaoa A royal necklace; *niho* is a pendant from the tooth of a *palaoa*, or "sperm whale."

Niumalu Where the author lived after leaving Lihue. At the time of his residence there it was a place, like Waimea, that was removed from the burgeoning development of Lihue.

noho lio Saddle.

noni tree The fruit, leaves, and flowers of this tree are used for medicinal purposes.

`opelu A variety of fish.

o`oma Stirrup cover.

o´opu Black goby, a seasonal fish.

oa Rafter.

oahi A stone used to attract *`opelu*.

ohana Family.

ohia, ohia lehua A kind of tree and wood used for building.

Ohu Hookano (or **Alfred Ka`ohu Hookano**) A cowboy of the Gay and Robinson ranch and brother-in-law of Kala Kapahu.

oi´hana kahuna An office of the priesthood.

oki piko A ceremony in which a baby's umbilical cord is cut.

olena ginger A plant once used medicinally; raised and used by Leinaala at Niumalu.

oli Chants.

olona plant The bark of this plant is used to make cord.

ono Delicious, deliciously.

opae Small freshwater shrimp, supposedly favored by the ancient Menehune.

opihi Limpets.

opu lio The strap around a horse's belly that secures the saddle to its back.

`pu Silencing.

pa Pertains to sheathing for a house.

pa´a kai ula ula Hawaiian salt; *pa´a kai* is "salt" and *ula* is "red." Often made by the old-timer Eugene Makaaila.

pahee Dart throwing.

pahu The wooden frame inside a saddle.

pala Parlor.

pali Cliff.

Paliuli Gorge where Willy Kani and Roland Gay lived.

pali wawae Stirrups.

panini Common wild cactus.

papa Surface.

papa kanaka The people of Hawaii nei.

papa kuʻi poi Poi boards, used in making poi from taro.

Papalekoa Name of one of the parcels of land on the Blackstad homestead in Waimea.

pau Wrap cloth.

pepe Baby (a modern term).

pepehi Literally, "deep groove"; a particular design of *iʻekuku* used in making *kapa*.

Philip "One Leg" Fortardo An old-timer from the author's youth who lost his leg in a factory accident.

piko The knotted navel.

pili To cling.

pili grass A native grass that turns to straw and takes many years to decay; traditionally used in the construction of dwellings.

Pipito Makuaole One of the last living mountain men. He resides in the Makaweli Valley, the place of origin of his ancestors. The author spends time with him in his youth (see chapter 7).

po pau ole Realm of endless night, the place where unclaimed spirits go.

pohaku Stone.

pohaku kahe ule Literally, "stone-split-penis"; this is the stone used for the procedure of sub-incision in ancient Hawaiian culture, a procedure similar to circumcision.

pohaku kikeke, pohaku kani Bell stones (see chapter 4).

pohaku luheʻe Stone sinker.

Pohaku pepe A rock ledge near Camp One where a burial cave was located; a *pohaku pepe* is a stone believed to be possessed by a baby (see chapter 4).

Pohaku uila Lightning stone.

poi dog An interbred Hawaiian dog.

pola Raised platform on a double-hull canoe.

pou A kind of post or pole used in building.

pou hana A post set at each end of a house to support the ridgepole.

pou kihi The corner post of a house.

pou kukana The post between the *pou hana* and the *pou kihi*.

puʻolo A secured bundle.

puʻu Hill.

puʻuone To mold in sand.

puʻuhonua A place of spiritual refuge.

puaʻa A pig.

Puhiʻula The legendary red eel of Alekoko fishpond.

pule Prayer.

pulehu Barbecued.

pupu Snacks.

Queen Liliuokalani The last ruler of the Kingdom of Hawaii.

Roland Lalana ka pahu kani o lono Gay (or **Roland Gay**) One of the author's *kapuna* who lives in Paliuli near Willy Kani.

Russell P. Gallo A contractor who is one of the author's close friends and mentors during his time in Lihue (see chapter 8).

Samuel M. Kamakau A well-known Hawaiian historian and scholar.

tabu Forbidden.

taro Plant grown throughout the islands; the leaves and tubers are eaten and used in a variety of ways.

ti leaf Leaves used to "package" food for cooking.

tutu Grandmother.

uha'loa plant The source of a solution used in mummification.

uhane A spirit of the present life, similar to an *unihi pili* (see chapter 1).

ule A type of notched joint used in building.

unihi To withdraw.

unihi pili A deified spirit in its role in the afterlife.

uwepa Horsewhip.

waa'kau'kahi A single-hull or one-passenger canoe.

Waimea The town where the author grew up.

Waimea Canyon The wild area explored by the author with the old-time *kupuna* he come to know well during his high school years (see chapter 7).

Waimea Valley The valley where the author grew up, carved by the Waimea River.

Wakea A first-century chief, the procreator of the Hawaiian people.

wauke tree Paper mulberry tree.

wawae'e Weed used to heal the lining of the lungs.

William Kanaka nui Kualu (or **Kanaka nui**) One of the mountain men of the author's youth (see **Kanaka nui**).

Willy Kani (or **William Kapahu kani o lono Goodwin**) A *kupuna* with whom the author spends a great deal of time in his youth. He introduces the author to the burial caves of the ancients and is one of the first kupuna outside of his mother to lead him to recognize the *'aumakua* within himself (see chapter 4).